Corporate Portals Empowered With XML and Web Services

T0348775

Corporate Portals Empowered With XML and Web Services

Anura Gurugé

Digital Press

An imprint of Elsevier Science
Amsterdam • Boston • London • New York • Oxford • Paris • San Diego
San Francisco • Singapore • Sydney • Tokyo

Digital Press is an imprint of Elsevier Science.

 Recognizing the importance of preserving what has been written, Elsevier Science prints its books on acid-free paper whenever possible.

Library of Congress Cataloging-in-Publication Data

ISBN 1-55558-280-X

British Library Cataloguing-in-Publication Data

A catalogue record for this book is available from the British Library.

The publisher offers special discounts on bulk orders of this book.
For information, please contact:

Manager of Special Sales
Elsevier Science
200 Wheeler Road
Burlington, MA 01803
Tel: 781-313-4700
Fax: 781-313-4882

For information on all Digital Press publications available, contact our World Wide Web home page at: http://www.digitalpress.com or http://www.bh.com/digitalpress

Printed and bound by CPI Group (UK) Ltd, Croydon, CR0 4YY

Transferred to digital print 2012

To Danielle and Matthew Gordon

Contents

Foreword

Imagine a high-profile retail store in a shopping mall with its windows boarded up. Shoppers will walk past rather than walk in. Couple this with the situation in which all the other stores have highly enticing window displays. It does not take much thought to realize that the lack of a "store front" puts many companies at a serious competitive disadvantage. The Web, in many respects, is viewed as a giant, global shopping mall. The need, therefore, to have a "store front on the Web" that draws the attention of potential customers and encourages existing customers to make repeat visits is critical. The ability to "window dress" on the Web is achieved through the use of the very product that this book so comprehensively describes. Portals provide a window, from the Web, that displays everything a company desires to communicate. It also provides customers with an easy and highly effective means of interacting with the company, whether it is for making a purchase, obtaining support for a product or service, or just looking for more information.

Of course, portals are not just for targeting consumers. They are currently in more extended use with internal audiences (employees) and business partners. Most companies will test their first portal deployments on their own employees before venturing into the public domain via the Internet. Although they provide other benefits, the key focus of internal portals is on improving employee productivity. Providing employees with a single view of information, delivering easier access to internal applications, and allowing access to the Web are just a few of the benefits delivered by a well-designed corporate portal.

The experiences I have had with many companies have shown that the majority of portal deployments were for internal use. Some of the most successful deployments were targeted, at first, at a very specific set of employees and then were extended to wider audiences as their success was demonstrated. This staged roll-out approach may seem obvious, but it is not always followed. Many businesses are looking for their portal to deliver ROI in as short a period of time as possible. As a result, they look to target as many internal users as possible and embark on a project with an unmanageable scope.

I have seen many successful projects targeted at the developers (or engineers) who work on the product development side of the business. Providing a consolidated access point to development tools, libraries, project schedules, and (through collaboration software) other developers, portals deliver productivity improvements as well as quality control during the development process. The portal can then be extended to new audiences (e.g., test groups), and personalization can be used to customize the portal environment depending on which type of user (developer or tester) logs on.

Regardless of which audience a portal is targeted at, the success of the deployment is dependent on how well the deployment is planned. There are many dependencies for a successful portal, some technically oriented, some focused on usability, and others dealing with cultural issues. All these issues should be taken into account during the planning phase. In addition, the portal content—or should I say the content that the portal provides access to—is a key parameter for success. The ideal situation is for a company to provide enough content through the portal so that the users (internal or external) establish that portal as the home page on their browsers. This way, whenever the browser is started, it immediately navigates to the company Web site, allowing the company to deliver important information to its target audience. This is critical for enhancing brand awareness, highlighting targeted promotions, accelerating the adoption of new products, delivering important corporate information to employees, establishing tighter relationships with business partners, and much more.

As we progress through 2002, business integration appears to be the high-priority topic on the minds of the leading CIOs. Many recent studies show that in 2002 the majority of IT spending will focus on business integration projects, where companies are looking to pull together the disparate IT systems inside the enterprise and provide the capability to connect with customers and business partners. The portal is one of the key integration points in projects such as this, and it will play a major role as companies integrate their systems.

In this book, Anura Guruge has managed to successfully cover all the areas required for even the most extensive portal deployments. With coverage of security, performance, personalization, Web services (including XML and other relevant technologies), and systems management, to name a few, the reader is presented with all that is relevant to this important strategic initiative. Each area is explained in a way that can be understood by non-technical audiences.

Presenting the details in a manner that can be understood by more general audiences is critical for many reasons. Since the budgets associated with large portal deployments can be extensive, the budget-approval process will involve many line-of-business executives who are, in general, nontechnical. In addition to this, the business benefits associated with portals can be significant, and it is thus important for the lines of business to understand this technology in order to translate it into competitive advantage.

It is important to note that this book is not primarily an explanation of the terminology and technology associated with portals. There is a much larger focus on the application of portals and how they can be used to optimize existing areas of the business and allow businesses to enter new markets. With chapters dedicated to knowledge management, supply chain management, and customer relationship management, the reader is guided through important applications that target audiences ranging from internal employees through business partners and on to customers.

There is no doubt that portals are here to stay. We just need to look at the market to validate this. I have lost count of the number of companies selling portals and related software products. There are a large number of vendors that specialize in portals, and all the large software platform vendors (IBM, Microsoft, Oracle, BEA Systems, and Sun) have a portal offering as part of their portfolio. Also, the market for portal software continues to grow at a healthy rate. In 2001 the overall enterprise software market grew only by 4.3 percent compared with 2000. Portals, however, grew by nearly 60 percent over the same period of time. With about 35 percent of the world's top 3,500 companies planning to buy portal software in 2002, there is no sign of this trend slowing down in the near future.

My recommendation for any business, regardless of what industry it is in, is to take a very serious look at portals and the business benefits offered. It is too risky to ignore this area of Web technology. This book provides the best starting point I can think of for getting an understanding of the many facets associated with portals and their relevance to modern businesses.

—Stuart McIrvine
IBM, Program Director
of Marketing for WebSphere
Integration Middleware

Preface

For IT management, these are challenging times with constant pressure to minimize costs, provide more services and do so faster. Corporate portals, empowered with XML and Web services, can really help you succeed in this charter. This book will help you work out how to best utilize portal technology to meet your needs.

This book is a guide to contemporary (i.e., post 2002) corporate portals, where a corporate portal in this context is considered to be a pivotal Web-centric resource both for external and in-house users. It even tries to make this exciting and inspiring. It provides you with a non-partisan, objective, factual, and accurate executive view of how best to design, implement and run contemporary corporate portals that profitably exploit XML and Web services. In addition to always describing the pros and cons of a given approach, technology or method this book always tries to list well known products, from multiple vendors, that could be used to realize the functionality in question. The 10-item Q&A section at the end of each chapter provides a quick and easy way to ensure a quick recap of the pertinent topics and make sure that you have not "misplaced" anything—especially if you were interrupted, as it is likely to have been the case, multiple times during the course of reading a chapter.

This book is not meant for an overtly technical readership that is looking for a "bits-and-bytes" guide to building new portals. If you know what you can do with a JavaScript that you cannot do with Java then this book is really not for you though you may want to skim through the illustrations and look at a few of the definitions to give you some ideas and hopefully inspiration as to what can be achieved in terms of corporate portals with today's technology, especially when it comes to Web services. A quick story here may help to clarify exactly what this book is striving to achieve.

A couple of years ago I used to have a business where I delivered, by boat and jet ski, take out food to people living on islands or picnicking for the day in their boats, on this relatively large lake in New Hampshire, that I call home. One evening I was coming back from a delivery when I was waved down by a group of college age kids driving around in what we refer to around here as "dad's boat." They were a bit "disoriented" (to use an euphemism) and wanted to know how best to get to Jonathan's Landing in Moultonborough. I took out my map and started giving them precise directions using compass bearings, island names and buoys numbers. A few seconds into this, one of the young men interrupt me and said: "I don't want to be rude, but don't get technical with us. Just point." Well that is what I am doing with this book—trying to point you in the right direction, point out what you should be looking out for and pointing out what your final goal should be.

If nothing else, even if you just speed read through this book it will stop you from being blind-sided at meetings where issues related to portals, XML, and Web services are raised, discussed, or actioned. From experience, from both sides of the table, I know that this is the scenario where management can best benefit from the corporate equivalent of *Cliffs Notes* that address the specific technical issues being discussed. When it comes to next generation corporate portals this book is that set of it-will-make-you-look-good crib notes. This book is non-partisan and vendor neutral and freely cites, without any bias or prejudice, technology and products from as many germane vendors as possible. If there are any portal server vendors that I have not mentioned, and there are bound to be some given how wide this field is, it does not mean that I do not consider them to be viable. It just means that despite my best efforts they managed to remain below my radar screen.

If you are looking at this book the chances are that you either currently do not have a portal of any sort, have an employee-only in-house/intranet portal or has one that does not fully exploit Web services or XML. If you fall into any of these categories this is indeed the right book for you—even if you discount my innate partisanship. This book does set out to provide as comprehensive a view as possible, without getting overly technical, as to what is viable today when it comes to implementing secure but function-rich portals.

The advent of XML and Web services do truly usher in a whole new set of exciting, far reaching and potentially bottom-line enhancing opportunities in this arena. To claim that XML and Web services empowered corporate portals represent the next generation in this genre is not mere hype. XML and Web services take what was already a powerful and proven IT solution and makes it even more "interoperable," open, cost-effective and easier to implement. This is where this book comes into its own. Not only does it address all the issues pertaining to the planning, implementation and operation of a modern corporate portal, but it continually shows how and where XML and Web services can play an incisive role.

What is covered?

This book sets out to cover everything that an IT related manager needs to know about modern, consolidated, but partitioned, corporate portals that server both external and in-houses users. It addresses the latest trends when it comes to portal design, implementation and methodologies and in particular how XML and Web services can be exploited. It provides and up to-date and accurate description of Web services and shows how they do represent a new, Web-oriented way to create and utilize reusable building blocks of business logic that can be used by portals as well as other e-applications.

The various types of portals that exists, their evolution and the relationship between them is also examined in some detail. This is because there is still much confusion as to what and what cannot be achieved with a portal with this issue often clouded by folks talking at cross purposes using incompatible terminology. For example, the term corporate portal *per se* can be a source of confusion and misunderstanding. There are some that still think of corporate portals as employee-only portals while others, in-line with current thinking, use this term, as is the case with this book, to refer to consolidated but securely partitioned portals that serve all users—irrespective of whether they are internal or external.

Chapter 3 is devoted to portal architectures and technologies using an incrementally refined and expanded portal model to serve as an easy to follow guide. Chapter 4 builds upon the themes explored in chapter 3 but focuses on security, scalability and speed related issues. Chapter 5 then rounds up these technology focused chapters by looking at the issues pertaining to managing and monitoring portals—with special emphasis on content management. Chapters 6 and 7 then address portal related "applications;" in particular, knowledge management, customer relationship management, and supply chain management. Chapter 8 is devoted to Web services, with references to XML, and Chapter 9 is a summation chapter that ties together the themes, technologies, methodologies, and recommendations covered in the previous chapters.

There is a glossary and a list of acronyms at the back of this book, though I strive to describe (at least once) the terms, technologies, or buzzwords that are mentioned in the text at or near to the first time they are mentioned in order to make sure that you are not left in the dark, so to speak. There is also an index and a detailed table of contents.

Headings and subheadings are used extensively after the introductory prose to identify and delineate the topics being addressed. The table of contents, which does list all of the headings and subheadings, can serve as a detailed navigational map through this book. Given this structure, where each chapter starts off with an overview, many topics may appear multiple times within a chapter—typically with incremental levels of detail or refinement. Each chapter ends with a 10-item Q&A section that sets out to recap the important issues addressed in that chapter.

Navigating through this book

This book, of course, is structured to be read sequentially from chapter to chapter, page by page. If read in such a conventional manner, the issues, options, technologies, and solutions will be presented in a systematic step-by-step manner, replete with detailed figures. It could, however, also be used as a reference guide where the reader pursues a particular technology or theme—for example, the role of Web services vis-à-vis corporate portals. If you intend to use this book as a reference guide, please use the index or the table of contents as the optimum means of locating the topics being sought.

I hope you enjoy it. Thank You.

Anura Gurugé
Lake Winnipesaukee,
New Hampshire
August 2002

Acknowledgments

The production of this book was greatly aided by two intrepid souls, viz. Stuart McIrvine of IBM and David Johnson of Cisco, who reviewed and critiqued each chapter as soon as it was written. They provided invaluable insights and did their best to keep me honest and accurate. Stuart, who also very kindly agreed to write the Foreword to this book, is a Program Director for IBM's WebSphere Integration solutions and used to look after the WebSphere Portal offering. His feedback was thus always incisive, germane and well reasoned. David and I go back a long time. We worked closely together in the early days of Web-to-host when David was the buccaneering Director of Marketing for OpenConnect Systems. Now as a Strategic Account Manager at Cisco, David in addition to being a daily user of Cisco's renowned corporate portal also was involved with many accounts using portals and pioneering the use of Web services. David, as ever, kept me on my toes and stopped me from going astray when it came to describing the nascent technologies. Despite their gallant efforts any errors, omissions and shortfalls you may still discover in this book are, alas, my fault and I will take all blame for them. Thank you Stuart, thank you David. Without the two of you I really would have struggled to pull this book together.

Theron Shreve the publisher of this book, for whom I had written for when he was at Auerbach, restored by faith in this somewhat idiosyncratic genre. He, aided by his assistant Pam Chester, was gentle, supportive, honorable and furthermore, always good for a "free" lunch (as long as it was Chinese). Alan Rose, the production manager for this book, and an ex-professor of English literature at UNH, performed miracles and was himself a miracle as far as I was concerned. He did not just make the oft angst ridden production phase painless—he actually managed to make it fun! I would in reality look forward to getting proofs back from him. Thank you Alan. You were great.

Thanks are also due to a few select individuals at some of the companies I deal with for their continued help and support over the years. These include my "bro" Carlson Colomb once with Aviva but now a Director at Webmotion; Michel Lefebvre a rare hero at NetManage; Mark Lillycrop for so long at Xephon but now with his own consulting firm called Arcati, Fiona Hewitt the incomparable editor of "TCP/SNA Update" for Xephon; Tim Clark once at Tavve but now a network management entrepreneur at large; Jim O'Connor still at Bus-Tech; Kathleen Riordan at IBM; Tod Yampel of ResQNet; Susan Verrecchia of the eponymous Verrecchia Group; Larry Samberg now with Broadcastle.com; Xavier Chaillot and Rana Aluraibi of Hummingbird; Marcus Dee of **look**software; Adrienne Stevens of Southern New Hampshire University; Deborah Leduke of McIntosh College and David and Cynthia Macfarlane of Mac-Durgin Business Systems.

It would be remiss if I did not also mention a few friends. Susanne Weldon Francke (sometimes also my lawyer) and Dr. Gary Francke keep an eye on me on a daily basis. Robert Rosenbaum is still related, albeit one degree of separation further, via the goldens while Larry and Eileen Samberg, as well as Jo-Ann Nealon, could always be counted upon for friendship and generosity. Kinney and Jean O'Rourke of the Black Cat and Rotary added a new facet to my life by getting me into Rotary. I probably would have needed to have my right foot amputated this Summer if not for Brenda Kennedy who happened to be a nurse.

I also need to thank my father as well as Dr. Tom Westerdale, still going strong at Birkbeck College who taught me how to write, though he should no longer be held responsible to the bad habits I have succumbed to. Matthew Gordon, now 10, and with his name now appearing in at least four books was not as persistent as he was last time around about me getting this book completed, though I will admit that he checked on the status of this book much more often than the publisher. Danielle, now a young lady of 13, still lights up my day, while Ulysses, my latest golden retriever, has made sure that I do have to go running at least once a day. Thank you all.

Corporate Portals: What, Why, and When?

Corporate portals function as gateways, in an "open sesame" manner, to widespread e-business. This is a given, regardless of one's attempts to dodge it, deny it, or defy it. This connection and correlation between corporate portals and e-business can be justified in many ways at many levels. To start with, however, a simple and somewhat intuitive explanation will suffice. A corporate portal, by definition, is supposed to be a corporation's strategic, electronic interface to the Web or, at a minimum, to Web technology–based private networks (e.g., extranets). It serves both external and internal users. It becomes a high-profile, strategic extension to a company's mission-critical operation.

E-business, whether it be e-commerce, customer relationship management, supply chain management, or professional services automation, is all about doing business over the Web. Consequently, in much the same way that call centers facilitate telephone-based business transactions, corporate portals open the way for secure, authorized e-business. Corporate portals reduce internal costs.

Corporate portals simplify, streamline, and expedite the entire process of interacting with a corporation. They provide an inviting and secure Web-based interface to a diverse range of corporate information, services, and applications. Corporate portals permit people to directly interact with a corporation to conduct authorized business or gain necessary information without having to deal with a company representative. Corporate portals thus heighten company efficacy and promote increased productivity. They reduce operational costs while increasing company reach.

Corporate portals can increase corporate competitiveness through better information dissemination and the provision of more incisive services.

FedEx's groundbreaking online package-tracking service, which debuted in 1994 and is discussed in more detail later, is a good example of the latter. Corporate portals can dramatically boost user satisfaction by eliminating the delays and frustrations associated in dealing with a harried call center. They thus facilitate customer retention and foster customer loyalty.

The burgeoning importance of eXtensible Markup Language (XML) and XML-centric Web services in post-dot-com e-business further accentuates the role of corporate portals. The pivotal XML enabling methodologies include incisive schemes such as universal description, discovery, and integration (UDDI), a new type of search and broadcast capability for the Web. Together these XML initiatives set out to automate the procurement, promotion, franchising, and delivery of products and services over the Web (i.e., functions already associated with corporate portals). Future corporate portals will thus continually cater to two types of audience—humans and automated, programmatic "clients." Authorized and validated business processes can thus occur with little, if any, human intervention. If you succeed in building a better mousetrap, UDDI and the other associated XML schemes will thus ensure that the world will indeed beat an electronic path to your portal without your having resort to too much traditional advertising.

Corporate portals are not new. Interactive, transactional corporate portals, as opposed to static, one-way "home page" Web sites, were relatively numerous by 1997. Corporate portals were thus around to play an inadvertent part in the dot-com fiasco. The dot-coms, in general, exploited the inherent worldwide reach and the credibility that comes with a snazzy corporate portal to promote their cause and solicit business. It should, however, be emphatically stressed, just in case there are any lingering misconceptions, that the demise of dot-coms can in no way be attributed, even tangentially, to their use of corporate portals. Blaming corporate portals for the woes of dot-coms would be akin to blaming credit cards for fostering fraud. The dot-coms, if anything, illustrated the innate power and possibilities of corporate portals.

The global economic slowdown that occurred in the wake of the dot-com meltdown in reality further empowered corporate portals, as corporations rediscovered that portal technology was indeed a sure-fire way to reduce operational costs while increasing the scope and range of their services. The anthrax scares that occurred in the midst of this period provided additional impetus to minimize mail-based transactions. Some corporations—in particular airline, credit card, and telephone companies (e.g., AT&T)—are openly acknowledging the advantageous cost economics of portal-based transactions. These companies are offering tangible incentives, such as gift certificates from Amazon.com, to people who commit to conduct most of their future interactions with these companies via their corporate portals rather than by telephone or mail.

Financial institutions and active investors have also known, for quite awhile, about the palpable cost savings possible with portal-based transactions compared with prior schemes—in particular, with "1-800" call-center operations, where calls may have to be transferred back and forth between customer reps and brokers qualified (or licensed) to execute the necessary trades. Online trading via the portal of a financial institute (e.g., Charles Schwab) has always been considerably less expensive, not to mention faster, than calling a broker to conduct that same trade. The reduced fees, in this

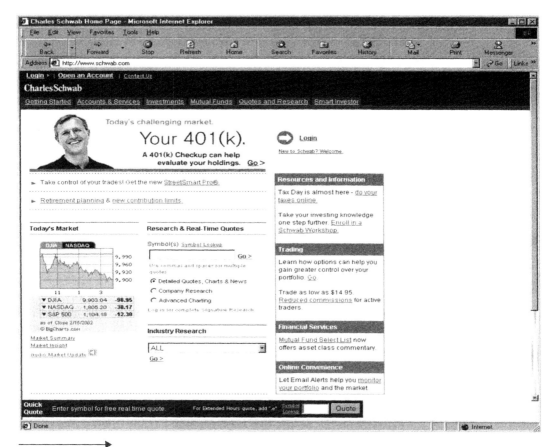

Figure 1.1   *The welcome page to Charles Schwab's highly successful corporate portal, which was initially implemented in 1996.*

instance, reflect the lower costs being incurred by the corporations. In this context, Charles Schwab & Company's portal, www.schwab.com, launched in 1996, serves as a great example of a personable, full-function, user-friendly corporate portal that always strives to ensure a warm, satisfying user experience.

Figure 1.1 depicts the "welcome" page of Schwab's portal. The numbers associated with this portal clearly attest to its success. In October 2001, more than 4.3 million customers maintained online accounts through schwab.com, with this portal averaging over 40 million hits a day. Online trading now accounts for nearly 80 percent of Schwab's total trading volume with over 169,000 online trades a day, on average, resulting in more than $8.5 billion in transaction values in a typical week. While it is true that this is a top-end, crème-de-la-crème corporate portal sustained by some hefty resources, these statistics do show, incontrovertibly, that it is no longer possible to stall the installation of a corporate portal by citing security, stability, and scalability concerns.

Corporate portals are thus, indubitably, on the ascent. XML and Web services, by accommodating authorized programmatic transactions in parallel to human interactions, will further broaden the potential, power, scope, and horizons of corporate portals. These XML-empowered corporate portals, with their additional functionality and interoperability capabilities, will ensure that e-business in general gains the traction and momentum it needs to break clear of the dot-com doldrums and establish a new, fortified beachhead vis-à-vis worldwide commerce.

1.1   What are corporate portals?

A corporate portal is a Web-based, fully automated emulation of a highly proficient, well-motivated call-center operation. A corporate portal is an elegant and efficient way to conduct most, if not all, business interactions hitherto transacted using telephones or faxes. Hence the association with call centers. An alternative name for corporate portals, during the early days, circa 1998, was "Internet call centers." Another often-used name is "self-service portals." Both of these alternative names clearly convey what a corporate portal is supposed to be.

Corporate portals ensure that anybody who has any interest in a corporation, whether it be customers, partners, suppliers, prospects, investors, employees, retirees, or well-wishers, always has immediate and ready access, 24/7, to all necessary information and services. XML and Web services will further extend the scope of corporate portals to include automated interactions with applications running on external computers, thus facilitating pervasive and productive e-business. Obviously, all of these interactions, whether involving humans or software, are always transacted over the Web (or a Web technology–based private network). Today's portal technology is also invariably client-type agnostic. Thus, ready access from mobile wireless devices such as Palm Pilots or even smart cell phones is not usually an issue and represents a fast-growing trend in portal usage. By 2005, voice-based interactions via digitized voice messages across the Web will not be uncommon.

Corporate portals eliminate "non-value-added" administrative intermediaries from the business transaction loop. With a corporate portal one does not have to deal by phone with a corporate intermediary seated in front of a PC and laboriously punching keys in order to obtain information or execute a transaction. Instead, one can, using a standard Web browser, directly obtain the necessary information without hindrance or perform the requisite transaction without being put on hold. That is the essential advantage of a good corporate portal. Corporate portals eliminate delays, frustrations, and inefficiencies—not to mention the infuriatingly annoying "press 9 to hear these options again" voice-response systems. Corporate portals expedite business interactions. They add agility to a corporation's business process cycle. They make people happy by giving them control and not wasting their time.

FedEx.com, another pioneering and well-implemented corporate portal, provides a compelling example of how portals can significantly expedite the time taken to execute a necessary transaction. Package tracking, especially if one is expecting money or gifts, has always been a valuable service regularly sought by corporations and individuals. Prior to the advent of www.fedex.com in 1994, most people had to call up 1-800-GoFedEx to obtain delivery status. Though FedEx tried hard to be responsive, there was no guarantee that you would always get straight through to a customer representative once you had successfully negotiated the inevitable voice-response front end. Then you would have to slowly enumerate the air-bill number and make sure that it had been correctly typed in. The FedEx portal revolutionized and turbocharged this whole process.

Provided you have access to the Internet, the FedEx portal enables you to track packages faster and get more detailed information about the path traversed by the package from the time it was picked up. Figure 1.2 provides a snapshot of the package-tracking function on FedEx's portal. This portal also enables you to do other things that had previously required a call to 1-800-GoFedEx, such as scheduling pickups or ordering more supplies. FedEx.com

Figure 1.2   *The package-tracking function on the FedEx portal, which debuted in 1994. A package-tracking function such as this is an ideal candidate to be made into a Web service.*

was the first of its genre, and FedEx, quite rightly, gained considerable competitive advantage by heavily promoting the advantages of portal-based interactions. Competitors had no choice but to follow FedEx's lead.

Online package-tracking applications are ideal candidates to be made into self-contained, self-describing, self-advertising Web services. In this respect, Web services can be thought of as a new breed of highly XML-centric Web applications. Other e-applications on the Web will be able to easily locate, invoke, and make use of these package-tracking Web services. Consequently, packaging-tracking functionality could be seamlessly embedded within other applications—for example, within an e-commerce order-status query application. Today, such e-commerce applications (e.g., amazon.com) provide you with an air-bill number and a hot link to the shipping company's portal so that you can manually track the package as a separate, disjunct task. Web services will automate this whole process and provide you with tracking information as an integral, inline part of the order-status query application.

1.1.1   Focal point for corporate information

A corporate portal is a secure, Web-based focal point of access to a broad range of corporate information, services, applications, and expertise. It will serve both internal and external users. Typically, all of this content and these services and applications are customized and personalized to the needs of different users or user groups. Thus, it is possible for partners and suppliers, for example, to have access to information and applications that are not made available to customers or prospects. Similarly, it is possible to ensure that employees have access to proprietary information and employee-specific applications (e.g., benefits management) that are kept hidden from and out of the reach of all other users.

This type of highly targeted personalization can be realized using user ID and password-based user authentication, digital certificates, or some form of user-identifying "cookie" (or applet) methodology. The explicit authentication approach, with or without digital certificates, obviously provides considerably greater control, privacy, and security than possible with a cookie scheme. Secure socket layer (SSL) and lightweight directory access protocol (LDAP) are pivotal technologies widely used to implement robust authentication schemes for corporate portals.

Personalization is one of the key features that differentiates a portal from a corporate home page. A Web page displayed by a portal (i.e., a portal view) typically consists of separate, autonomous windows, which are referred to by some as "portlets." Each window provides access to different content, services, or applications. Each of these windows can be personalized so that the entire portal view is explicitly customized to specific users.

A corporate home page, typically a corporation's first venture in establishing a public Web presence, does not generally offer personalized content. The other big difference between a corporate portal and a corporate home page lies in the bidirectional, self-service, transactional capabilities that are more or less a prerequisite for a portal to be a portal. A home page, at best, directs visitors to a call center or gives them an impersonal e-mail interface by which to contact the company. Consequently, personalization and self-service transactional capabilities are the two key features that clearly distinguish a corporate portal from a corporate home page.

Corporate portals are, in essence, private, company-specific variants of the Internet portals à la AOL, Yahoo!, and Lycos, which popularized and commoditized Web usage. Internet portals, which continue to flourish, thus serve as an ideal model for developing welcoming and productive corporate portals. The concepts, methodologies, technologies, and issues are essentially the same for both types of portals despite the differences in their targeted audiences. There are obviously some basic differences when it comes to scalability, security, and personalization concerns. While a corporate portal will never need to handle the traffic volumes encountered by AOL, a corporate portal that provides authorized access to sensitive data will typically have much greater security, authorization, and validation concerns.

Internet portals, nonetheless, are an invaluable incubator and proving ground for technologies and ideas that can be profitably used within corporate portals. Many of the innovations found on corporate portals have their roots in these large-scale, public portals. Therefore, anybody involved with implementing and sustaining a corporate portal should frequently peruse the major Internet portals to look for any new approaches, trends, or services that could be offered on their own company's portal. It should be noted that these public Internet portals, by necessity, have their own corporate portals. Figure 1.3 reproduces the "splash page" of Yahoo!'s corporate portal, showing the expected links for investors, advertisers, and potential business partners.

1.1.2   A logical portal serving both internal and external users

Corporate portals are also referred to directly or indirectly by a variety of other names, such as enterprise portals, e-business portals, intranet portals, and self-service portals. In some instances the different names are used to differentiate employees-only portals from those open to customers, suppliers, partners, and the like. Many still think of a corporate portal as being an employees-only portal (i.e., an intranet portal). Within this taxonomy, the term "enterprise portals" applies to those that can be used by external entities.

Today, arguments about the exact definitions of these terms are somewhat immaterial. Most mid-tier and larger corporations already had employees-only portals by 2000. The emphasis now is on the external-focus

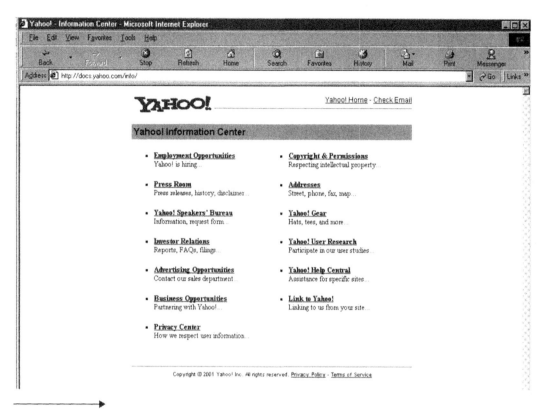

Figure 1.3   *Even companies with large public Internet portals such as Yahoo! have their own corporate portals to interact with investors, potential business partners, and prospective employees.*

portals to energize e-business, extend customer reach, enhance company productivity, and reduce transaction-processing costs.

Contemporary portal solutions (i.e., portal servers) offer rigorous authentication and strict rules-based access control to ensure that the same portal can, in theory, be safely used for both internal and external clients. Nonetheless, the exasperating and never-ending exploits of hackers, fraudsters, computer-virus creators, and disgruntled ex-employees guarantee that many a senior IT professional still has sleepless nights worrying about the security of vital corporate assets. Thus, most IT professionals, understandably, still want as many firewalls as possible between their intranets and the outside world. Consequently, having separate portal servers strictly demarcated between internal and external access with a firewall-enforced demilitarized zone (DMZ) in between is still common.

Figure 1.4 shows the general architecture of the split, internal-versus-external portal approach currently preferred by corporations. Despite the

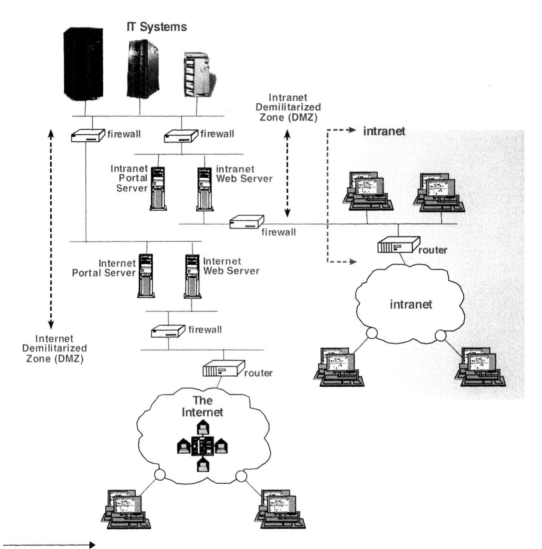

Figure 1.4   *The separate intranet and Internet split-portal approach currently preferred by corporations to maximize demarcation between resources accessible by in-house users versus those open to external users.*

firewalls separating them, the internal and external portals, obviously, share much of the same requirements, technologies, and, most likely, content. Therefore, it makes sense to think of them as being logically one, even though physically partitioned.

This book favors the concept that a corporate portal is a single logical entity serving both internal and external communities via the conventional portal methodologies for user authentication, access control, and personalization. The physical separation of the servers, though important in some discussions, does not have to continually get in the way. Consequently, the term "corporate portal" in the remainder of this book will refer to logical, "horizontal" portal implementations serving both internal and external users, even though the actual portal implementation may involve separate demarcated servers with a DMZ between them.

1.1.3   Aggregation, syndication, search, and collaboration

A corporate portal offers content aggregation, content syndication, search services, collaboration schemes, and access to applications (including Web services). "Content aggregation" in this context is the assimilation of information from diverse sources according to the personalization criteria for the target user and the presentation of it in the form of a navigable Web page replete with title bars, edit buttons, and scrolling controls. Content syndication permits diverse data from external sources, in multiple different formats, to be elegantly dovetailed into a corporate portal's overall framework in a consistent and systematic manner. Today, corporations can get a plethora of up-to-the-minute, topical information feeds pertaining to their line of business, ranging from scrolling stock tickers to breaking news from a variety of established "Web content retailers" (i.e., content syndicators).

Electronic Web content syndication of this type is but the Internet equivalent of the external material sourcing practice very successfully employed by newspapers for many decades for items such as comics, columns, and crosswords. Some of the content syndicators that can provide highly-pertinent feeds, including wireless-specific content, for corporate portals include YellowBrix.com (which includes the old iSyndicate), Factiva.com (a Dow Jones & Reuters company), Moreover.com, NewsKnowledge.com, and Hoovers.com. Web content syndicators are making a concerted attempt to deliver more and more of their content in XML form, using schemes such as news industry text format (NITF), XMLNews (which is a subset of NITF), publishing requirements for industry standard metadata (PRISM), rich site summary (RSS), and open content syndication (OCS).

A powerful and smart search capability is a prerequisite for a good corporate portal. Given the wealth of information that a portal contains, users will not be able to quickly locate specific information or services without the aid of an incisive search mechanism. Corporate information made accessible via a portal is likely to be located on a variety of different platforms, each with its own type of database and file structure. A portal's search mechanism thus needs to be able to deal with heterogeneous data sources ranging from legacy databases to XML documents stored on LINUX servers. It also needs to be able to conduct searches on multiple distributed sources, in parallel, and then combine and collate the results—ideally according to a ranking of relevance. This type of distributed search is referred to as a federated search. The major commercial portal server offerings from the likes of IBM, Oracle, iPlanet, and BEA include integrated search engines. In addition, the well-known Internet search engines such as Google, AltaVista, and NorthernLight now readily license their search-engine technologies to be used inside corporate portals.

Collaboration and application access are the other two key features of a representative corporate portal. E-mail, bulletin boards, and chat rooms with instant messaging are some of the basic forms of collaboration that can be offered by a portal. Calendering, customized for authorized groups spanning employees, partners, and suppliers, is a valuable and popular service. The next logical step is to offer browser-based, interactive, bidirectional, multimedia conferencing capabilities, such as those offered by WebEx.com, to facilitate cost-effective interactive virtual meetings, product demonstrations, and customized miniseminars across the Web.

Team collaboration tools are another much sought after and quick ROI option. Such tools are epitomized by such products as QuickPlace, from electronic collaboration stalwart Lotus, and BrightSuite, from DCA-Soft.com. Collaboration tools enable people scattered around the globe to coordinate tasks, schedules, decisions, and resources and conveniently share ideas, issues, and documents. They permit the controlled coauthoring of complex documents and enable lessons learned during a project to be captured, distilled, and distributed. Pertinent and topical information about collaboration and knowledge-management technologies and solutions can be found at www.collaboration-tools.com.

Application access vis-à-vis a corporate portal, though a multifaceted issue given the wide range of application types, user interfaces, platform diversity, and the application vintages involved, is typically not a stumbling block—anymore. A wide range of proven technologies from at least 200 companies are available to adapt any application, regardless of its original characteristics, for gainful use within the contexts of a portal. Web services, as will be discussed later, further simplify application location and invocation.

The online ticket-ordering option for the Guthrie Theater in Minneapolis at www.guthrietheater.org, shown in Figure 1.5, provides an irrefutable example of how even very old applications can be dramatically revamped

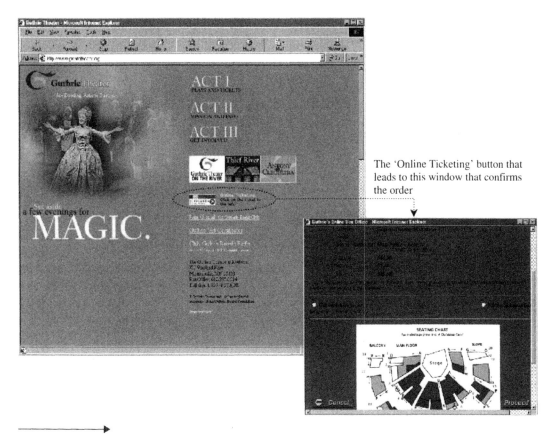

The 'Online Ticketing' button that leads to this window that confirms the order

Figure 1.5   *The online ticketing application on the Guthrie Theater portal shows how even an application developed in 1980 can still be gainfully utilized in the context of a portal.*

for a new lease on life on the Web. The back-end ticketing application at the core of this highly successful online initiative was originally purchased by the theater in 1981 to run on an IBM S/34—a very distant, indirect predecessor of the IBM AS/400 it is running on today. It is worth noting in this context that PCs as we know them now did not come into being until August 1981. Consequently, this application, now being used on the Web to sell over $35,000 of tickets online a month, predates PCs—never mind "www."

1.1.4   What is XML all about?

XML is a platform and programming language–independent scheme for sharing data in an unambiguous and consistent manner. XML is a meta-markup language for documents—in particular, documents containing structured information. Most documents have some level of structure in that the information they contain is invariably made up of content (e.g., text, graphics) and "context" (e.g., headings, tables, captions). XML's forte is its ability to clearly and cleanly describe the context and meaning of the data vis-à-vis that document.

HyperText Markup Language (HTML), the basis for defining nearly all Web pages until about the middle of 2001, in marked contrast to XML, does not concern itself with the meaning or context of the data it is dealing with. Instead, HTML focuses purely on how to display content. HTML is a content-formatting scheme; XML is not. Hence the fundamental difference between XML and HTML is that the former is a means for specifying the meaning of data and does not in any way deal with how the data should be presented, whereas the latter is all about data presentation and possesses no means to describe the meaning of the data being presented.

XML was never intended to be an enhancement or replacement for HTML. XML documents are typically displayed on a Web browser or a handheld device by associating a style sheet with the XML document. In some cases this can be achieved by simply using standard cascading style sheets (CSSs); CSS is a methodology that has been around since late 1996. Two other strategic ways to add formatting information to XML documents are the eXtensible Stylesheet Language (XSL) and Extensible HTML (XHTML). These schemes are described in Chapter 8. Figure 1.6, using a very simple example involving the contact information for a person, differentiates XML from HTML.

Sample HTML	**Sample XML**
`<p><b>Mr. Anura Guruge</b>` ` ` `Principal` ` ` `i-net guru` ` ` `4 Varney Point Road, Left` ` ` `Gilford, NH 03249` ` ` `USA` ` ` `anu@wownh.com</p>`	`<contact_info>` `<name>` `<salutation>Mr.</salutation >` `<first-name>Anura</first-name>` `<last-name> Guruge</last-name>` `</name>` `<title>Principal</title>` `<company> i-net guru</company>` `<address>` `<street>4 Varney Point Road, Left</street>` `<city>Gilford</city>` `.......` `</address>` `<e-mail>anu@wownh.com</e-mail>` `</contact_info>`

Figure 1.6   *A very simple example involving fragments of HTML and XML, using the contact data for a person, to highlight the similarities and differences between these two markup languages.*

Data (i.e., content) are included in an XML document as strings of text. The data are bracketed by XML text markup, which sets out to describe those data (i.e., give those data context). The basic building blocks of an XML document are called "elements"; an element is a specific unit of data along with the XML markup describing those data. The XML markup, in much the same way as HTML, is in the form of tags, with the tags appearing within angle brackets. XML, unlike HTML, is a metamarkup language. This means that XML does not contain a fixed set of tags and elements that has to be used by everybody. Instead, with XML you can define the elements you want as you go along. With XML you can design your own customized markup languages for limitless different types of documents. Thus, you can have elements specific to organizations and industries. This flexibility and extensibility is what the "extensible" part of XML refers to.

XML was formalized by the World Wide Web Consortium (W3C), www.w3.org, in February 1998. XML is derived from the Standard Generalized Markup Language (SGML), which became an ISO standard (ISO 8879) around 1985. SGML is the standard for defining descriptions of the structure of different types of electronic documents and has been widely used by the U.S. military, the U.S. government, and the aerospace industry during the past decade. HTML is also a derivative of SGML. SGML, by design, is very detailed, powerful, and complex. It was too unwieldy to be easily adopted for the Web and e-business. XML is "lite" SGML; it retains enough of the SGML functionality to make it useful but removes much of the optional and redundant features that make SGML so convoluted.

Since XML documents are always in text form, they can invariably be read and deciphered by humans. However, in order for an application to be able to successfully process an XML document it needs to know what the various elements represent. In other words, the application needs to know what the tags mean. Since the meaning of a tag can differ, significantly, between different organizations, countries, and industry sectors, an application really needs to know what each tag means within a specific "application domain." This is the rub when it comes to XML.

The fact that you have a well-formed XML document does not guarantee that it can and will be correctly interpreted by any and all applications. There are two different mechanisms available to facilitate the mutual understanding of XML documents: Document Type Definitions (DTDs) and XML Schemas. These mechanisms are described in Chapter 8. Industry and application-specific DTDs and XML schemas are already available, and many new ones are in the process of being defined, with ebXML (for electronic business XML for e-business) and tpaML (for Trading Partner Agreement Markup Language) being but two pertinent examples.

The rationale for XML, the reasons for its phenomenal popularity, and the politics behind all of the current hype surrounding XML are discussed in section 1.2.2.

1.1.5   What are Web services?

Web services are a new breed of Web applications. They are heavily XML oriented and based on protocols and definition schemes formalized in the 2000–2001 time period. The term "Web services" is thus something of a misnomer and somewhat confusing, since it invokes visions of key "backbone" services to facilitate Web transactions rather than readily conveying the concept of modular, XML-centric applications. A catchy term alluding to their XML centricity, such as "x-apps," might have been more helpful.

Web services are modular, self-contained, self-describing Web applications that can be published, readily located, and easily invoked across the Web. They now provide a standard, strategic, and consistent way to package business processes and make them available over the Web to interested and authorized parties. Whereas XML permits data to be shared, Web services permit business logic to be shared and reused. The potential and appeal of having the package-tracking applications offered by the likes of FedEx and UPS as Web services were discussed previously.

The possibilities of making other popular Web applications into Web services are endless and exciting. Just a very few, at random, include stock-quote applications, specialized search applications, "get-directions" applications, credit-card validation applications, and "find-the-cheapest-flight" applications. Applications such as these, when available as Web services, can be readily invoked and gainfully utilized by other applications (or other Web services) across the Web. A Web service "application" in essence thus becomes a reusable, remotely invoked, business-logic "object"—rather like a large JavaBean, where a JavaBean is a client-side Java object to facilitate reuse of program functionality. In a manner similar to object-oriented technology, Web services can thus significantly expedite new application development by obviating the need to reinvent functionality previously developed by others. The availability of feature-rich functionality in the form of Web services also enables new applications to offer additional capabilities.

Web services will have a profound impact on corporate portals. For a start they will help expand the business services available via a portal.

They will compress the development schedule for new applications and enable more incisive functionality to be added to your applications. If the applications being offered through your corporate portal are aimed at a wide external audience, then they should be packaged as Web services. The self-describing and self-advertising aspects of Web services will ensure that these applications are now readily visible and available to authorized entities—including other applications or Web services. Your corporate portal will become a bidirectional gateway for offering and accepting Web services.

In addition to XML, the key enabling technologies associated with Web services are simple object access protocol (SOAP), Web Services Description Language (WSDL), and universal description, discovery and integration (UDDI). SOAP, a W3C specification à la XML, is the preferred messaging protocol for Web services. SOAP is a platform and programming language agnostic. SOAP is XML based and as such is extensible. It is a simple, light-weight mechanism for exchanging structured and typed information (typically in the form of XML) between peers in a decentralized, distributed environment. Figure 1.7 provides a high-level view of the end-to-end Web services architecture, and Figure 1.8 shows how the Web services enabling technologies relate to each other.

SOAP is typically used over HyperText Transfer Protocol (HTTP), which is the protocol most often used between Web servers and Web browsers. SOAP, however, is not tied to HTPP. It can also be used across other transport schemes, such as native TCP (as in TCP/IP) and Simple Mail

Figure 1.7
The basic architecture of Web services showing the relationship between a Web service publisher, Web service subscribers, and the UDDI registry.

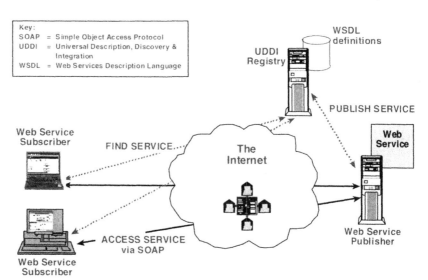

Figure 1.8
The basic relationship between the Web services enabling protocols.

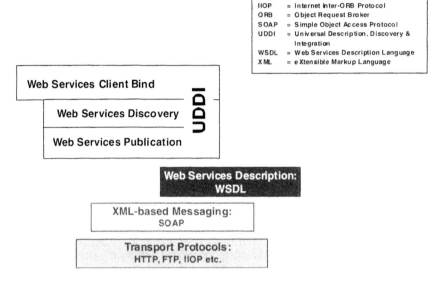

Key:
FTP   = File Transfer Protocol
HTTP   = HyperText Transfer Protocol
IIOP   = Internet Inter-ORB Protocol
ORB   = Object Request Broker
SOAP   = Simple Object Access Protocol
UDDI   = Universal Description, Discovery & Integration
WSDL   = Web Services Description Language
XML   = eXtensible Markup Language

Transfer Protocol (SMTP) as used by Internet e-mail and IBM's message-queuing MQSeries. SOAP is considered to be pivotal to the success and proliferation of Web services.

WSDL is an XML derivative for describing the functionality of Web services. WSDL satisfies the "self-describing" characteristic of Web services. Web services describe their operational model, interfaces, parameters, and binding requirements using WSDL. This WSDL-based definition of interfaces, parameters, and bindings ensures that a Web services "client" can readily invoke a remote Web service, programmatically, regardless of how or where the Web service is actually implemented.

The goal of UDDI is to create a platform-independent, Web-centric, open framework for describing applications, discovering businesses, and integrating business services. In other words, it sets out to create and maintain a worldwide machine-readable "yellow pages" for e-business. UDDI enables businesses (or individuals) to describe themselves in a standard and consistent manner so that other businesses can easily determine whether they could profit by conducting e-business with that company (or individual). UDDI, in effect, is a universal, Web-centric product and service advertising and syndicating mechanism. UDDI is XML-based and uses SOAP as its transport mechanism.

In addition to be being self-describing, thanks to WSDL, Web services are expected to be published on the Web so that they can be readily located and transparently invoked. UDDI is responsible for handling the publishing function as well as the locate and "bind" functions. The UDDI Publish function deals with how and when the provider of a Web service registers that "application," as well as itself as the provider of that Web service. The UDDI Find function addresses how a Web service "client" locates the description of a Web service or a provider of Web services. The UDDI Bind function then deals with how a client application connects and interacts with the appropriate Web service after locating it on the Web via its description.

1.2   Why do you need a corporate portal?

The simplest but most telling answer is that a corporate portal will help you, incontrovertibly, to reduce operational costs. This is not mere hyperbole or conjecture. The typical ROI for a medium-sized corporate portal (e.g., a corporation in the Fortune 1500 to 2000 range) is two years. This, moreover, is without even taking into account the increased business, the wider customer reach, improved user satisfaction, and enhanced competitiveness that also invariably come with having a good corporate portal. The major direct cost-saving opportunities afforded by a corporate portal are by now well established, proven, and beyond debate. The top ten of these, in no particular order, include the following:

- Realizing significant reduction in call-center operation costs through staffing cuts, reduction in operational hours, and call-center consolidation in the case of multiple call-center operations

- Minimizing transaction-processing and data-entry costs (e.g., accounts payable, order processing, or material ordering) by permitting direct online interactions

- Generating huge savings in remote-access costs by enabling mobile and remote employees to securely access all necessary corporate resources, across the Internet, via the portal—which, in some cases, can result in as much as a 95 percent lowering of costs

- Tangibly decreasing all costs associated with mail, mail handling, mailrooms, and express delivery services (e.g., FedEx) by reducing the need for both incoming and outgoing correspondence

- Diminishing the spending associated with advertising, public relations, and investor relations, with the portal now serving as the primary means of disseminating corporate information and news

- Creating a marked drop in inbound (i.e., 1-800) and outbound telecommunications charges as well as the ability to dispense with now unneeded call-center equipment

- Lowering the printing, production, and distribution costs connected with company brochures, annual reports, product data sheets, investor reports, and other such collateral by publishing all of these documents, including those requiring online authorization prior to access,

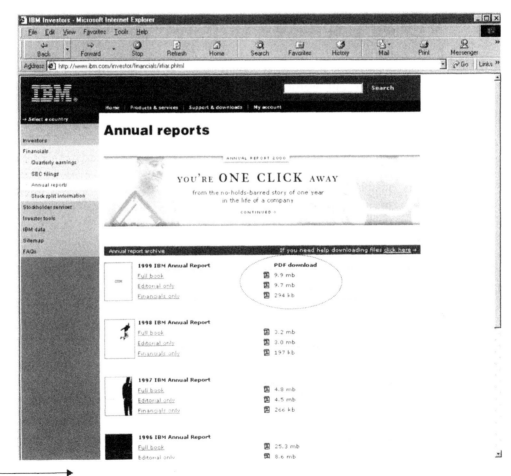

Figure 1.9   *IBM's portal showing how Adobe Acrobat PDF documents can be gainfully used to deliver high-quality, high-resolution documents in their original format.*

on the portal as downloadable, high-resolution Adobe Acrobat "portal data format" (PDF) documents, which can then be printed by the user. Figure 1.9 shows a portal offering corporate documents in the form of PDFs.

- Reducing the costs involved in filing, electronic capture, archiving, and disposal of paper documents (e.g., bills, invoices, statements) by promoting paperless transactions, including electronic check payments, through the portal. Figure 1.10 shows electronic check payment of credit-card accounts as offered by the Discover card corporate portal.

- Decreasing the operational costs connected with customer and product support groups by encouraging "first-level" support via the Web— if necessary, using Microsoft as a model for such online support

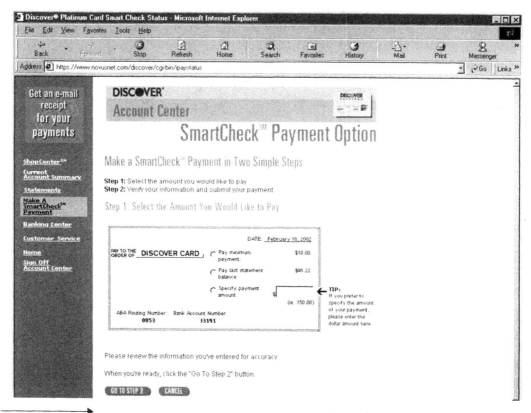

Figure 1.10   *Electronic check-payment scheme available on many portals—in this instance, the Discover credit card.*

- Eliminating nonstrategic remote offices and offering customers and prospects additional services, possibly at a lower cost à la the discount online trading philosophy

In addition to these palpable and quantifiable direct cost-reduction possibilities, a corporate portal can significantly improve the sacrosanct bottom line of a company in numerous other ways, including:

- Increased productivity within departments that have to deal with outside parties (e.g., accounts payable, purchasing, order processing) by reducing the number of telephone call interruptions they receive

- Better overall efficiency across the company by ensuring that most administrative tasks, especially those related to benefits management, stock option administration, time or project management, and supply ordering can be quickly, effectively, and decisively performed via the portal

- Reducing overhead and expediting the approval process for routine tasks (e.g., check requisitions, p.o. requests, invoice acceptance) by ensuring that the whole process, including any external interactions, is strictly electronic and is coordinated using collaborative tools provided by the portal

- Improving corporate cash flow by encouraging online payments by customers as well as leveraging portal-based just-in-time production and supply-chain management techniques

- Minimizing lost opportunity costs by ensuring that no business is lost because customers or partners despair of trying to get through to a company representative

- Fostering strong customer loyalty (and attracting new customers) by respecting their time pressures and enabling them to do more things more quickly and simply than ever before (e.g., pay bills, change addresses, renew subscriptions, transfer assets)

- Gaining access to a much wider customer, partner, and supplier base, around the world at no additional marketing cost, to increase business and potentially to get needed supplies on better terms

- Exploiting the automated, extensive, and "standardized" data interchange capabilities offered by XML and Web services, within the framework of the portal, to continue reducing operational costs by further leveraging paperless, online b2b e-business processes for as many tasks as possible—thus bypassing voice mails, hard-to-read faxed statements, and redundant data entry

- Reducing lost opportunity costs and improving productivity at the managerial and executive levels by guaranteeing rapid, up-to-date access to all key corporate data by enabling employees, remote offices, mobile workers, partners, and suppliers to enter critical business data into the appropriate MIS systems via secure and user-friendly "front-end" interfaces provided by the corporate portal

- Further maximizing the investment in current IT applications and wring additional ROI out of them by extending their useful life by reusing their proven business logic within the portal—if necessary with HTML, XML, or Web services front ends.

1.2.1   A big investment with a positive ROI

A simple but indelible lesson I learned at my local post office in Laconia, New Hampshire, clearly demonstrates the cost savings inherent in automating and eliminating the paperwork associated with even a relatively simple transaction. The U.S. Postal Service (USPS), in marked contrast to other agencies (e.g., the U.S. Internal Revenue Service), does not charge a surcharge or convenience fee on top of the purchase price to cover the 3 percent to 8 percent commissions that credit-card companies charge for each transaction. The USPS absorbs this commission cost regardless of the dollar value of the transaction.

This seems incongruous, because in essence it translates to buying our first-class stamps at a "discount." When asked about this apparent anomaly, a friendly postal worker went on to explain that it is cheaper for the post office to accept credit-card payments, even for $5, than to handle cash or a check. At the end of the day, checks and cash have to be counted by at least three different people and their amounts reconciled. Then there is all the paperwork related to depositing this money in the bank. On the other hand, the credit-card transactions, once swiped in, are handled centrally without the need for as much manual intervention at each post office. The cost savings of this are greater than the commissions paid to the credit-card companies.

Now extrapolate this cost-saving model to your business. Determine the number of paperless transactions that could easily be performed over a portal and the amount of revenue you could collect directly by accepting payments in credit-card or electronic check form via the portal (see Figure 1.10). The cost-saving opportunities and possibilities should be numerous and obvious. The exact ROI for implementing and sustaining a portal and the time taken for the ROI to become positive will vary, depending on the nature and size of your business; as mentioned previously, two years is common for a medium-sized business. You should by now be getting a comfortingly warm and fuzzy feeling that this is one IT project that is unlikely to backfire in terms of ROI, given the multiple cost-saving possibilities coupled with all the ways to increase the reach and scope of your business.

Implementing a corporate portal is not a trivial, low-cost undertaking. To think otherwise would be imprudent to say the least. For a start, building a portal will involve a sizable investment in equipment (e.g., servers), infrastructure software (e.g., a portal server), security software, Internet connection, and development tools. This "capital" cost, however large, will nonetheless be equaled if not exceeded by the cost of planning, designing, prototyping, implementing, and testing the portal. A lot of this cost will, understandably, go toward obtaining and customizing the necessary content, applications, and services. All of this, which could easily run into millions of dollars rather quickly, are just the start-up costs.

The costs involved with a corporate portal will not abate once it is up and running. For a corporate portal to be productive and successful it has to be continually updated, maintained, monitored, and nurtured. Content needs to be updated as necessary. New applications and services need to be provided per a preestablished schedule. The workload and traffic statistics of the portal need to be monitored, at least weekly, to ensure that performance expectations are being met and that users are not being frustrated by sluggish response times. Most important, the business milestones associated with the portal—whether they be the number of successful transactions per day, the amount of revenue generated per week, or just the number of overall hits per hour—need to be assiduously tracked, charted, and reported.

To achieve all of this you will, of course, require an unequivocal mandate from senior management, designated people, and a realistic budget. The corporate portal has to be seen and accepted as a major component of the company's operational plan. It will become a key part of the overall IT functions. Marketing and sales will rely on it. In reality you will need a team dedicated to maintaining the portal. Since your corporate portal will end up being a superset of what was your original Web site, this portal team will invariably include your current Web maestros and designers. But since a portal includes applications and services, you will need access to programming resources as well. The bottom line is that a corporate portal is a big investment.

The capital and operational costs of a portal, though indubitably steep, are still reasonable compared with the costs of running a call center. And that is the crux. A corporate portal allows you to do more with less, the less applying specifically to head count. That is where the big cost savings come from to begin with. Thus, corporate portals exemplify the management mantra about the need to work smarter. A corporate portal is the smart way to get more done while reducing costs.

1.2.2   Why XML and Web services?

XML enables all types of information to be exchanged across disparate systems in an easier and better manner than was possible in the past. XML provides data from disparate applications and platforms with a standardized "interchange" format. With XML it does not matter whether the data were produced by a proprietary application and originally structured in a manner that could be interpreted only by that application. XML thus becomes a standard way to describe structured data irrespective of whether those data belong to a spreadsheet, an electronic address book, a CRM application, an operating system configuration file, a financial transaction, or a technical drawing.

A simple example will help put XML into perspective. Microsoft's Excel spreadsheet application is widely used in the business world as a ready means to store, represent, and analyze a wide spectrum of data types ranging from simple financial records to complicated supply chain management details. Though widespread, Excel, to Microsoft's chagrin, is not ubiquitous and never will be. Thus, sharing Excel spreadsheets, which are in a proprietary Microsoft format, with those using different applications can be a challenge, though, to be fair, there is a plethora of various application-specific "filters" to facilitate such interworking.

Converting the Excel data to plain text, though always an option, is not optimum since this strips the data of their inherent structure and context. Using this example, assume that you would like to exchange data between an IBM mainframe–based manufacturing scheduling application, a supplies control program running on a UNIX server, and an Excel spreadsheet that keeps track, in real time, of customer orders. Even though writing the necessary conversion tools is an option, this still makes this whole process application specific and hinders your ability to introduce different applications into this processing chain. This is where XML comes in and saves the day.

Microsoft Excel 2002, as found in Microsoft Office XP, supports bidirectional XML. You can now save Excel spreadsheets as XML documents, replete with all of the formulas used in the spreadsheet and definitions of how the data are formatted within the spreadsheet. Excel can also open XML documents that include data that are appropriate for a spreadsheet. XML thus facilitates data interchange in an application-independent and extensible manner. This is why XML is so crucial to the future of corporate portals. XML ensures that the applications and services implemented within a corporate portal will not be hampered when it comes to importing or exporting data.

Thanks to XML, it will be possible for your ERP applications to exchange pertinent data, automatically, with your suppliers' order processing applications. Using XML, your partners' CRM applications running on PCs could automatically update your master customer records database maintained on an IBM AS/400 minicomputer—even though each partner is using a proprietary CRM application obtained from a different vendor and you have just migrated your database from NT to the AS/400 as a part of the portal implementation.

XML will also, in time, add meaning and structure to the Web page content of corporate portals to facilitate, at a minimum, meaningful information searches and the ability for some of these data to be automatically accessed and processed by applications running on other portals (e.g., a partner's or supplier's portal). Today's HTML-centric Web page content is devoid of context. Hence, a search for a keyword such as "bill," using any of the popular Web search engines (e.g., Google.com), will return thousands of entries covering people's names (e.g., Bill Gates), laws (e.g., Bill of Rights), theater play lists, and monetary notes. IBM's search engine suggests trying the keyword "chip," which can result in topics spanning microchips to chipmunks, interspersed with entries for chocolate-chip cookies and people named Chip.

XML-based content will eliminate such confusion and enable quicker, more incisive, and automated access to pertinent information. So rather than having HTML-based Web pages, future corporate portals will rely more and more on XML-defined Web pages. Technology such as eXtensible Stylesheet Language (XSL) will then be leveraged to format and present those data, attractively, for human consumption.

The bottom line here is that XML sweeps aside the incompatibility hurdles that have hitherto hampered genuine any-to-any data interchange between disparate applications. XML, as it becomes more and more pervasive and entrenched, will eliminate today's lead times and costs when it comes to interfacing your applications with those of your suppliers, your partners, and even your customers. XML will make the data interchange requirements of corporate portals a reality.

1.2.3   Why Web services?

What XML is for structured data, Web services are for applications. Whereas XML permits data to be readily shared across disparate platforms, Web services enable applications to be shared across disparate and distributed platforms. Web services, which are highly XML-centric, thus complement XML. Ironically, however, Web services also minimize to an extent the need for data interchange. With Web services, rather than having to move data from one application to another, you have the option of directly using the native application.

It is the availability of interactive, transactional applications and services that differentiate corporate portals from plain, information-only Web sites. Hence the significance of Web services. Web services standardize the process for "publishing" easily locatable and readily accessible applications on your portal. Web services also provide you with the capability to easily reuse the business logic of existing applications relative to the Web. In this context you can think of the Web services enabling protocols as Web-specific, middleware schemes for locating and invoking remote, reusable business logic "objects"—a business logic object in this case could be a modular application in its own right. Thus, the Web services enabling protocols are a kind of Web equivalent to previous object invocation schemes such as CORBA, Microsoft's DCOM, and the Java-oriented RMI.

A package-tracking application, as previously discussed, is a good candidate to be made into a generic reusable Web service. This would obviate the need for others to develop their own versions of this functionality or be forced to refer users to an external site (e.g., FedEx or UPS) so that they can check on the status of a delivery. If your portal could benefit from having a built-in package-tracking capability, you would now seek to obtain this functionality as a Web service. You would be able to buy the Web services application and implement it on one of your servers. However, given the inherent remote invocation capabilities of Web services, you may instead opt just to subscribe to the application. More than likely you will have this functionality as a part of an overall order-processing application. Consequently, the remote invocation can be totally transparent to the end users.

In a similar vein, Web services could obviously be used to obtain a plethora of core portal-related functionality. Security-related functions such as user authentication immediately come to mind. But the possibilities are immense and unlimited. If you intend to accept payments via credit cards, you could obtain all the necessary credit-card approval functionality as a Web service that could be transparently embedded into your order-processing application. Web services could also be used to handle international currency-rate conversions, shipping-rate calculations, language translation, and customer-satisfaction surveys.

The self-description side of Web services, achieved using WSDL, simplifies the process of locating and identifying the applications that will best suit your needs. In much the same way that you can get syndicated content for your portal, as discussed earlier, you will soon be able to get "syndicated" portal functionality in the form of Web services. A company called Web-Collage (www.webcollage.com) is already offering a service whereby it will take existing Web applications and turn them into Web services. The bottom line here is that Web services, in essence, will be the long-term, strategic means by which your portal will provide applications and services in the future, starting around 2005.

1.3   When should you implement a corporate portal?

"As soon as possible," is the short and quick answer to the above question. However, it is unlikely to be that simple; if it was, you would most likely already be in the throes of implementing your portal. Implementing a corporate portal is not an undertaking to be taken lightly on a whim. A corporate portal will change your company's business model. These changes will percolate through the company and impinge upon many groups within the company. In addition, sustaining the portal will require active cooperation from multiple departments ranging from accounting to sales. Consequently, you should not even think about implementing a portal until you have a clear and concrete mandate from the highest management levels of your company.

Such a mandate will be the culmination of what will inevitably be an iterative, protracted justification and rationalization process. Senior managers, though appreciating, viscerally, that the company's long-term future is indeed contingent on having a successful portal, will require constant reassuring as to its technical and economic viability. Although they would have heard, seen, and read about the success other organizations have had with portals, they will still be anxious and edgy and want guarantees that the risk exposure is minimal and accounted for. They will want to see what the competition is doing and demand various presentations and reports from in-house and external experts as well as the key vendors.

More than likely you will end up having to create a rigorous, full-blown business case specifically for the portal to adequately address all of the management-level concerns. Preparing such a business case is actually a good idea. It will force you to be crisp and clear about the business goals, anticipated costs, intended ROI, and the implementation schedule. At a minimum it will take you six months to develop an acceptable business case. If you are lucky, you could then look for a final approval cycle of about three months—but that in turn could be at the mercy of a variety of other external factors, such as budget cycles, board meeting schedules, and the obligatory company reorganizations. So if you are starting from scratch, it is going to take you in excess of nine months before you have the mandate, and hopefully the budget, for your portal.

1.3.1   A corporate portal is mission critical

When planning a corporate portal you have to constantly keep in mind that it is going to be a key mission-critical asset. Think about your other mission-critical IT applications and all of the issues related to ensuring their integrity, resilience, and performance. Your corporate portal will require as much, but most likely considerably more, care and attention as your most important mission-critical application. The reason for this is obvious. The corporate portal will become the gateway to your other mission-critical applications. If it malfunctions, and that includes unacceptable response times, then you are compromising access to everything behind it.

One of the few bad things about a portal is that having a poor portal is worse than not having one at all. A sluggish, unreliable portal with missing pages and links will alienate users, whether customers, partners, or suppliers, and will result in lost business and customer defections. Consequently, as with other widely used mission-critical applications, you have to devote painstaking attention to all aspects of a portal's implementation, from selecting the right server platform to testing and retesting all of the functionality, to make sure that they will not let you down.

Your Web site, though important, is probably not mission critical in the strictest sense, because a couple of hours of downtime is unlikely to result in a tangible loss of revenue. Any unscheduled downtime on your portal, however, could impact your bottom line and, even worse, result in threats of litigation. The latter is most likely if your portal deals with time-sensitive financial transactions such as online stock trading. A portal failure or inordinately sluggish performance could result in users not being able to execute trades in a timely manner. If this happened during a time when the market was particularly volatile, your customers could legitimately claim that they lost money because your portal was not working. If this is a potential vulnerability, then you would have to work with your legal department so that you could get users to accept service-level agreements that indemnify your company from certain types of litigation.

Given this mission criticality, it is best that you have somebody with considerable proven experience in maintaining mission-critical applications on your portal team—even if it is just as a part-time devil's advocate. Ensuring the near 99.99 percent uptime sought for mission-critical applications is both a science and an art. One apparently innocuous detail overlooked during the planning and implementation stage—for example, having a firewall or Internet connection that is a single point of failure—could prove to be fatal. People with hands-on experience in maintaining mission-critical applications are usually adept at quickly detecting potential weak links and working out ways to get around such problems.

1.3.2   A phased implementation

A corporate portal will be implemented in phases. It is not unusual to allocate one to two years for such a phased implementation, given the tasks involved and the need to guarantee mission-critical operation. The corporate portal will also naturally evolve and mature during this period, being nudged and prodded by user demands as well as in-house requests. Typically, a corporate portal will be built on your existing Web site. If you already have an intranet portal, you may start with that as your basis. In many cases, however, the Web site is a better starting point from a security standpoint, because you already permit external, Internet-based access to it. If you start with your Web site, you will take what is already there in terms of content and then start adding new transactional functionality in a planned, systematic manner.

Adding functionality for business partners is invariably a good and safe place to start—given that they, in theory, are supposed to be on your side. Partners, in addition to being a more self-contained and definable user group to deal with, are also likely to be supportive, accommodating, and eager to proffer constructive criticism. It is a good way to check out critical core features, such as user authentication, search engine efficacy, and the implications of using XML to represent certain content. If you are planning to offer Web services, use your partners as a testbed at this juncture. You could keep others away from the functionality that is being tested in one of two ways.

One option is to use a "private" (i.e., unpublished) URL at the origination of your partner section. Then you can control who will participate in the testing process by selectively providing this URL only to the chosen partners. A major advantage of this approach is that the whole world does not need to know that you are in the process of implementing a portal. You can thus control when partners, suppliers, customers, and investors will hear about your portal plans. But this might, however, not be a big issue. Implementing a portal is a good thing, and most people will be waiting for you to do so. The only negative is that you might get more requests than you want from people wanting to help you test the new functionality.

The other option is to rely on user authentication to control access to the functionality being tested. With this approach, you would go ahead and add a "partner" button (or link) on your existing home page. This button would take users to the partner section. They would not, however, be able to enter this section without a user ID and password. A key justification for this approach is that it implements and tests the exact processes and paths that will be used by the production system. The disadvantage is that anybody visiting your Web site will be able to see that you are implementing a section for partners. Partners not previously privy to this information may take umbrage. But you could get around that by saying that the partner section is still not ready for external access.

The bottom line is that implementing a corporate portal is not going to be a quick-and-dirty rush job. Instead it will require lots of foresight and planning. The implementation, by necessity, will also need to be phased. This will ensure that the overall design and technology can be tested and refined with a limited number of friendly users. During this phased implementation the portal will mature and evolve. That is normal and positive. If you are starting today with a blank sheet, then make sure you have at least 12 months for planning and implementation before you commit to having a mission-critical portal ready for production use by customers.

1.4   **What have others done with portals?**

Though industry research firms are predicting a huge surge in the number of corporate portals that will be implemented in the 2003–2006 time frame, it is important to remember that there were already thousands of slick, full-function corporate portals in production at the start of 2001. In reality, corporate portal technology and methodology, excluding XML and Web services, are highly proven in that these portals have been around since the mid-1990s. The FedEx portal went online in 1994, and Charles Schwab introduced its two years later.

Financial firms, banks, and travel companies were in the forefront when it came to pioneering and popularizing corporate portals. These industry sectors, with their heavy dependence on "1-800" call centers, were obviously ideal candidates to immediately benefit from the customer reach and automated transactional capabilities of portals. Looking at any of the big names within these sectors will, of course, provide you with examples of sophisticated and sprawling corporate portals. Thus, fidelity.com, the portal for the financial services behemoth Fidelity Investments, as shown in Figure 1.11, is expansive and covers a lot of ground, including sections that deal with specific international geographies.

Though these top-tier corporate portals indubitably validate the promise of portals, they may in many cases be just be slightly too "grand" to serve as templates for what you want to achieve. The corporate portals of smaller companies in each of these fields may be more appropriate. Hence, look at

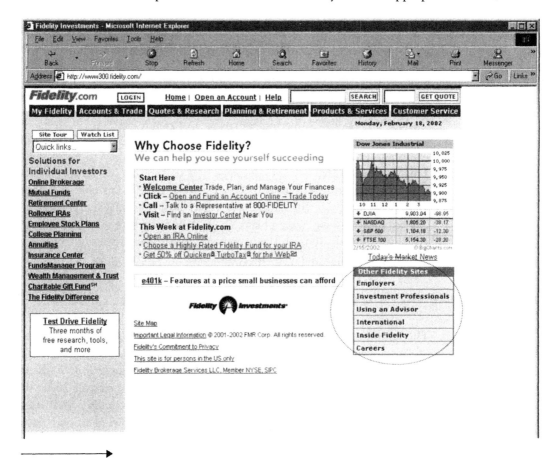

Figure 1.11   *Fidelity Investments's expansive corporate portal with links to other portals including geography-specific portals.*

the likes of janus.com, massmutual.com, suntrust.com, or citizens-bank.com. Note that the latter two offer multiple separate logon options based on customer type or the function you are trying to perform. You may, however, decide to offer a unified logon process and then steer the users to the right section within the portal once they have been authenticated and checked in. This is the advantage of looking at existing portals. They will provide you with ideas and inspiration and show you what works and what might not.

The corporate portals of companies that are in the "business," so to speak, are also good examples—though once again the portals of the likes of IBM or Sun fall into the category of "grand." The portal of networking leader Cisco is worth a visit. Cisco, with its vested interest in furthering Web-based business, was an early and vocal advocate of portal-based electronic transactions, whether it be for accepting orders, providing technical support, or closing the firm's financial books at the end of each fiscal quarter. The portal of Jacada, an Israeli company specializing in leveraging host system assets, is another good example of a portal in that it has clearly defined areas for customers, partners, investors, and prospective employees. Yet again, these just happen to be examples that I am familiar with. You should look around and find your own favorites.

There is just one other site that you may wish to visit: navarre.com. Navarre Corporation out of New Hope, Minnesota, is one of the largest distributors of consumer software, music, DVDs, and home videos to traditional retailers (e.g., office supplies giant Staples) as well as to Web-oriented "e-tailers" (e.g., Amazon). Navarre was a pioneer of Internet-based, portal-centric b2b e-business. The firm had an active portal at the start of 1999 through which it was channeling supply chain management and funds-transfer activity. Vendors (e.g., music companies) that wish to distribute their wares through Navarre have no choice but to conduct most of their transactions, including inventory-level management, through the portal.

1.5   What do you have to lose?

Not having a corporate portal will diminish your competitive edge. Time, more so than ever before, is a scarce and precious commodity for most people. Portals are one of the few and guaranteed ways that they can "buy" themselves some time within their busy schedules and allow them to better utilize other facets of their lives. Portals eliminate being put on hold by call centers. Portals obviate the need for office visits. Portals do, irrefutably, make people's lives easier.

People have realized that good corporate portals can simplify their lives. Doing business over the Internet is no longer a novelty or a scary experience. People are getting more and more used to relying on the Web to get things done. Consequently, if they had to choose between a company that offered a slick and helpful portal versus one that still expected you to deal with a call center for all your needs, most would opt for the convenience of the portal approach. That is why a good corporate portal is so vital for maintaining your competitive edge.

Credibility is the other thing that you can lose by not having a corporate portal. The loss of credibility could, in addition, be twofold. Your company, as a whole, could lose credibility within the industry and the market, with partners, suppliers, investors, and customers wondering why you don't have a portal when others of your ilk do. The loss of credibility could, however, also reflect on your IT department. While it is possible that your portal plans are being undermined by budgets, politics, paranoia, or reorganizations, there will be some, both within your company and outside, who will assume that the lack of a corporate portal is due to the IT department's not being able to get its act together.

The bottom line is that not having a corporate portal is not really going to be a viable option going forward. In the mid-1990s the big issue was that of implementing a Web site so that a company would have a presence on the Web. Some companies were quicker to do this than others. Today this is a given. It is hard to find a company of any reasonable size that does not have a Web presence. Some of the TV commercials that IBM did a few years ago featuring mom-and-pop cottage industries from around the world drove home this point, and there is still a lingering memory of Tuscan olive oil producers promoting their wares over the Web. Corporate portals are the next inevitable evolutionary step in this Web assimilation process for corporations.

1.6   What can you gain?

To answer the above question by saying "fame, fortune, and kudos" seems trite, but it certainly does capture the upside rewards of implementing a corporate portal. The downside risks involved with implementing a corporate portal, given today's technology and expertise, are small, definable, and, as such, confinable. The upside rewards will always outweigh the downside risks by a wide margin. Franklin Delano Roosevelt's well-known restatement of a sentiment originally expressed by the Duke of Wellington— "The only thing we have to fear is fear itself"—always appears to be apropos when discussing the need for corporate portals.

Given that the tangible and intangible advantages of corporate portals have been already discussed in some detail, it is best to reprise some of the key factors using credible, external sources. SAP, the ERP giant with 36,000 installations and 10 million users of its various software offerings, identifies the following as the real business benefits of implementing an enterprise portal:

- Increased productivity

- Accelerated resolution of business issues with reduced effort

- Improved user experience and individual efficiency because of role-based information

- Improved customer, partner, and supplier relationships thanks to collaboration within and beyond organizational boundaries

- Streamlined, single point of access to important data regardless of time, location, or device

- Improved queries through federated searches that allow users to extract relevant results much faster and to see results in context

You can, of course, get similar confirmations from other major vendors such as IBM, Oracle, Computer Associates, and BEA. But it is beneficial to look also at what some of the smaller companies in this sector (e.g., Plumtree, Vignette, and Corechange) have to say. Notice that the message, across the vendors, despite their different vantage points, is remarkably consistent and thus reassuring. It would be best to let Vignette have the last word with its pithy summary of what the firm sees as the advantages of corporate portals: Streamline operational costs, increase customer satisfaction and loyalty, and drive revenues through long-lasting relationships.

1.7 Why have people procrastinated?

Justifiable concerns about security have been the primary reason that many have shied away from implementing corporate portals in the past. Though security threats, unfortunately, continue to increase rather than decrease, fears about security exposures cannot be used forever as the excuse for not offering a portal. This goes back to the discussion about upside rewards versus downside risks. Obviously, thousands of companies, many with sensitive assets, already have corporate portals, and quite a few have had portals for a good number of years.

The challenge, when it comes to security, is to identify and implement the security measures that address your unique requirements. The good news is that there is no shortage of security technology and proven solutions, whether it be for firewalls, user authentication, encryption, or single sign-on. The popularization of Web services is likely to further increase the options available for obtaining the security functionality you need, as vendors, including the likes of Microsoft with its Passport initiative, start to offer proven security solutions in the form of Web services.

When it comes to portal security, one size is unlikely to fit all. You will have to carefully determine what your exact security needs are and what steps you should take to implement security measures that meet, if not exceed, your requirements. However, keep in mind that there is a danger that you could become overzealous and possibly even paranoid. It may be prudent to hire some credible external consultants to recommend suitable security strategies that could then be evaluated by your in-house experts. Get multiple perspectives and options so as to cover the security issues from as many different angles as possible. Look at some of the portals mentioned in this chapter and see what kinds of security they offer. Refer to section 4.1 for further details on security options. The bottom line when it comes to security is that while it is indeed of paramount concern, there is enough proven technology around to ensure pretty good, if not totally infallible, security.

Post-Y2K depression, the IT equivalent of the postpartum affliction, was another bona fide factor that hampered the implementation of corporate portals. After the energies and moneys expended on Y2K compliance, most IT departments needed and were entitled to a hiatus from any new major IT initiatives. The dot-com implosion, which was closely followed by the worldwide economic slowdown, did not help matters. But much of this is now history, and corporate portals are high on IT, as well as corporate agendas.

Budget constrains were another impediment, and some were related to the Y2K "overspend." Management, however, is now beginning to realize that corporate portals are a way to reduce overall corporate expenditure without sacrificing services offered or customer reach. There is a growing realization, thanks to all of the successful portals around, that corporate portals will allow you to do more with less expenditure. In essence, the ROI potential of corporate portals is promising and palpable.

Technology was never a bottleneck when it came to realizing corporate portals. The good news is that the necessary infrastructure technology continues to grow and mature and to become even more affordable. New technologies such as XML and Web services further enhance the potential of corporate portals. The bottom line is that there really are no genuine impediments, either technical or business related, to postpone the implementation of a corporate portal. The necessary technology is highly proven and readily available from multiple credible vendors. The business case is unimpeachable. A corporate portal will, at a minimum, reduce costs, increase productivity, maximize reach, foster customer loyalty, enhance revenues, bolster customer satisfaction, and accelerate the speed of business transactions and decisions.

1.8   Q&A—A time to recap and reflect

Q: What is a corporate portal?

A: A corporate portal is a secure, Web-based, easy-to-use, focal point of access to a diverse range of corporate information, services, applications, and expertise—to both internal and external users. It is the foundation for creating a sound and extensive Web-based corporate operation. It is in effect a Web-based, fully automated emulation of a utopian, 24/7 call-center operation where customers, partners, prospects, suppliers, and investors will always be able to get what they want without ever being put on hold or made to jump through hoops of a voice-response system. It is the optimum way to conduct most of the business transactions previously transacted using telephones, faxes, or express mail.

Q: How does a corporate portal differ from a "home page" Web site?

A: A corporate portal differs from a static, "home page" Web site in two fundamental ways: personalization and transactional capability. The content, applications, and services available via a corporate portal can and will be tailored and personalized to meet the exact demands of specific users or user groups, who will be identified through an authentication process or via a "self-describing" scheme involving some kind of "cookie" (or applet) technology. Corporate portals also enable authorized users to conduct bidirectional self-service transactions—query account balances, make payments using credit cards or electronic checks, order goods or services, or check the status of an order delivery, among other things.

Q: Do corporate portals facilitate e-business?

A: Yes. Corporate portals provide a uniform, streamlined, and extensible framework for e-business. While it is possible to implement certain e-business processes (e.g., supply-chain management) without having one, a corporate portal will add structure, cohesion, and consistency to a corporation's overall e-business strategy. Rather than doing each e-business initiative in piecemeal fashion, a corporate portal can be used as a common infrastructure, replete with core services (e.g., authentication, host data access, company news broadcast) for all current and future e-business projects.

Q: Is a corporate portal different from an enterprise portal?

A: Yes and no, depending on the somewhat arbitrary use of these terms. The term "corporate portal" is being increasingly used to describe an integrated portal offering that can serve both internal and external users. This book assumes that a corporate portal is a single, logical entity with powerful security, personalization, and content-partitioning capabilities that ensure that it can be safely used by multiple disparate user audiences spanning both corporate employees and nonemployees. The term "enterprise portal" is used by some to describe portals that are reserved for external entities—as opposed to the intranet portals that are for in-house users. What is important here is to have a clear and consistent understanding as to what the term means in a particular context. If in doubt, seek clarification as to the scope of the portal being referred to by these terms or for that matter any of the other terms, which include self-service portals, enterprise information portals, e-business portals, and the like.

Q: Weren't corporate portals the cause of the dot-com collapse?

A: Most assuredly not. While most dot-coms, by their very nature, relied heavily on corporate portals to promote their message and gain business, the failure of the dot-coms was the result of poor business models rather than anything to do with the nature of corporate portals. Corporate portals are being successfully and profitably used by companies of all sizes around the world, ranging from the ultra large to small start-ups. If your company has a viable business model and plan, a corporate portal will invariably help you extend the reach of your business, reduce costs, and foster strong relationships.

Q: What are the benefits of a corporate portal?

A: A corporate portal, at a minimum, will reduce operational costs, increase corporate reach, enhance competitiveness, bolster customer loyalty, improve productivity, expedite business processes, and accelerate decision making.

Q: Why is there a need for XML?

A: XML provides a platform and programming language–independent scheme for sharing data among applications and corporations in an unambiguous, consistent, and extensible manner. Whereas HTML deals with the presentation aspects of data, XML focuses on the meaning and context of data—especially structured data. XML can eliminate the proprietary nature of commercial applications and ensure that data from one application can be understood by a totally different application, even if the two applications are from different, competing vendors. XML thus sweeps away the incompatibility issues that in the past precluded easy data interchange between disparate applications.

Q: What are Web services?

A: Web services are a new breed of Web applications that are heavily XML centric and are based on protocols such as SOAP, WSDL, and UDDI. They are modular, self-contained, self-describing Web applications that can be published, readily located, and easily invoked across the Web. They provide a standard, strategic, and consistent way to package business processes and make them available over the Web to interested and authorized parties.

Q: What are the key functions provided by portals?

A: The key functions typically offered by a corporate portal include content aggregation, content syndication, search services, collaboration schemes, and access to applications (where the applications could be in the form of Web services).

Q. Are corporate portals just a passing fad?

A: No. For a start corporate portals have been in gainful production use since the mid-1990s (e.g., FedEx, Charles Schwab). Furthermore, following Y2K, the rate at which companies are installing corporate portals has been steadily growing and is not showing any signs of peaking. Rather than considering portal a fad, most people in IT now recognize the value and potential of corporate portals. All of the necessary technology to implement corporate portals is mature, robust, readily available, and affordable. Corporate portals are still in the ascent.

2

Types of Portals

Mistakes are the portals of discovery.

—James Joyce

Portals, irrespective of their type, to paraphrase the famous adage about beauty, are essentially all the same under the skin. In other words, much of the perceived variation among different types of portals is mainly on the surface. Although the content, structure, and presentation of portals may vary dramatically, through design and necessity, the underlying precepts, infrastructure, and mechanics of a portal are basically the same for a corporate portal, an Internet call center, a business-to-employee (b2e) intranet portal, a b2b extranet portal, a business-to-consumer (b2c) e-commerce portal, or a self-service portal.

There are basic core functions, such as aggregation, personalization, search, collaboration, and security, that any portal must provide for it to be a bona fide portal as opposed to a "home page" Web site. The exact level of functionality of these core services that will be needed for a given portal may certainly vary among different portal types. This is particularly true when it comes to security, authentication, collaboration, and personalization. An intranet or extranet portal may typically require more security and personalization than a self-service portal dealing with public-domain information (e.g., a state or local government or county court portal). On the other hand, a self-service portal, which deals with personal finances and allows people to pay their bills through it, may require as much security and personalization as an employees-only intranet portal.

The point here is that there will always be functional commonality across portals no matter what they are called. It is important to appreciate this commonality, since corporate portals, especially the new generation of XML-centric and Web services–capable ones, will begin to consolidate what were previously positioned as different portal types into a single unified entity—exploiting authentication-based personalization.

Although it's not obvious until you start to work through the details of implementing a portal, even specialized value-added functions previously associated with one particular portal type can now have applicability across a much wider range of portal types. Take the now rather familiar "shopping-cart" product-ordering functionality shown in Figure 2.1, using Amazon.com as the example. Most would assume that shopping-cart functionality, typically sold as an add-on "store-front" or commerce feature within the

Figure 2.1   *Classic "shopping cart" functionality associated with e-commerce portals, shown here using Amazon.com as the example.*

portal framework solution, would be restricted to b2c e-commerce portals and possibly to some b2b e-business portals.

One would not normally associate "shopping-cart" functionality with employees-only, in-house, intranet portals. Benefits administration and management are now one of the most popular and productive applications for intranet portals. Any company with 250 or more employees that maintains a fully fledged intranet portal is also likely to offer its employees different options when it comes to benefits in terms of dental plans, insurance schemes, health club membership, and the like. HR people refer to these choice-laden schemes as menu-style benefits. Employees are, in effect, shopping to pick the best permutation for their needs. It is really no different from picking books at Amazon.com or selecting vitamins at GNC.com. Rather than trying to implement a scheme to handle benefit administration, you could take a standard "shopping-cart" feature and easily customize it to elegantly handle menu-style benefits—with élan.

Accepting and processing credit cards is another function that one normally associates with e-commerce portals rather than with b2e intranet portals. But even this is changing. More and more corporations now encourage employees to acquire company logo products (e.g., golf shirts), company memorabilia, and even company products (if appropriate) via the internal portal. Some even offer special promotions through partners such as discount cruises or trips to Disney World. To facilitate such in-house commerce, what are still basically b2e intranet portals are now beginning to devote a section for what is, in effect, a full-function, b2c e-commerce operation.

What all of this shows is that the old demarcation lines used to pigeonhole portals based on their functionality are beginning to blur. Portals are becoming multipurpose and multifunctional. The new generation of corporate portals will be the epitome of such multipurpose, all-in-one portals. So rather than maintaining separate discrete portals with duplicate content and functionality for different user communities (e.g., partners, customers, prospects, investors), you can now significantly reduce cost and complexity by moving toward a single, consolidated but partitioned portal. XML and especially Web services can facilitate this consolidation.

XML's ability to unambiguously describe the meaning and structure of data—in a presentation-independent manner—can and should be exploited to minimize the need for data replication. Today it is not uncommon for corporations to replicate the same data in multiple forms and formats to meet the demands of specific applications, user communities, or end-user devices (e.g., using WML for mobile devices). If a corporation maintains separate portals, then data replication is inevitably further exacerbated. The rationale for the replication is to customize the data.

With XML you could realize this type of customization by adding a new layer of end-user–specific structure (or partitioning) on top of the original data. Take, for example, a set of product specifications. While there will always be a core set of common product information required by all parties, there will also be specialized and privileged information (e.g., costs, suggested retail pricing, internal part numbers, maintenance schedules) that is primarily of interest to (and targeted at) specific user groups such as partners, prospects, existing customers, field support, and personnel. With XML you can now maintain all of these data in one place without any replication, using XML tags to categorize and partition the data. You could then use eXtensible Stylesheet Language Transformations (XSLTs), a standard-based adjunct to XML, to publish these data in a customized form to suit the needs of specific user groups.

XSLT, which is described further in Chapter 8, is, in essence, a simple but powerful scripting mechanism replete with variables, function calls, and loops, based on the concept of style sheets. With XSLT you can identify specific structures in an XML document using a pattern-matching mechanism specified as templates within the style sheet. When a match is found corresponding to a specific template, transformation rules defined for that template are used to generate the necessary output. Thus, by using different style sheets you can easily and conveniently generate different, highly customized views of the underlying data—in multiple formats (e.g., HTML and WML) to boot. Although XML is manifestly cumbersome and adds significant overhead to data maintenance, this ability to minimize data replication is one of its many redeeming attributes.

The concept of using XML to simplify portal content management and delivery started to gain traction around 2001, and it is now cited as one of the key uses for XML. The issue here is that of biting the bullet. The initial switch to XML-defined data will be time consuming and involve a relatively steep learning curve. The good news, however, is that there is no need to convert all of your data and content to be XML based in one "do-or-die" push. This is not Y2K.

Existing data can coexist alongside XML-defined data. Thus, the migration toward XML can be selective, gradual, and carefully staged. You can start with the data that are most often accessed by partners, suppliers, and affiliates. This is likely to deliver the best ROI vis-à-vis the investment in coming to speed with XML. Another option, assuming your company is committed to standardizing on XML, is to mandate that all new applications being developed or any new data types (or content) being created must be XML oriented. Furthermore, tools for facilitating XML conversion are on the ascent. Large database vendors such as IBM and Oracle are already offering XML "extender" capabilities, and Microsoft's Excel 2002 (within Office XP) supports both the exporting and importing of XML-based data.

In parallel with XML, Web services, in effect the next breed of Web applications, will also help companies consolidate and streamline their portal operations. Given that Web services typically rely on XML-defined data, they can be used, even more effectively than XSLT, to deliver highly personalized, user-specific results based on authentication and personalization criteria. Web services could also be developed to offer different sets of customized services to different user groups. Thus, the same Web service—for example, an online e-catalog of products—could be used by employees, partners, prospects, and customers, with each group having access only to a specific set of functions.

The bottom line is that there are no technical or implementational imperatives for a company's having to create and maintain multiple types of portals. Proven technology—in the form of portal server frameworks from the likes of IBM, SAP, BEA, Oracle, iPlanet, and Plumtree, just to mention a few—is readily available for building secure and scalable consolidated corporate portals that can, with panache, serve both internal and external user communities. To eliminate the potential for misunderstanding and to provide a historical backdrop for appreciating how corporate portals have evolved since 1996, the remainder of this chapter looks at the different portal types in existence today. It should, however, always be remembered that a primary goal of this book is to encourage and promote the migration toward consolidated corporate portals that profitably exploit the data-sharing and data-targeting capabilities of XML and Web services.

2.1 "Public" versus corporate portals

The biggest hurdle when talking about different portal types has to do with conflicting definitions and perceptions emanating from some of these definitions. Thus, to avoid confusion, the safest course is to carefully define what we mean when talking about different portal types as we go along. Inevitably, the most significant distinction is that between "public" and internal (or "public" and corporate) portals.

Ironically, the definition battles can start right at this juncture based on one's view of what a public portal is. If your portal experience is primarily

Figure 2.2
*Excite is a
quintessential
example of a public
Internet portal.*

with the huge Internet portals à la Yahoo!, Lycos, Excite, MSN, Netscape, or AOL, you may think of these, quite rightly, as being public portals. Figure 2.2 uses Excite to illustrate the composition of a typical public Internet portal of this type. It is certainly difficult to argue with this definition, given that these Internet portals (also called Web portals) are indeed the epitome of public portals. They openly welcome any and all Web users without regard to their identity, affiliations, or motives. They are the Internet equivalent of public libraries; anybody can walk in and sample the goods on display. Though nearly all of these Internet portals now offer optional, members-only personalized content and services to foster brand loyalty, their primary charter is to be open to all comers.

Thus, a public portal to some is an "open-house" Internet portal, best characterized by Yahoo! or MSN. However, those who have been closely embroiled with corporate or enterprise portals for the past few years may define public portals as the opposite of intranet portals (i.e., company portals with an Internet interface that are accessible to the general public). By this criterion, FedEx.com or Schwab.com are public portals. This definition

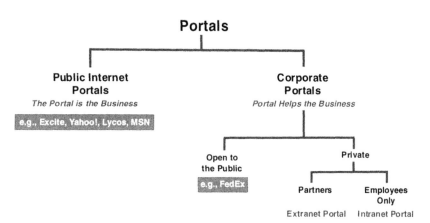

Figure 2.3
The basic taxonomy of portals showing the separation of corporate portals from public Internet portals.

also has merit and is obviously logical. The only way to resolve this is to expand the definition of what constitutes a public Internet portal as opposed to a corporate portal open to the public. Figure 2.3 sets out to define the basic taxonomy when it comes to portals and to highlight the difference between public Internet portals and corporate portals with external interfaces.

There is a fundamental and clearly identifiable difference between public Internet portals and general publicly accessible corporate portals, based on their business model, that can be used to provide an unambiguous and consistent demarcation between the two types. In the case of a public Internet portal such as Yahoo!, the organization's primary business is the portal per se. This is true even of MSN as a network, despite its ownership by Microsoft.

A portal in itself, however, is never the primary business rationale of a corporate portal, no matter whether the portal is accessible to the general public or not. The FedEx.com portal, despite its public popularity, is not the driving force behind FedEx. This is true even of Amazon.com, the granddaddy of dot-com ventures. Although its business presence is confined to the Web via a sophisticated e-commerce portal with some advertising links, its core business is that of selling books, electronics, and entertainment titles. On the other hand, the main business of Yahoo! or Excite is that of selling advertising, syndication, and affiliations on its portal. This business model–based distinction between public Internet portals and publicly accessible corporate portals is easy to apply and difficult to misconstrue. Hence, this business model–based definition is used in the remainder of this book when it comes to differentiating Internet portals from corporate portals.

Other criteria could be used to differentiate public Internet portals from corporate portals. Corporate portals are invariably corporation specific; they revolve around the corporation they represent. They are unlikely to devote any real estate to topics that do not directly further the corporate mission. Thus, it is unlikely that you will find headings for horoscopes or relationships on a corporate portal—unless, of course, the portal happens to be associated with a company that actually markets astrology-related products or is involved in match-making. But the message here should be clear and obvious. The overriding mission of a corporate portal that is open to the

Figure 2.4   *iVillage.com is a good example of what is referred to as a vertical, public Internet portal.*

public is to promote the corporation's products, services, image, and beliefs. By marked contrast, the express purpose of a public Internet portal is to deliver as much diverse content as possible to attract and retain a wide cross-section of Web users.

Since public Internet portals cover such a broad spectrum of general-interest topics and services, they are sometimes referred to as horizontal portals. By this definition corporate portals become vertical portals, or vortals, since their focus is narrow and confined to their specific business goals. However, these horizontal-versus-vertical definitions are not as clear-cut and watertight as the previous definitions for demarcating public portals from corporate portals. The reason for this is that there are some public Internet portals that are targeted at specific constituents. iVillage.com, a very successful portal aimed at women, shown in Figure 2.4, is a good example. iVillage is deemed by some to be a vertical portal, though given the depth and breadth of its content, not to mention its business model, one could also call it a horizontal portal—albeit with slightly specialized content.

This iVillage example illustrates how definitions commonly applied to portals can be confusing and misleading. Figure 2.5 builds on the framework set out in Figure 2.3 to introduce the concept of horizontal and vertical portals. Guru.com (for self-employed professionals), cars.com, boats.com, and telegraph.co.uk (the publisher of the British telegraph newspaper) all fall into the category of vertical public portals.

Figure 2.5
Extending the portal taxonomy developed in Figure 2.3 to include the concepts of horizontal and vertical portals.

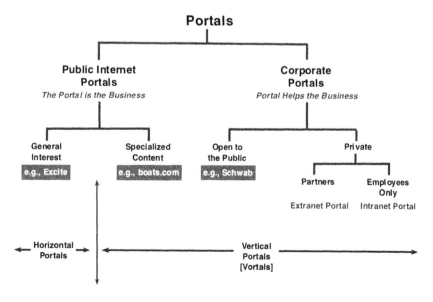

2.2   Types of corporate portals

While the mid- to long-term goal is to move toward single, consolidated, multipurpose corporate portals, today there are many different types of corporate portals with a bewildering array of names. As with many emerging IT technologies, this implementational diversity in essence reflects technological evolution coupled with cautious adoption of technology. The main fear when it came to corporate portals, understandably, was that of general public access across the Internet. Hence the first two generations of corporate portals, spanning the 1995–1999 time frame, were primarily employees-only intranet portals, though there were some notable exceptions (e.g., FedEx.com and Schwab). Today, intranet portals are also very accurately described as b2e portals, with this term gaining currency after the widespread use of the terms b2b and then b2c.

Restricting corporate portals to in-house users and possibly selected partners made sense in the early days of this technology. Security risks were minimized, and techniques and technology could be tried out on captive and for the most part friendly users. Moreover, this was also the period when intranets in general were the vogue and corporations, despite their previous preferences when it came to networking, were rapidly converging on highly LAN-oriented, router-dominated IP networks. Since intranet portals dominated the corporate culture, these portals were naturally referred to as corporate or enterprise portals. This explains the confusion that arises when the term "corporate portal" is now used to refer to portals whose scope is no longer restricted to corporate employees and preferred partners.

The first generation of intranet portals focused on ensuring universal connectivity across the company and providing uniform access to a fast-growing body of Web content. Transactional functionality was initially limited to simple operations such as telephone directory look-up or vacation request submission. Soon, however, executives, suitably primed by the vendor community, discovered the power and potential of b2e portals when it came to administrative and HR-related functions.

It did not take long before b2e portals became the basis for highly efficient electronic timekeeping, benefits administration, expense report filing, in-house job placement, 401(k) monitoring, and supplies-ordering applications. Particularly in the case of high-tech companies that once offered lucrative stock options, another widely used and much cherished portal application was a company-provided interactive stock option management and trading system. Some companies that relied heavily on IBM (or compatible) mainframes or IBM AS/400 (now iSeries) minicomputers for their IT needs also provided access to applications running on these systems from their intranet portal using various Web-to-host solutions. (IBM now refers to its latest mainframes as the zSeries.) The initial Web-to-host solutions, which were all Web browsers invoked to ensure neat integration with the intranet model, came in two primary varieties:

1.   Java- or ActiveX-based "thin-client" emulators (e.g., IBM's host on-demand), which would be cached on a user's hard drive after being dynamically downloaded from a Web server whenever a new release was installed on the server.

2.   Zero footprint, "on-the-fly" host-to-HTML solutions (e.g., Net-Manage's OnWeb), which converted host terminal data streams (i.e., 3270 in the case of mainframes and 5250 for AS/400s) to HTML, and vice versa, so that portal users could directly interact with host applications from a standard Web browser window.

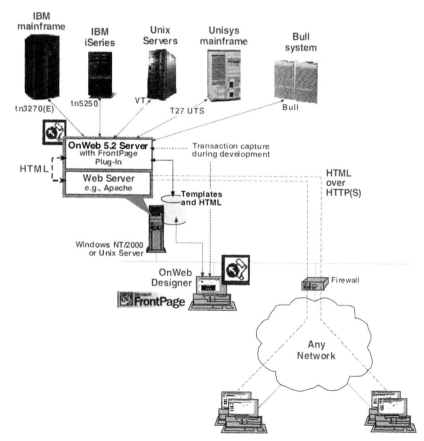

Figure 2.6
The general architecture of a contemporary Web-to-host solution— in this instance NetManage's OnWeb, which performs host-to-HTML conversion, replete with an optional Microsoft FrontPage "plug-in" to expedite the creation of graphical Web pages to serve as the new host interface.

Figure 2.6 shows the relatively simple and straightforward architecture of a contemporary host-to-HTML conversion solution, and Figure 2.7 illustrates the highly rejuvenated, "point-and-click" graphical user interfaces possible—albeit with some degree of customization needed—with current Web-to-host solutions. Today there is a third option when it comes to providing host access from a corporate portal. It is referred to as "host integration" or "enterprise application integration" (EAI). Whereas the "thin-client" and "zero-footprint" approaches are still screen-oriented terminal emulation schemes, despite their Web browser affiliation, the focus of host integration solutions is to enable proven business logic from existing host applications to be gainfully reused within new e-applications or Web services. Web-to-host technologies, including host integration, will be discussed further in section 3.4.

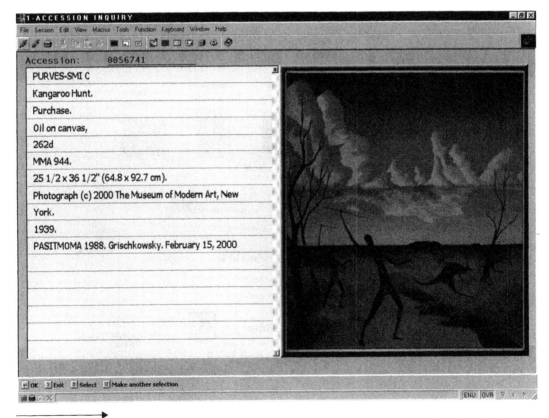

Figure 2.7   *A highly customized and rejuvenated IBM AS/400 "green screen" used by The Museum of Modern Art in New York, showing the degree of user interface modernizing now possible with Web-to-host solutions.*

The second generation of b2e portals, built on the growing expertise and expectations stemming from the first batch of implementations, started to offer increasingly specialized functionality. Two key types of b2e portals that gained prominence during this period were called collaborative portals and business intelligence (or decision-processing) portals. The term "enterprise information portals" (EIP) gained popularity as a collective umbrella term that spanned both of these two new types of portals.

2.2.1   XML to aid collaboration

Collaborative portals, per their name, specialize in helping corporate employees locate, organize, share, and—where appropriate—update a variety of unstructured workgroup information sources such as e-mail, office documents, spreadsheets, calendars, meeting minutes, product specifications, and customer contact information. XML would have been a great boon at the time these portals were being developed, but it was still in the process of being formulated out of SGML. Consequently, many of these initial collaborative schemes were realized using proprietary, product-specific techniques.

Collaboration tools, as discussed in section 1.1.3, are now integral components of corporate portals. Rather than developing a portal specifically to enable in-house collaboration, as was the case a few years ago, now you would implement a multipurpose, integrated corporate portal in which collaborative capabilities are included on a horizontal basis across the entire portal. Collaboration tools will thus no longer be confined to employees only. Partners, suppliers, customers, prospects, and investors will have selective access to appropriate collaborative tools—with e-mail becoming a ubiquitous medium for communications. New collaborative tools will exploit XML and Web services.

The whole rationale for XML is to facilitate data interchange—the crux of any collaborative scheme. In today's corporate culture, with its emphasis on mergers and acquisitions, it is not unusual to have disparate client platforms and applications within the same organization. When the scope of collaboration is extended to encompass partners and suppliers, the potential need for cross-platform interoperability becomes even greater. XML-based tools can permit cross-platform and cross-application collaboration in such heterogeneous environments.

It is, however, important at this stage to stress that XML, despite its strengths and backing, is not a guaranteed or automatic panacea. XML's fundamental weakness is that data interchange is contingent on a mutual understanding on both sides of the exchange of the data-describing tags. For example, an XML tag that is defined as <first_name> needs to be understood and appreciated in exactly that form, with not even the slightest variation, by the recipient application. If the recipient application was expecting to find <firstname> instead, no data interchange will occur. However, it should also be noted that there are various organizations such as the Organization for the Advancement of Structured Information Standards (OASIS)—now endorsed and supported by the United Nations (UN)—that are working diligently and feverishly to define common XML "vocabularies" to promote the unimpeded exploitation of XML. Visit www.xml.org/xmlorg_registry to learn about the common vocabularies now available for specific industry sectors such as accounting, aerospace, financial services, construction, automotive, software, food services, and others.

Whereas the goal of XML is to promote data interchange (albeit subject to the "mutual understanding" caveats), the rationale for Web services is to provide self-describing, easy-to-locate, platform-independent applications that can be shared and used by a diverse population of users. Consequently, when evaluating collaborative tools for a corporate portal you should now pay particular attention to their XML and Web services–related capabilities and plans for future releases. The large players in the portal arena (e.g., IBM, SAP, BEA, Oracle, and iPlanet) are already offering XML-capable collaboration capabilities. But also look at XML-specific offerings from Data-Glider, Macadamian, SiberLogic, IPNet, Vitria, and others.

The goal of business intelligence portals is to enable corporate executives, managers, supervisors, and analysts to make better and more timely decisions by giving them unhampered access to as much pertinent corporate data as possible. Consequently, these types of portals specialize in supporting a diverse range of information types with powerful indexing, cross-linking, and search capabilities to facilitate and expedite data access and analysis. The key business intelligence–related data available on such a portal typically encompasses detailed financial breakdowns, supply-chain performance, sales reports, market analysis, competitive profiles, manufacturing statistics, inventory status, customer relationship trends, and product support analysis. To aid analysis and decision making these portals invariably offer a variety of business intelligence–related tools for online analytical analysis (OLAP), report generation, and data mining.

As with collaborative portals, business intelligence portals are unlikely to remain as specialized portals as corporations forge forward with XML-capable portals. Business intelligence tools, like collaborative tools, will become horizontal services available to a broader range of users—albeit on a restrictive, "need-to-know" basis enforced via the standard personalization features. XML, from what has already been said before, can obviously play an increasingly significant role in this arena going forward—with the usual proviso that XML's success is always contingent on the use of mutually agreed-on vocabularies.

2.3   Partitioning a corporate portal

The ability to converge on a single, consolidated, multipurpose corporate portal that serves both internal and external users is obviously contingent on being able to build and maintain unbreachable and uncompromisable watertight compartments between the various user communities. Figure 2.8 extends the portal type taxonomy developed in Figures 2.3 and 2.5 to show the convergence in the corporate portal arena toward partitioned, multipurpose portals.

With firewalls now being mandatory for any type of Web-oriented network, today's IT professionals, regardless of their area of expertise, are conversant with the concept of access validation and access restriction. Firewalls, though they will be liberally deployed around a portal server to ensure some degree of separation and isolation of corporate assets from the

Figure 2.8
The trend toward consolidated but rigorously partitioned corporate portals.

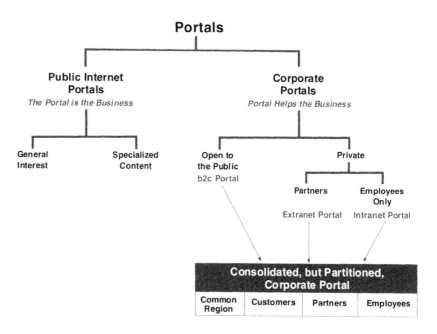

outside world, are not the answer to corporate portal partitioning. Effective but flexible corporate portal partitioning is best realized by using authentication and portal personalization in tandem.

2.3.1 User authentication

All of today's major off-the-shelf portal server solutions offer personalization and security functionality, with authentication usually included as one of the security options. In addition, trusted and respected names in network security, such as RSA Security, Tivoli, and CheckPoint, offer powerful, policy-based authentication systems that can be used in conjunction with portal servers. Most of the authentication systems, in particular those from the security specialists, offer multiple options for identifying and validating users. These include user-ID and password schemes, client-side digital certificates, and RSA's highly acclaimed and award-winning, "two-factor" SecurID token-based authentication.

Digital certificates are an electronic credential issued by a trustworthy organization such as a large company (e.g., IBM or Microsoft) or a security-specific entity (e.g., VeriSign or Tivoli SecureWay Trust Authority). The digital certificate vouches for an individual's or business's identity and authority to conduct secure transactions over the Web. In essence, they replace traditional user IDs and passwords. The public key infrastructure (PKI), which is rapidly becoming the accepted standard for ensuring Internet encryption and security, is the basis for digital certificates. Digital certificates that are defined by the X.509 standard are discussed further in section 4.1.

At the start of 2002, RSA's two-factor SecurID user authentication was already being used by over 10 million Web users around the world. It is referred to as two-factor authentication because it requires users to identify themselves using two unique factors, one on top of the other. One of the factors would be something they know (e.g., password or PIN), and the other factor would be something they have. Automated teller machine (ATM) cards, though not based on RSA's SecurID, are an easy-to-understand example of two-factor authentication; your personal PIN is the factor that you know, and the ATM card with its encoded magnetic stripe is the factor that you have.

In reality, RSA does offer an ATM card–type system based on a chip-embedded smart card and a smart-card reader that is connected to the user's PC. Such a smart card–based system, though offering exceptional security, is obviously somewhat cumbersome, complicated, and costly. It is, nonetheless, a viable option. It could be used selectively to safeguard your most sensitive information with the smart cards, the readers being restricted to specific, privileged users. RSA's SecurID, however, can be used effectively without the need for this smart-card system.

RSA's SecurID system, in general, works with a user-specific secret password and a token. The password is the factor that a user knows, and the token becomes the factor that the user has. The token is a time-synchronized code that is periodically generated, typically every minute, starting with a unique seed code supplied by RSA. RSA can determine the validity of the token based on the time-sensitive code entered by the user. A valid token proves that users have access to the "factor" that they are supposed to hold. In effect, this token becomes the equivalent of the magnetic stripe on an ATM card. In order to be successfully authenticated a user must enter this continually updated code (i.e., the token) and a user-specific secret password. RSA tokens can be generated using RSA-supplied hardware gizmos, as shown in Figure 2.9, or using RSA-supplied software that can run on standard PCs, Palm handheld PDAs, or even smart telephones.

Since it is essentially an extension of normal password-based security schemes, users can be taught how to use two-factor authentication relatively easily and quickly. In the case of the software token schemes, the users may only have to enter their personal password (or PIN), since the client-side security software will automatically generate the token, append it to the user-entered password, and send this combined key, suitably encrypted, to the security server for authentication. Despite its simplicity from an end-user perspective, two-factor authentication is obviously a significantly more powerful security scheme than a password-only (i.e., one-form) authentication scheme. Large and high-profile high-tech companies such as Cisco have been successfully using two-factor authentication, initially with hardware tokens but with a rapid transition to software tokens since around 1995 to partition and safeguard their employee-only intranet portals.

RSA SecurID Key Fob
(SD600)

RSA SecurID PINPad (SD520)

RSA SecurID Standard Card
(SD200)

Figure 2.9   *Illustrated are some of the hardware token–generating gizmos supplied by RSA Security for its SecurID "two-factor" authentication scheme, although the trend today is to use RSA-supplied software token schemes that can be installed on PCs, Palm Pilots, or even smart phones.*

By now it should becoming clear that there is enough proven and sophisticated authentication technology on the market from highly trusted sources such as RSA Security to enable the watertight partitioning of a consolidated corporate portal. It is thus possible to partition a portal so that it can be shared by different internal and external user communities with varying degrees of "need-to-know" status, access privileges, and affiliation affinities. It should be noted at this juncture that you have the further option of using multilevel (or multistep) authentication, whereby users may have to be authenticated more than once, using different authentication mechanisms, when they need to access sensitive information.

Security concerns, though sacrosanct, ultimately cannot become an impediment to progress and productivity. As any cop or burglar would point out, it is either impossible or too cost prohibitive to make anything totally, unassailably secure and burglar proof. The best that you can hope for is to make thievery as difficult and time consuming as possible. That is the bottom line when it comes to corporate portal partitioning using authentication. Keeping separate portals isolated with firewalls offers no more intrinsic additional security than a well-designed consolidated portal partitioned using adequate authentication schemes.

If you truly believe that somebody could successfully breach your authentication schemes (especially a two-form scheme) and gain unauthorized access to your portal, then you have to ask yourself: What stops this same ingenious person from hacking into my intranet portal? Claiming that you keep your intranet portal secure by keeping it totally isolated from the Internet is, unfortunately, not the right answer anymore. Restricting Internet access is regressive and counterproductive. The Internet is, indubitably, the most effective and least expensive way to provide mobile users, telecommuters, remote office users, wireless users, and after-hours users with portal access. Virtual private networking (VPN), which provides highly proven security and protocol tunneling so that Internet bandwidth can be gainfully and securely used for private, corporate use over a leased line, is another way to realize portal access across the Internet. Once you have an Internet interface, which in the end is inevitable, your security exposure, despite initial impressions, is really no different whether you maintain a separate intranet portal or move toward a well-designed partitioned portal.

2.3.2 Personalization

Personalization is the other technique for effectively and creatively partitioning corporate portals. Once you have used authentication to unequivocally determine the identity of a user, you can leverage personalization to enrich the portal experience for that user and ensure that the user establishes an affinity with the portal, its contents, and the customized services. In the case of nonprivileged general public users visiting the nonsecure, public-domain areas of the portal, simple cookie technology could be used to identify the users on repeat visits and offer them a semipersonalized experience based on information gleamed and recorded on a prior visit. (A cookie is a widely used mechanism to store specific information about a portal or Web site user in a small file on the user's computer.) In some instances, where security is not paramount, a cookie scheme, which will automatically and transparently submit a previously entered user ID and password, can be used to provide more specific personalization to repeat, but nonprivileged, users.

Personalization is all about ensuring that users continually have ready access to authorized information, services, and applications that are of particular relevance to them. Public Internet portals such as Excite and Lycos are the masters of personalized content, albeit on an optional basis subject to the wishes and initially stated preferences of the user. Cookie technology is used to identify the user and, in some cases, to maintain the user's preferences.

Some e-commerce portals, most notably Amazon.com, also excel at personalization; Amazon's, however, is based on carefully tracking and analyzing user interest, behavior, and buying patterns recalled from previous visits. If you buy any books, DVDs, CDs, or software from Amazon.com, the portal will ensure that you are made aware, with no room for uncertainty, of other similar offerings on your subsequent visits. It might even take the liberty of sending an occasional unsolicited e-mail about new titles that correspond to your current "profile," given that it has your e-mail address from when you last ordered an item. This type of automated and transparent user-behavior tracking for personalization is referred to as "implicit profiling," because the user is not directly engaged in stating preferences and requirements. Information gathered in this way is also used for data or Web mining purposes, referred to as "collaborative filtering." Consequently, the Excite or Lycos approach, in which the user is asked to specify preferences via a questionnaire, is known as explicit profiling.

There are two other types of profiling that can also be used to good effect in personalizing corporate portals. One obvious and essentially mandatory approach is to personalize the portal based on user type and relationship with the company. The other is to personalize based on specific, historic data pertaining to a user. Typically, both of these techniques could be used in tandem to complement each other. Thus, existing customers, as a group, will automatically get different personalization—and personalization options—from, say, partners. Then the historic-data angle can be used to personalize further within each of these broader categories. For example, partners and customers could get geography- or industry-specific personalization on top of product- or service-oriented personalization. There are many options along with the powerful and proven personalization technology to make it real—quickly, easily, and without slowing down the portal experience.

The same user type and historic data–based personalization also applies, even more so, to employees. Employees in HR will start off with a "category" of personalization different from, say, employees in sales and marketing. Within each department further personalization, based on stringent authentication, can be done on level of responsibility, title, grade, or whatever. Possibilities abound. Figure 2.10 contains a high-level schematic of how authentication and personalization can be used in tandem to partition a corporate portal.

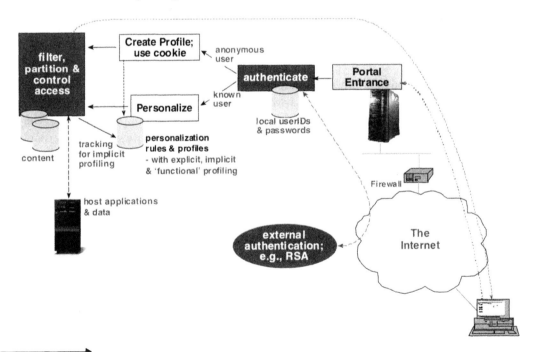

Figure 2.10   *High-level schematic of how authentication and personalization can be used to partition and control portal access.*

The one big danger in getting too carried away with personalization is that of intimidating users. You do not want to give the impression that you are impinging on the privacy of users—even if you are! Privacy is a valid and very sensitive issue, one with some significant legal ramifications. Big corporate portals now invariably have a detailed section devoted to their privacy policies, and some even have a disclosure of the technologies they use to track and profile users. Figure 2.11 depicts the start of IBM's description

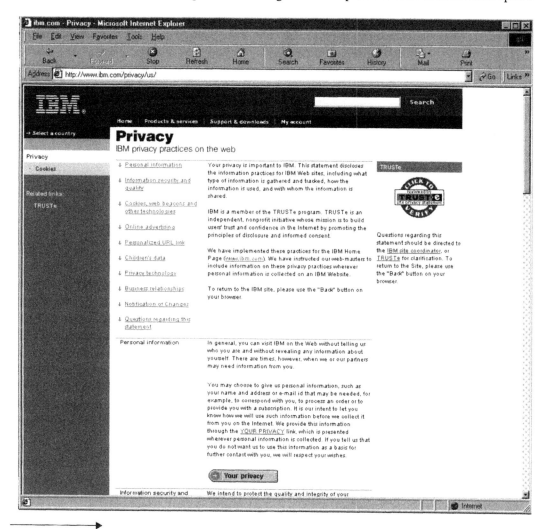

Figure 2.11   *Example of a portal privacy statement, in this case using IBM as a good example. Note the entry about "cookies" on the top left, just under the word "Privacy" appearing within the white bar.*

of its privacy policies, replete with a link that describes the use of cookies near the top of the left-hand navigation bar. So when planning personalization schemes for your corporate portal, it's a good idea to visit other sites and check what they offer as well as their statements about privacy policies. It would also be prudent to get your legal resources involved in formulating, reviewing, and stating your privacy guidelines vis-à-vis your portal.

Portal personalization products (e.g., the personalization and interaction management feature of BEA's WebLogic Portal and IBM's WebSphere Personalization) are typically rules based and goal oriented. There is usually a "rules engine," which determines and manages the content and services offered to each user based on existing profiles and rules. If implicit profiling is to be used, the rules engine will be complemented by a "recommendation engine," which will track user behavior using sophisticated statistical techniques and then update the personalization rules so that a user can influence the user experience on subsequent visits. Personalization is discussed further in the next three chapters.

2.4   B2e portals

Intranet b2e portals are now an essential and taken-for-granted mainstay of corporate culture on a par with cubicles, PCs, and water coolers. While dispensing chilled water or hot coffee is not something that can be, as yet, conveniently realized using a portal, b2e portals, nonetheless, now serve much of the corporate social functions that for so long had been indelibly associated with water coolers. The adage about guess what is going to be talked around the water coolers tomorrow should, in reality, now be changed to guess what is probably already being passed around on corporate portals right now. It is inconceivable to imagine a North American or western European company with over 250 employees that does not have a b2e portal of some type. Employees, especially if they have worked at other companies that had them or have friends that talk incessantly about theirs, now expect b2e portals as a corporate benefit that they are entitled to.

You can't blame employees for wanting b2e portals—or in future, employee-specific regions within consolidated corporate portals. B2e portals help keep employees informed, simplify many of the tasks they have to perform, and above all give them a strong communal affiliation. B2e portals can instill corporate identity in individuals and thus enhance loyalty. A well-designed and maintained b2e portal becomes a community in its own right that employees can relate to, and it will even invoke some level of ownership, even for employees who are not in any way directly associated with maintaining the portal. A b2e portal is thus a very powerful and valuable corporate asset. One could even call it an icon. It is not something that should be given low priority or ignored.

Once in place, a regularly maintained b2e portal has the potential of becoming the unofficial psyche of the company. It can and should be used to set the tone and pace for the company. It should reflect, albeit subtly, the company's aspirations and values. It can be used to boost morale and motivate employees. A b2e portal is one of the most powerful and effective "employee-conditioning" tools ever devised. Some companies are gainfully using video over IP, within the context of b2e portals, to convey "view-from-the-top" up-beat management briefs as well as to permit eye-to-eye contact via interactive video conferencing. Consequently, don't ever fall into the trap of thinking that a b2e portal is just an IT system or a corporate marketing instrument. Always keep in mind that a b2e portal is also an HR-related asset. Hence it is a good idea to have your HR management, at the highest level, proactively involved with the b2e portal initiative from day one.

The business rationale for b2e portals is and always will be that they enhance employee productivity and facilitate better and faster decision making. Though it is difficult to find any strong empirical data to conclusively validate these assertions, all the indications from large companies that have been using b2e portals for some time now are that they do certainly appear to live up to their expectations. Intuitively one can appreciate how a b2e portal, especially with the right tools, might streamline information access, promote up-to-date data interchange (e.g., sales reports), simplify data analysis, facilitate collaboration, eliminate paperwork, and expedite in-house transaction processing (e.g., expense report processing). Obviously, these benefits become greater for larger companies with employees dispersed across the globe. A b2e portal is a 24/7 corporate presence.

Internet access maximizes the effectiveness of a b2e portal and ensures universal, "no-added" cost access to employees around the clock and from anywhere in the world. Security obviously is the concern, and strong authentication is the answer. With an Internet interface traveling employees, telecommuters, remote office workers, and employees at international subsidiaries all have easy and cost-effective access to the portal. It also encourages employees to log on from home—in the evenings, on weekends, and the first thing in the morning.

With a compelling and cooperative portal with an Internet interface, you will get zero-cost, after-hours work from your employees, typically to do with collaborative and e-mail–related tasks, usually with little or no complaints. Any complaints that you hear, ironically, are likely to revolve around portal outages and the inability to log on to the portal at 6:00 A.M. to check e-mails and study the meeting calendar for the day. Suffice to say that b2e portals tend to cast a mesmerizing, mystical spell over their users.

This also means that the portal needs to be monitored and sustained on a 24/7 basis. It becomes another high-availability, mission-critical IT resource. Initially, you will just need somebody to keep an eye on it and know how to bring it up if there is a server failure of some type. But this could change rapidly, especially if you have locations spread across different time zones. There might be a justifiable request for regular content refresh. The good news is that this type of around-the-clock nurturing is easier to justify the more people you have accessing the portal. Having consolidated portals with the b2e portion occupying just one region of it will address this issue of amortizing the portal upkeep costs over a larger populace of users.

While an Internet-accessible b2e portal will encourage after-hours work, there is also no question that information and services-packed b2e portals do result in employees spending more time than absolutely necessary surfing the portal, justifying all the time spent on the portal as being work related. If the employees have Internet access, they could be using this time, instead, to surf the Web. So in a way it is better that they stay around the corporate portal rather than venturing far and wide. And this is where the water cooler analogy kicks in again. A b2e portal can be a distraction and a diversion, but the goal is to provide enough time-saving functionality (e.g., time sheets, expense reports, vacation requests, benefits administration, 401(k) management, performance evaluations, supply ordering) to compensate and overcome the "goofing around the portal" overhead.

The concepts of business intelligence portals and collaborative portals have already been discussed, and the opportunities for using portals for knowledge management, supply chain management, and customer relationship management will be addressed again in Chapters 6 and 7. There are really no hard-and-fast rules as to the level and amount of information that should be maintained on a b2e portal. In the end, the information available through the portal will be gated only by the effort required to structure those data and provide the necessary links to them. This is something that can evolve.

Start with a core set of content and then slowly but surely start adding to this in a structured and systematic way. This core set of information will most likely include in-depth product and service descriptions, company policies and procedures, corporate contact information, company-specific news, competitive information, company financial data (if applicable), lists of upcoming events, and job postings. Depending on corporate strategy and based on what has been stated about XML previously, you may decide to make some of this information XML qualified, per industry-standard vocabularies if possible, to facilitate more extensive sharing in the future.

When it comes to the services to be provided on b2e portals, there is, fortunately, a very simple rule of thumb that can be used. In essence, any often-performed task that requires paperwork to be completed, intra-company telephone calls to be made, or people wandering the corridors should be considered a candidate for automation via the portal. Collaborative functions, such as calendaring, are a must and are guaranteed to be enthusiastically received. Vendors (e.g., Plumtree) are already rushing to deliver some of these core portal functions in the form of Web services. Again, this could be something that evolves. All services and applications don't have to be in the form of Web services to begin with. That can be a goal.

2.5   B2c portals

The term "b2c" is supposed to designate business to consumer. Hence, the term is most often associated with e-commerce portals such as Amazon.com, buy.com, jcpenny.com, and landsend.com. However, there is no reason to restrict b2c just to e-commerce portals. A more realistic and representative approach would be to think of b2c portals as encompassing all business-to-customer portals—with customers in this context meaning both existing customers and prospective customers. This would mean that b2c portals could be thought of as also covering public-access self-service portals. Anything that is addressed today with a "1-800" call-center operation is thus a candidate for being handled via a b2c portal. The tremendous possibilities of such portals when it comes to banking, credit cards, financial services, insurance, travel reservations, package tracking, utility companies, and cargo transportation have already been referred to.

Atlas Van Lines, Inc. (www.atlasvanlines.com), based in Evansville, Indiana, is the fourth-largest carrier of household goods and special products in North America. It is also at present the fastest growing major mover within this industry space. Atlas has been proactive, for quite a few years, in creatively leveraging the Web to fuel its growth by enabling it to easily extend its reach to prospective customers and by the provision of business-attracting automated services (e.g., online request for an estimate). Figure 2.12 illustrates some of the online services currently available on the Atlas b2c portal. Notice that there is a mix of services, ranging from purely informa-

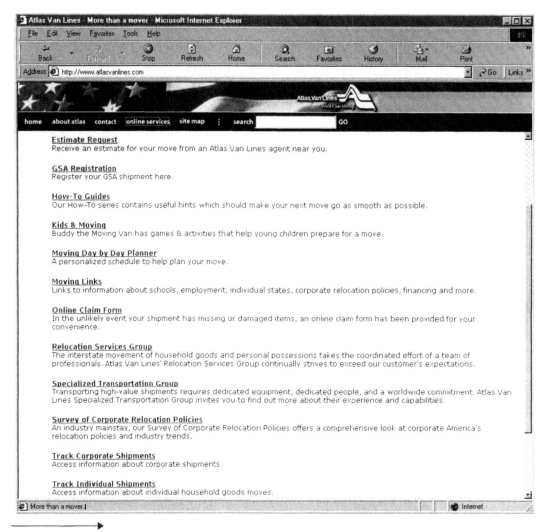

Figure 2.12   *The online services offered by Atlas Van Lines on its b2c portal.*

tional items (e.g., how-to guides) to self-service applications (e.g., agent locator or online insurance claim submission).

For security purposes as well as to ensure customized services, some of the online options offered require some type of authentication. For example, the individual shipment-tracking option that enables people to check exactly where their household goods are during a long-distance move requires that customers enter their last names as well as the registration numbers from their bill of landing. Insisting on this type of authorization, in addition to making the information lookup easier, makes eminent sense, since you really wouldn't want any unscrupulous character to easily get access to the exact whereabouts of your worldly goods.

Other services that do not involve sensitive information—for example, the moving-day planner—rely simply on user identification rather than authentication. This portal is a good example of a b2c portal that is not devoted explicitly to e-commerce. Now compare this site with that of one of its competitors, National Van Lines at www.nationalvanlines.com. This will show you how various companies, operating in the same industry space, will differ widely in terms of how they set out to exploit the Web via b2c portals. A good, service-laden b2c portal with crisp performance is a valuable sales and marketing asset that will increase business, attract new customers, and enhance customer satisfaction. A poor or excruciatingly slow b2c portal will result, inevitably, in customers defecting to competitors. In addition to Atlas and National, there are quite a few other moving companies with b2c portals. Some of these are slow, nonintuitive, or error prone. Capacity planning to ensure adequate scalability, as described in the next two chapters, is thus imperative if a b2c portal is to succeed, as is careful design and continuous, rigorous testing. Companies such as Atlas that follow these precepts and end up with better portals will prevail over those whose portals do them an injustice.

Compared with other marketing and direct sales approaches, gaining a competitive edge via a slick and sophisticated b2c portal is relatively inexpensive, especially when you factor in that a b2c portal will allow you to justifiably downsize your call-center operations without sacrificing customer satisfaction. Thus, innovation and creativity abound. Companies such as Lands' End and National Decorating (www.nationaldecorating.com) offer instantaneous live help at the click of a button via either an instant messenger scheme or telephone. Figure 2.13 shows the Lands' End Live "talk to us!" feature. Some sites offer online remote assistance in navigating the portal, whereby a customer service rep can take control of a user's browser and guide the user through the portal.

In nearly all cases a company considering a b2c portal is already likely to have a primarily informational home page Web site. The b2c portal will usually evolve from this initial Web presence through the introduction of transactional, self-service functions. The need for authentication will depend on the sensitivity of the information involved. In the case of a standard "e-catalog" find-an-item application, whether it be for airline tickets, investment CD rates, books, or apparel, authentication is unlikely to be required. However, if the catalog perusal leads to an e-commerce order, an account, which could be used on repeat visits, will have to be set up.

Figure 2.13   *The Lands' End Live "talk to us!" feature—another innovation vis-à-vis a b2c portal.*

In some instances you may elect to impose some level of user-ID/pass-word–based registration and subsequent authentication in order to track user patterns, instill a sense of community, and collect statistics. Many online newspaper and media portals favor this approach. Though the infor-mation that they are parlaying is not obviously confidential, the need for authentication adds a certain cachet to the transaction from the consumer's perspective and at the same time provides the content provider with some concrete user statistics. This need to log on, if it is not automated via a cookie approach, also has the effect of preventing users from "portal hop-ping" within a given category—in this case news portals. Given that they know that more and more portals will stop them in their tracks and get them to register (or log on), they tend to just go to their most favorite and go through the logon process just once. Thus, logon schemes can serve as a convoluted but effective way to garner portal loyalty.

Although XML can be effectively used in b2c portals, its relevance isn't as great as with b2b applications, given that XML is a program-to-pro-gram—as opposed to program-to-human—data interchange methodology. Hence justifying the overhead of XML qualification for b2c portal–specific data could be problematic. Accordingly, it would be best to devote your initial XML efforts to b2b ventures. Some of these data will also have b2c applicability. That would not be a problem, because you could use XSLT, as discussed earlier, to render the XML-qualified data to consumers in HTML or WML form.

On the other hand, b2c portals are already a fertile arena for Web services. The possibility of delivering some of today's popular Web applications, such as package tracking, in the form of Web services has already been discussed. In reality any and all applications associated with a b2c portal, whether it be an "e-catalog," a calculator figuring out how much wallpaper you need, an estimator of moving costs, or a trip itinerary planner, can be in the form of Web services. Going forward, this will undoubtedly be the trend and expectation when it comes to b2c portal applications.

2.6   B2b Portals

B2b portals should be the basis for future e-business. B2b portals can be used for two distinct purposes:

1.   To interact with existing partners, distributors, and suppliers when it comes to all aspects of supply chain management (SCM) and mutual customer relationship management (CRM)

2.   To identify and locate new business opportunities replete with new business partners, distributors, and suppliers

The identification and location of new business ventures should not be confused with trying to locate or attract additional partners, distributors, or suppliers. Any b2b or corporate portal will, as a matter of course, have a link or button in an appropriate section (e.g., "about the company" or "partners") that tells people how to go about contacting the company in order to become an accredited partner. The new-business aspect has to do with finding new contracts, new markets, new territories (e.g., China), or new technologies. While it is technically possible to address both these objectives from a single b2b portal, there is typically a demarcation as to how these are addressed from a portal standpoint. In effect you end up with:

1.   Company-specific b2b portals (or b2b regions with a corporate portal)

2.   Industry- or business-specific "public" b2b portals

The concept of company-specific b2b portals for dealing with existing "partners" and supply chain management issues is readily understood, and most large companies (e.g., Cisco, Disney, Boeing) already rely heavily on b2b portals as a means of executing streamlined, efficient, and highly cost-effective business transactions. Navarre.com, discussed in Chapter 1, is a good example of such a corporate-specific b2b portal.

The industry- or business-specific portals, in contrast, are the b2b equivalent of public Internet portals. Their business, much like Yahoo! or Excite, is that of running and maintaining a b2b portal. The goal of such portals is to act as a communal market and clearinghouse for companies involved in a specific industry or market (e.g., automotive, China, aerospace, Middle East, aluminum, or Japan).

Fibre2fashion.com, as shown in Figure 2.14, is a typical example of such an industry-specific portal, in this case for all things to do with apparel. Also look at freshfromtheweb.com, a b2b portal for worldwide agricultural products. Note that these b2b portals encourage membership and that logon options are prominently displayed. Inevitably, given the interest in b2b, there

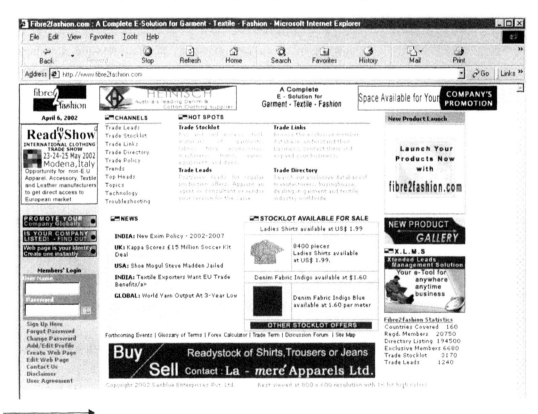

Figure 2.14   *Fibre2fashion.com, one of many b2b portals for the apparel industry.*

are b2b "index" portals such as b2btoday.com and b2byellowpages.com. Though b2b per se has yet to live up to expectations set during the dot-com era, when it comes to real business volumes, industry-specific b2b portals and b2b "index" portals continue to proliferate and expand.

There are also "closed user group" b2b portals restricted to the "high rollers" within a given industry. Large "component" consumers, such as car manufacturers, chemical companies, electronics firms, and telecommunications companies, typically spawn b2b portals aimed at their suppliers. Some of these sites are auction sites with suppliers submitting best-and-final bids for items requested by a customer or with a customer making bids for goods posted by suppliers. The public auction sites such as eBay and Amazon provide a good model as to how to structure and operate such closed user group auction portals.

A company-specific b2b portal will typically be an access-controlled subset of that company's b2e portal, possibly with the inclusion of some functionality (e.g., e-catalog) associated with b2c. Authentication will be paramount for security, tracking, and personalization. Thus, logons are an indelible feature of b2b portals. Thanks to authentication and personalization, content and services can be partitioned and offered on a "need-to-know" or "need-to-use" basis. B2b portals are being increasingly used to provide controlled access to selected enterprise resource planning (ERP) applications, so that partners can directly and dynamically share or update information (e.g., billing records, inventory status, manufacturing schedules, credit limits) without having to contact an in-house representative. Such direct ERP access improves productivity on both sides and hastens information interchange.

Since most ERP systems are implemented on host systems of one sort or another (including UNIX servers and minicomputers), some form of Web-to-host technology is invariably utilized to deliver the necessary access. Host-to-HTML conversion (a.k.a. host publishing) is one obvious and easy way to implement such access. All the major Web-to-host solutions offer options whereby the user interface presented to the partners can be extensively modernized and customized. Other approaches such as host integration could be used to add new "front ends" to the ERP applications to enhance their applicability and scope. The various options available in this arena are addressed further in section 3.4.

XML will also play an increasingly important role in the future when it comes to b2b portals and ERP, SCM, and even mutual CRM. Whereas Web-to-host access is primarily geared toward human clients, XML-based data interchange will be for application-to-application interactions. With the expected spread of XML during the coming years, partners will no longer have to log on to your applications per se to use them. Instead, XML-qualified data will be exchanged between your applications and corresponding applications maintained by your partners. The partners will then gain access to your data, most likely following additional processing and merging with other data, via their applications, so to speak. As repeatedly mentioned, any such XML-based data interchange is contingent on the use of mutually agreed-on vocabularies. Visit sites such as www.schema.net, www.xml.org/xmlorg_registry, and www.biztalk.org to get a feel of the industry-specific XML vocabularies already defined.

Web services, as the next generation of Web applications, will also play a key role in the future vis-à-vis b2b portals—or, to be more precise, the b2b region of a consolidated corporate portal. Software vendors are already talking about delivering some of their current applications in the form of Web services. In time, new releases of all popular ERP, SCM, and CRM applications will offer a Web services option. Therefore, when it comes to b2b it is best to start planning for Web services right now.

2.7   Wireless portals

Wireless-specific portals, such "Fidelity Anywhere," are no longer as hot as they once were. This is, however, not a reflection on the continuing growth in the wireless Internet access market. It reflects the fact that people have realized that wireless devices, given their growing significance, are best handled as a part of a standard corporate portal rather than via specialized portals. This eliminates the need to maintain and update separate content. It obviates concerns about the timeliness of data (i.e., how up-to-date these data are compared with data available on the "main" portal). The issue with wireless devices is that they don't have the bandwidth, the presentation area, or the navigational capabilities to deal with today's increasingly sophisticated and graphics-laden portals. Portal designers, understandably, still tailor their goods for PC users, but this, fortunately, is no longer a stumbling block.

All of today's popular portal server solutions understand the importance of supporting wireless clients and accordingly provide content conversion and filtering tools to ensure that the same content and services can be accessed by both wireless and wired clients. In addition, there are powerful and extensible tools such as IBM's WebSphere Transcoding Publisher (WSTP) and MobileSys MX for simplifying the complexity of wireless device integration, thereby promoting universal portal access.

WSTP facilitates the support of new device types and markup languages (e.g., WML) and thus allows portal designers to focus on running and maintaining a single consolidated portal that is client type independent. WSTP dynamically adapts existing content to meet the exact demands of specific wireless devices. Much of today's Web content is written in HTML rather than in the specialized markup languages required by the new wireless devices, whether they be PDAs, smart phones, or PocketPCs. WSTP solves this problem by dynamically bridging the different HTML structures, tailoring the content to the specific device, and conveniently delivering the customized content to the user.

WSTP already includes standard content transformations, known as transcoders, for the following:

- HTML to WML

- HTML to iMode (a variant of compact HTML)

- HTML to Handheld Device Markup Language (HDML)

- XML to XSLT

- JPEG images to GIF and wireless bitmap

- GIF images to JPEG and wireless bitmap

All of the current indications are that in the future XML cum XSLT will be the strategic and accepted way to handle wireless devices relative to a corporate portal. You could have different XSLT transformations to handle different types of wireless devices or even have different groupings within a class of wireless clients with some groups, based on their needs, getting more content and services than others. Obviously, the use of XML for wireless integration is contingent on having the necessary content in XML-qualified form. That is the rub.

On the flip side, however, there are those who strongly believe that wireless integration is indeed one of the "killer apps" for justifying the move to XML. The compromise here is to factor wireless into your XML plans. If you are indeed thinking of moving toward XML to facilitate b2b and minimize data replication, then the ability to easily integrate wireless devices via XML gives you additional justification. The bottom line is that wireless support is indeed important, but you do not need a wireless-specific portal to accommodate these mobile users. Instead, wireless support can be provided as a standard feature of your consolidated corporate portal.

2.8   Q&A—A time to recap and reflect

Q: Why are there so many different types of portals?

A: Much of the diversity when it comes to portals is historic and has to do with the way portal implementations and perceptions evolved. In the early days, circa 1996, most companies were only too ready and willing to create employees-only Intranet portals, which some people used to call corporate or enterprise portals. Some of the early e-commerce sites such as Amazon also started to appear around this time. The initial e-commerce sites, much like the now defunct dot-coms, were independent ventures in their own right as opposed to extensions of existing, established businesses. This spawned the concept of b2c portals, which were kept separate from b2e portals primarily because of security concerns. Then came b2b portals to cater to partners, distributors, and suppliers, followed by a short-lived interest in wireless-specific portals—though it would have been possible to extend and partition an existing b2e portal to cater to these new user groups. The bottom line is that the different portal types reflect different business goals and implementational bias within what was a new and quickly evolving industry, as opposed to any major differences in underlying technology.

Q: Do the different portal types differ in terms of infrastructure and functions offered?

A: Not really. All portals, regardless of what they are typecast to be, share similar infrastructural frameworks and are expected to offer a core set of common functionalities, including content aggregation, personalization, search, collaboration, and security. Consequently, the same portal server from such vendors as SAP, IBM, Plumtree, iPlanet, Hummingbird, and others could be used to build different types of portals. Even some of the specialized functions associated with just e-commerce portals, such as shopping-cart functionality and the ability to accept and process credit cards, are now being gainfully utilized in other portal types, including b2e portals. The differences between portal types are really just skin deep and have to do mainly with content, structure, and presentation.

Q: What is the future trend in terms of corporate portals?

A: Rather than the same corporation maintaining separate b2e, b2c, and b2b portals, there will be a move toward all-in-one, unified, consolidated corporate portals. These consolidated portals will be securely partitioned through the use of authentication, personalization, and possibly XML technology. The partitioning will ensure that the different user groups can gain access only to preauthorized content and services. You can thus get the best of all words with a consolidated but partitioned corporate portal. The consolidation will eliminate content and service replication and greatly simplify portal maintenance, not to mention reducing capital (i.e., equipment) and operational costs. The authentication-based partitioning, on the other hand, will enforce security and privacy and make sure that users can see and do only the things for which they are authorized.

Q: How does a public portal differ from a b2c portal?

A: Yahoo!, Lycos, MSN, or Excite typify the accepted norm for a public portal—or, to be more precise, a public Internet portal. The primary business of a public portal (even in the case of MSN) is that of the portal per se. A public portal makes money through advertisements and promotions. A b2c portal, in marked contrast, is not the driving force behind the parent corporation. The b2c portal is a tool to further the company's primary business, which would not be that of maintaining a public portal. Even Amazon's b2c portal, though its only window to the world, is not the business that the company is in. Amazon, though utterly reliant on its b2c portal, is in the business of selling books, music, software, electronics, and other things. So a public portal is its own business whereas a b2c portal is a tool to further another business.

Q: What is a vortal?

A: A vortal is another name for a vertical portal. Corporate portals are examples of vertical portals in that their focus is narrow and confined to the business interests of that corporation. On the other hand, most public Internet portals are referred to as horizontal portals, since they cover a broad spectrum of diverse, general-interest topics. However, it is possible to have some public portals that fall into the vortal category—such as iVillage—in that they are targeted at specific user groups (women, in the case of iVillage).

Q: Is today's authentication technology really strong enough to permit partitioned, multipurpose corporate portals?

A: Yes. There are multiple, highly proven authentication approaches including user ID and password schemes, client-side digital certificates, and "two-factor" token-based validations. Many large and very public corporations have been using "two-factor" authentication for many years to safeguard their Internet-accessible b2e portals from unauthorized access. They typically have a single portal presence (i.e., the same Web address or URL accessed by all users) on the Internet that serves employees, prospective customers, partners, suppliers, investors, competitors, existing customers, analysts, or casual passers-by. There is, however, a logon function to enforce "two-factor" authentication. Until you successfully log on, you are in the general-public, b2c region of the portal. The only way to gain access to privileged and personalized content and functionality is by logging on to the portal.

Q: What is "two-factor" authentication?

A: Two-factor authentication requires users to identify themselves using two unique factors, one on top of the other. One of the factors would be something they know (e.g., password or PIN), and the other factor would be something they have. Automated teller machine (ATM) cards are an easy-to-understand example of two-factor authentication; your PIN is the factor that you know, and the ATM card with its encoded magnetic stripe is the factor that you have. RSA's SecurID system, one of the most widely used two-factor authentication schemes, works with a user-specific secret password and a token. The password is the factor a user knows, and the token becomes the factor the user has. The token is a time-synchronized code that is periodically generated, typically every minute, starting with a unique seed code supplied by RSA. In order to be successfully authenticated a user has to enter this continually updated code (i.e., the token) and a user-specific secret password. RSA tokens can be generated using RSA-supplied hardware gizmos or RSA-supplied software that can run on standard PCs, Palm handheld PDAs, or even smart telephones.

Q: Are there different ways to achieve personalization?

A: Yes. There are two broad categories, referred to as implicit and explicit profiling. Explicit profiling relies on either asking the user to specify preferences or determining preferences based on the user's attributes (e.g., relationship to company, job responsibility, or seniority). Implicit profiling, on the other hand, is based on tracking and analyzing a user's behavior from prior visits. B2c sites are fond of using implicit profiling to steer users toward products and offerings that correspond to prior buying patterns or browsing interests.

Q: Are there dangers to using implicit profiling to achieve personalization?

A: Yes. Ruthless implicit profiling could potentially impinge on privacy. It is always best to have a stated and published privacy policy as it relates to your portal to alleviate user concerns about privacy. Privacy statements that can be used as frameworks for what you want to say can be found on most portals today, usually through the invocation of a small button located toward the bottom of the start page or the "about the company" page.

Q: Why is there an apparent shortage of wireless portals?

A: People responsible for maintaining corporate portals realized that there was really no need to maintain separate portals to accommodate the fast-growing population of mobile clients. There is enough off-the-shelf technology available to allow the same portal to be used by both wired and wireless clients. In the long term, if most of the content is XML qualified, then XSLT can be effectively used to deliver customized content to mobile users. Thus, the trend is not toward wireless-specific portals but toward multipurpose portals that can seamlessly support wireless clients.

3

Architectures and Technologies

Architecture begins where engineering ends.
—Walter Gropius

There is no single "industry standard" architectural framework for corporate portals—at least not yet. Nonetheless, all corporate portals irrespective of the orientation of their parent company, the nature of their content, or the way they are implemented always share a common set of mandatory core functionality. At a minimum, this core portal functionality must include:

1. Interface to the Web

2. User interface management (i.e., presentation services)

3. External data access mechanisms

4. Data management services

5. Security, authentication, and personalization

6. Portal development tools

7. Portal administration and management tools

The need for these discrete functional components, in which each component has logical and very specific relationships with the other components, ensures that all corporate portals start off with a common inherent structure. This basic common-to-all structural framework can easily be leveraged to serve as the foundation for a solid but extensible architectural reference for future corporate portals. Figure 3.1 illustrates a high-level view of a practical and flexible architectural reference for contemporary corporate portals that is built around the mandatory, prerequisite functional components required to realize a credible portal. The architecture shown in Figure 3.1 will be extended and refined during the course of this chapter.

Figure 3.1
*Basic, first-cut
architectural
framework for
contemporary
corporate portals.*

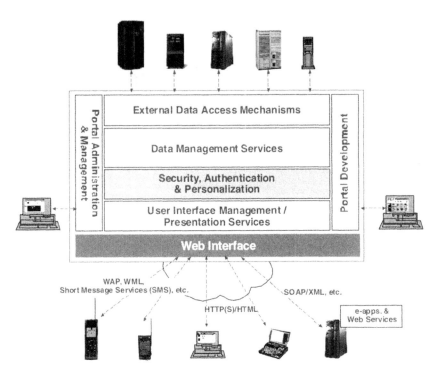

Functions such as aggregation, search, collaboration, syndication, document management, business-intelligence gathering, and workflow management can be systematically plugged into the data management services component to flesh out this architecture. Similarly, the Web interface component, which in practice would typically be realized using a Web-oriented application server, can be extended to include Web services enabling protocols such as SOAP, WSDL, and UDDI. The flexibility and incremental extensibility of this architecture is accurately reflected in most of today's portal solutions. Implementing a successful corporate portal does not have to be an all-or-nothing, do-or-die undertaking. You can start off small, just offering a few interactive services off your existing home page Web site. The portal can then be gradually and systematically expanded, as budgets and time permit, according to a master implementation plan.

Today there are two orthogonally different ways to set about implementing a corporate portal. You can either do it the difficult way by synthesizing ad hoc, à la carte programs; customized scripts; and individual services on top of a Web server; or the easy way, using one of the popular, off-the-shelf portal servers. In the early days (i.e., pre-1997) the involved and complicated development approach using Perl scripts and CGI programs was, obviously, the only way. Now, the integrated, all-in-one portal servers are a compelling and economical alternative.

Opting for a portal server–based solution also does not lock you into a rigid regime. The major portal servers, anticipating customer requirements, provide multiple ways to customize, enhance, and augment corporate portal implementations via plug-ins, APIs, and adapters. Web services are another, very contemporary way to extend the scope, functionality, and reach of a portal server. It is thus possible now to have the best of all worlds. You can start off by using a portal server, with its built-in repertoire of tightly integrated core services, such as collaboration, search, aggregation, and personalization, to implement the bulk of your corporate portal. You can then use plug-ins, scripts, and Web services to customize it further, refining it to meet your exact needs.

Thus, the conventional wisdom of today is not to "stick build" a corporate portal from scratch, unless, of course, you have a budget to burn. Instead, the recommended and preferred approach is to start with a good portal server as the underlying foundation and then build on that as you gain experience and expertise. Some of the better known portal servers, in no particular order, include IBM's WebSphere Portal family (e.g., Portal Enable), mySAP Enterprise Portals, Microsoft's SharePoint Portal Server 2001, BEA's WebLogic Portal, Plumtree's Corporate Portal, iPlanet's Portal Server, Hummingbird's EIP, Iona's Netegrity Interaction Server, Oracle9i Application Server Portal, Tibco's ActivePortal, CA's CleverPath Portal (née Jasmine Portal), PeopleSoft's PeopleTools 8.1 Portal, Sybase Enterprise Portal, Brio Portal, Abilizer Web Engine, Viador E-Portal, Bowstreet Factory, Epicentric Foundation Server, Corechange's Coreport, Verity K2 Enterprise, BroadVision InfoExchange Portal, and Enfish (once Knowledge-Track) Enterprise.

This list, though long, is by no means exhaustive. Its primary goal is to illustrate the range of representative, off-the-shelf solutions that are readily available from a range of vendors, big and small. Start by looking at the specifications for some of the products on this list online. You may want to begin with vendors you are familiar and comfortable with. Then check out some of the less-known names. Some of these vendors offer instructive online demos that succinctly illustrate the types of portals possible with current technology. Most include detailed documentation, typically in the form of white papers, about their architecture. The topics discussed in this chapter and the next will serve as a road map for navigating through some of these architectures.

A growing number of portal server vendors emphasize the role of Web services in future portals, with nearly all already offering some level of support for Web services. While the role of the likes of IBM, BEA, and Oracle in promoting Web services is well known, check out some of the smaller players such as Epicentric, Abilizer, Plumtree, and Tibco to gain a broader perspective and appreciation of how Web services can be leveraged going forward. There are two important messages to take away from this. The first is that there is near universal concurrence that Web services, whether they be Java-centric or .NET-based à la Microsoft, will indeed play an increasingly significant role within corporate portals in the coming years—with the only real variance in opinion being as to whether this is already in the making or is in reality two to three years down the road, despite the availability of the requisite, underlying technology. The other point is that using a portal server, rather than in any way impeding the potential deployment

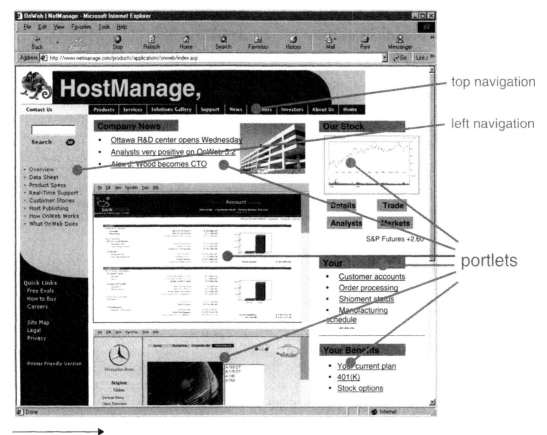

Figure 3.2   *The concept of portlets vis-à-vis a corporate portal.*

of Web services, will most likely facilitate and expedite the adoption of this promising new methodology for Web applications.

Portal servers, in an effort to simplify portal development and maintenance as well as to gain competitive differentiation from each other, have introduced many innovative, novel, and remarkably useful concepts and features during the past few years. Noteworthy among these are portlets, digital dashboards with Web parts, gadgets, breadcrumbs, skins, roles, domains, and iViews. Of these portal-facilitating schemes, the concept of portlets (or related concepts such as PeopleSoft's "pagelets") is probably the most pervasive as well as the most incisive. Portlets are endorsed and supported by IBM, BEA, Oracle, Sybase, Viador, and Verity, among others.

In the case of server solutions that support them, portlets become the vital building blocks for a portal. Portlets, in essence, are the active visible components that end users see within their portal Web pages. Figure 3.2 illustrates the concept of portlets relative to a portal page. A portlet, as shown in Figure 3.2, ends up owning a portion of the Web browser or wireless device screen through which the portal is being accessed. From a user's perspective, a portlet is a content channel or an application "window." The windows analogy is apt and helpful. On a Windows 9x desktop, each application interacts with the user via a window, with each window being a self-contained "workplace" with its own title bar, menu selections, and, if necessary, up-and-down "elevators" for scrolling through the window. A portlet offers a similar self-contained, workplace replete with the necessary controls vis-à-vis an overall portal view. Portlets and the other portal-facilitating techniques are discussed in section 3.2 after the overall architecture for portals has been fleshed out.

3.1   An overall architecture for corporate portals

The high-level architectural model for corporate portals shown in Figure 3.1, though simplistic, is valid, accurate, and representative. It shows the key components that have to be present in any credible portal architecture. Consequently, the various architectures postulated by the portal servers listed earlier are essentially all variations of this basic theme. Figure 3.3 illustrates IBM's original architecture, circa 1999, for its WebSphere Portal. The "types of portals" section at the top of this figure highlights that this portal server can be gainfully used to implement virtually any type of portal, with today's corporate portals in essence representing a synergistic synthesis of all of the types shown here.

Figure 3.3
*IBM's architecture,
circa 1999, for the
original WebSphere
Portal Server
product.*

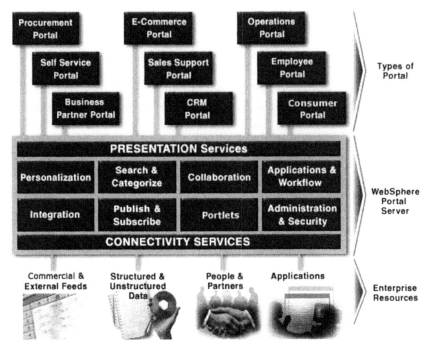

The presentation-services component of IBM's architecture obviously maps directly to the similarly labeled component shown in Figure 3.1, although IBM in this instance is rather remiss in not explicitly noting the role of a Web interface when it comes to realizing the end-user interface. In practice, IBM's current WebSphere Portal products include as part of their "bundle" IBM's Java-based WebSphere Application Server. In essence, IBM's portal servers are Java applications (or, to be more precise, Java servlets) that run on top of a Java application server. The application server in turn will connect with a standard Web server (e.g., IBM's HTTP server, Apache HTTP Server, Microsoft IIS) to interact with the portal users via transport protocols (e.g., HTTP or WAP) replete with the necessary end-to-end security. Protocols such as SOAP, WSDL, and UDDI will be supported and provided by the application server. Thus, in this case, the Web interface service for the WebSphere Portal products will be performed by an application server working in tandem with a Web server. BEA, Oracle, and Sybase, among others, use a similar, application-server-cum-Web-server approach to realize the Web interface component.

The connectivity services shown in IBM's architecture in the main relate to the "external data access mechanisms" component in Figure 3.1. However, it should be noted that any b2b e-business–related data interchanges will, in reality, occur across the Web via the Web interface, as portrayed in Figure 3.1. Access to remote data sources (e.g., a database at another of the corporate data centers), although it will usually be achieved using adapter technology provided by the "external data access mechanisms" component, may also actually take place across the Web, given the hard-to-ignore cost advantages of using Internet bandwidth as opposed to other non-Web alternatives (e.g., Frame Relay circuits, xDSL connections, leased lines).

3.1.1   Data management services

What the basic architecture in Figure 3.1 does not address compared with IBM's more detailed representation is all of the content publishing, content management, search, collaboration, syndication, and workflow-related functions. These functions, in the main, fall into the "data management services" component of the basic architecture. The mandatory functions that now need to be included to flesh out this architecture are as follows:

- Content management, which encompasses:

    - *Content publishing*—manual or automatic inclusion of data, in multiple disparate forms, for access by authorized portal users
    - *Content structuring*—such as portlet mechanisms or templates
    - *Content syndication*—the ability to subscribe to external data feeds using popular content-access standards such as RSS, OCS, PRISM, NITF, xmlnews, and so on (as discussed in Chapter 1)
    - *Content aggregation*—the assimilation and synthesis of data from diverse sources per the personalization rules for a specific user and the presentation of these data as an appropriate portal view
    - *Content delivery*—this includes the handling of both automatic "push" type schemes (e.g., continuously scrolling information ticker at the bottom of a portal view) as well as subscription services, which allow users to request periodic (i.e., scheduled) updates or to be notified if a designated event occurs (e.g., somebody updating a specified document or the company stock price exceeding a certain threshold)
    - *Content directory*—a comprehensive index that identifies and maps all of the data, services, and applications accessible via the portal
    - *Content categorization*—automated and continuous classification of portal content into pertinent categories, also referred to as taxonomies, using "Web-crawler" technology that periodically crawls through the portal information content, checking any metadata tags associated with that content and using this to update content directory

- Search, which includes federated searches

- Collaboration

- Workflow management, which enables users to monitor and control the flow of multistep transactions, possibly spanning multiple corporate IT systems, that are required to complete a specific business process (e.g., acceptance of an order, shipment of the ordered product, invoicing of the customer, and receipt of payment by customer)

3.1.2   Rules engine, directories, and external data access

Figure 3.4 extends the basic architecture shown in Figure 3.1 to reflect the functionality discussed previously. Although it is now a highly workable architecture, there are still some key functions that need to be included to ensure total veracity. For example, rules play an increasingly important role in the management and operation of corporate portals. Rules-based personalization was discussed in Chapter 2. This, though important, is, however,

Figure 3.4
The corporate portal architecture fleshed out to include the pertinent data management services functions.

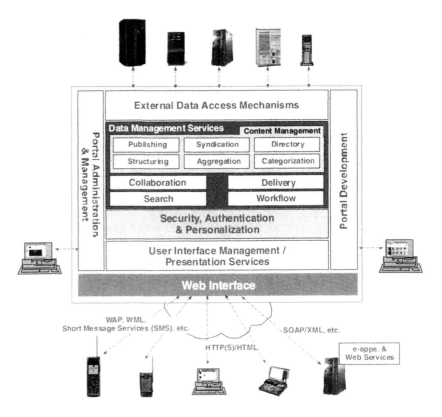

not the only gainful use of rules-based methodology within a contemporary corporate portal. Rules directories with appropriate rule-enforcing engines can also be used in the area of content delivery and subscription management, content categorization, and workflow management.

In the case of content delivery and subscription management, rules can be used to customize and update any push-based data as well as the auto-alert triggers. Rules-based alerting also can be extended to cover workflow processing. For example, a salesperson can be automatically alerted when the company receives payment for an order taken by that salesperson; this way salespeople can determine when they will get their commissions. Rules can also be effectively used for categorizing content, with a key advantage being that you can easily make sweeping changes to the categorization taxonomies simply by updating the relevant rules. Thus, it is important to have a rules component within the architecture. Logically, this component will have interfaces to the portal administration component, personalization, and the overall data management component.

Another important capability that a modern portal must possess is the ability to leverage and reuse information that is already maintained in existing user directories. This ensures that user information, including access right and entitlements, can be centrally administered and controlled. In addition to greatly simplifying and reducing the amount of work involved in directory maintenance, the ability to work off a single, central directory obviates out-of-synch, out-of-date directories—especially in today's highly fluid corporate workplace with its mergers, layoffs, acquisitions, and terminations. A portal directory component will invariably offer multiple options when it comes to directory usage. It will certainly offer a portal-specific directory, more than likely based on a standard ODBC-capable relational database management system, for customers who currently do not maintain a centralized user directory. In the case of customers who do, the portal-specific directory could be used for portal-specific user information, such as personalization settings, page-view setting, portlet settings, and content subscription data.

A portal server's directory component will typically permit multiple directories to be used in a federated scheme. This ensures that a portal can work with an existing directory scheme that is augmented by portal-specific information maintained in another directory. The interface to existing directories will, in most cases, be the lightweight directory access protocol (LDAP), which is an Internet era, industry standard. However, given the ubiquity of Windows desktops and the popularity of Windows NT-family servers, most portal servers will also try to support Microsoft's Active Directory. Some will also try to accommodate Novell's formerly market-leading Novell Directory Services (NDS) scheme—now referred as to as NDS eDirectory. The Java-centric portal servers will normally exploit the Java naming and directory interface (JNDI), which is an integral service within the Java 2 Enterprise Edition (J2EE) standard for interacting with LDAP-compliant directories.

The external data-access mechanisms component of a portal server architecture will focus on providing as many diverse adapters as possible to cover as many of the potential external data sources. Obviously, there will be adapters for database and file access, with at least one ODBC scheme in the case of the databases. Given the amount of corporate data that still resides on traditional data center systems (e.g., mainframes, AS/400s, and other minicomputers), there will invariably be multiple adapters for host (or "legacy") access. Some of the key options in this area are discussed in section 3.4.

Figure 3.5
The final version of an accurate and representative architecture for corporate portals.

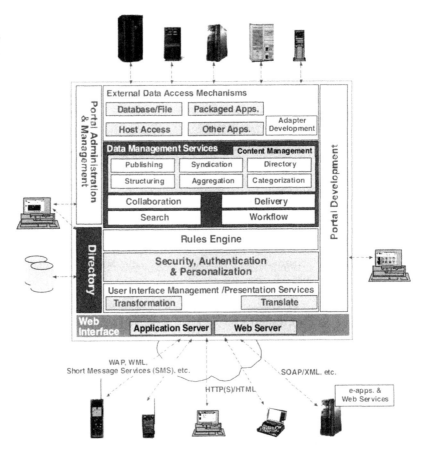

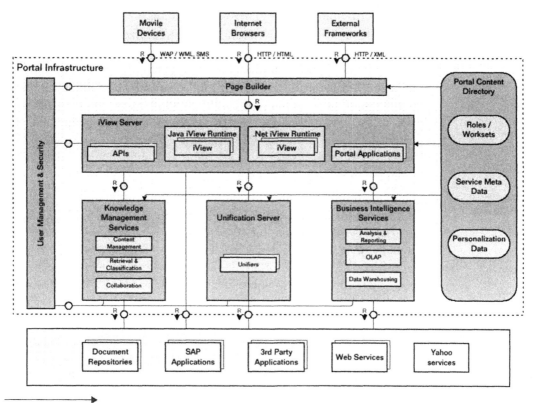

Figure 3.6   *SAP's portal architecture.*

With the widespread popularity of packaged ERP, CRM, SCM, knowledge-management, and process-control applications during the past few years, most portal servers offer application-specific adapters. An adapter development capability is invariably present to enable customers to create their own bespoke adapters. In the case of the Java solutions, the trend is toward making as many of these adapters conform to the new J2EE connector architecture (JCA) standard. Figure 3.5 builds upon the architecture shown in Figure 3.4 to include the functions discussed previously, while Figure 3.6 shows the portal architecture espoused by SAP AG.

3.2   **Portal-facilitating techniques: Portlets, gadgets, and Web parts**

Portlets, or similar mechanisms, are popular, high-profile features of many well-known portal servers in that they really do simplify portal design and maintenance and expedite content availability. There are numerous ways in which portlets simplify portal design and minimize the time taken to activate content. For a start, portlets provide modularization and function isolation. Each portal application will be associated with a specific portlet. Thus, each portal application along with its corresponding portlet can be developed, maintained, and updated independently. Each portlet is thus a self-contained autonomous entity. Hence, the e-mail inbox for collaboration will be one portlet, the calendar application another portlet, and the corporate address book will be yet another. The portal view aggregation function will bring together, in real time, the various portlets that correspond to a specific portal view.

The other key factor that makes portlets so attractive and compelling is the ready availability of prebuilt portlets—from the portal server vendor as well as from third parties. Since most of the servers that promote the portlet concept are Java-centric, they invariably offer a JavaServer Pages (JSP) portlet to serve as a strong and versatile workhorse for portal development. JSP is the Java equivalent of Microsoft's Active Server Page (ASP) server-side scripting scheme that debuted with the Windows NT–based Internet Information Server (IIS) 3.0 Web server around 1997.

JSP sets out to be a simple and fast way to create, and, more important, maintain Web pages that display dynamically generated content. JSP separates Web presentation from Web content. JSP is not an alternative to HTML. Instead, it augments HTML-formatted content by adding interactive, transactional capabilities to a Web page, incorporating the ability to use JavaBean technology to access external data sources including data-center host systems. JSP thus offers a way to quickly develop Web-based applications that, true to the Java promise, are server and platform independent. JSP technology is thus particularly pertinent vis-à-vis corporate portals—albeit only if you opt to pursue a Java-centric solution.

A JSP-based Web page will consist of static page content, JSP tags, JSP "scriplets," dynamic content, and, optionally, HTML formatting tags and possibly XML tags describing the content. The JSP tags are XML-like, while the "scriplets" that contain the logic as to how the output and resultant input should be handled are written in the Java programming language. JSP does not interfere with any HTML or XML that may be present. These HTML and XML tags are passed, unchanged, to the end-user device (e.g., a Web browser). At this juncture it is important to note that JSP, like ASP, is a server-side mechanism. Thus, there is no JSP per se that runs on a browser, PDA, or smart phone. By separating the page logic from its design and display, and, furthermore, by supporting JavaBeans as a reusable means for accessing external resources, JSP really does accelerate the development of contemporary Web content.

Given its capabilities, JSP is understandably popular with Java-savvy Web and portal developers. Having a JSP portlet as a standard feature of a portal server means that these developers can get a running start at creating a corporate portal. They develop standard JSP pages leveraging their expertise, experience, and favorite Java tools. When necessary they resort to JavaBeans to plug in interactive applications to the Web view. The JSP portlet and portal content "aggregator" take care of the rest. Consequently, JSP portlets are widely used to deliver information views, news updates, e-catalogs, and portal applications that require access to external resources. JSP portlets highlight the power, agility, and beauty of the portlet concept. In this instance, it shows how a portlet can be profitably used to capitalize on a popular Web development methodology (i.e., JSP). It also illustrates how you can have different JSP portlets, even within the same portal view, each handling a portal application.

Some of the other commonly available and highly useful portlets include the following:

- XSL portlet, which will automatically render XML-defined content using XSL Transformation (XSLT)

- WML portlet, which will automatically convert HTML to WML to accommodate mobile devices that support WML

- News portlet, with support for RSS or equivalent protocol, so that syndicated news feeds can be directly plugged into a portal view

- Collaboration portlets, typically specific to Microsoft Exchange, Microsoft Outlook, or Lotus notes, replete with e-mail, address book, calendar, and "to-do list" capability

- Database portlet for facilitating database access applications

- Instant messaging portlet that allows this capability to be easily offered within a portal—if necessary just to selected users

- Search portlets, typically in conjunction with a provider of a well-known search engine such as Alta Vista, so that powerful external search capabilities can be offered

- Application-specific portlets for the popular ERP, human resource, CRM, and SCM applications that greatly simplify the integration of these widely used corporate applications into a portal framework

The portal servers vendors that support portlets now have extensive online catalogs of all the portlets available for their servers. They also offer development kits or APIs so that you can build your own customized portlets. Oracle is already promoting the concept of building future portlets in the form of Web services. This makes sense given that Web services represent the next genre of Web applications. The bottom line is that if you opt to go with a portal server that supports portlets, make sure that you truly exploit the availability of prebuilt portlets to expedite your portal implementation cycle.

3.2.1   Digital dashboards, Web parts, iViews, and skins

A concept as innate and intuitive as portlets when it comes to facilitating portal development is obviously not going to have the field to itself in today's competitive and rather crowded portal server market. There will be the inevitable counterparts and even competitors. In many cases the difference is primarily in terminology, with the underlying concept being essentially the same. Microsoft, for awhile now, has advocated the concept of digital dashboards.

A digital dashboard is a portal view composed of various Web components (called Web parts) that can be combined and customized to meet the needs of individual users. Every digital dashboard is a standalone Web page containing one or more Web parts—where a Web part is an individual reusable object that contains data (with HTML and optionally XML tags) or script that presents information to the user. Microsoft's SharePoint Portal Server 2001, promoted as a "portal in a box," is totally digital dashboard–centric—so much so that the SharePoint server actually refers to portals as dashboard sites. It is, however, possible to implement Microsoft digital dashboards with other Microsoft products as well, in particular with Microsoft Office XP Developer, Microsoft SQL Server, and Microsoft Exchange Server. In the context of digital dashboards, Web parts, which are highly customizable, become the equivalents of portlets.

Not to be outdone by portlets, Microsoft provides a gallery of Web parts, including plugins for applications from the likes of SAP and Sibel. At present, Microsoft offers Web parts for business intelligence, CRM, ERP, information delivery (i.e., syndicated news reception from the likes of Hoovers and Factiva), knowledge management/collaboration, project management, and Microsoft applications. There is also a toolkit for building your own Web parts. Many of the Web parts in Microsoft's extensive gallery are from third parties and as such cover a lot of ground encompassing lots

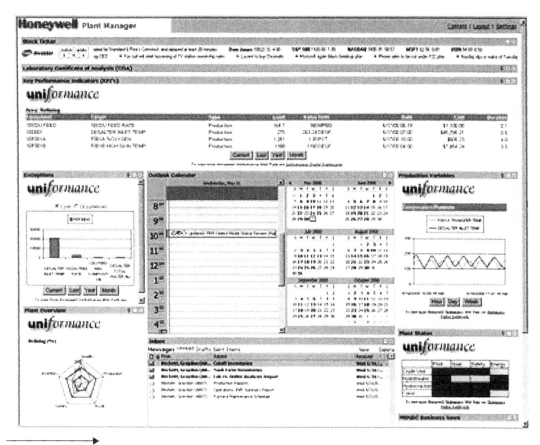

Figure 3.7   *A digital dashboard developed for Honeywell by Microsoft.*

of different applications from many vendors as well as data sources. Figure 3.7 shows a digital dashboard developed by Microsoft for the aerospace, automation, and transportation giant Honeywell; in it one can clearly see the calendar and e-mail Web parts.

Microsoft ASP constitutes the underlying technology behind digital dashboards in that a digital dashboard per se is an active server page (ASP). The ASP in turn references one or more Web parts. Each Web part is a self-contained module that is defined using HTML, XML, or a script. The script can be written in Microsoft Visual BASIC Scripting (VBScript) or Microsoft Jscript. The digital dashboard approach, with its reusable, customizable, and extensible Web parts, is a powerful and appealing paradigm for developing corporate portals. If you are partial to Microsoft technology and want to pursue a Microsoft-oriented portal approach, then start thinking about digital dashboards, Web parts, and SharePoint Portal Server.

iView, which stands for Integrated View, is SAP's equivalent of a portal. The SAP portal architecture shown in Figure 3.6 shows an "iView Server" as the second large horizontal box from the top, with the Java and .NET run times that occur within that server each showing multiple iViews. iView permits content and applications to be integrated into an SAP portal. SAP defines an iView as being a self-contained, XML-based presentation element. The explicit XML angle, which appears to be relatively new, is the only thing that makes iView somewhat different from the other approaches—in that portlets and Web parts, although supporting XML, do not expect everything to be XML based. SAP iViews gain access to data sources and applications via constructs referred to as iView Connectors.

Skins, a term popularized by BEA, are not portlets, Web parts, or iView equivalents—although they are something used by BEA portlets. Skins can be thought of as "themes," available with Microsoft Front Page, PowerPoint, or even a Windows desktop. A skin defines a particular look and feel for a portal view. Since a BEA portal view is made up of portlets, a skin will specify the fonts, colors, and icons to be used by a particular portlet—hence the reference to the concept of themes. Just as with a theme, you can now change the complete look and feel of a portal view or of a portlet by specifying a new skin. Others, of course, offer similar capabilities, unfortunately bereft of attention-grabbing names.

3.2.2   Domains, roles, gadgets, and breadcrumbs

Domains and roles, in essence, go hand in hand and are related to portal personalization. The concept of domains has been used in networking for a long time to denote a self-contained network. The Web reused this term, in a similar connotation, to refer to a unique Web address—the so-called domain name. A domain in the Web context is thus the last part of a Web address (e.g., the URL) that identifies that Web presence (e.g., cisco.com, irs.gov, w3.org). In the context of a portal server, a domain is the highest level of a particular portal.

If a company has only a single consolidated portal, then that entire portal can be a single domain vis-à-vis the portal server hosting it. If the company has multiple portals, as is the norm, then each of those would be a separate domain if they are all implemented on the same portal server. Another way to think about this is that everything that falls under the same portal Web address belongs to that one domain. Thus, if you use different Web addresses (i.e., URLs) for different portals within your company, then you have separate portal domains. The significance of domains vis-à-vis portals is that it partitions and defines the user community for a portal, which is really of importance only if you want to run multiple portals side by side on the same portal server. The domain concept, as in networking, allows you to use the same names and properties across multiple portal domains without conflict, even when they all share a common underlying server.

Personalization is invariably implemented by portal servers via some form of role-based mechanism. In effect, each authenticated portal user is assigned a unique role within the portal's domain—with unauthenticated users getting allocated default roles. The user's role then defines the portal experience for that user. This will include a user's portal view layout, the content within the layout, and the look and feel of the view—as well as that of each "portlet." Roles will also control content, service, and application access.

Roles can and should be defined hierarchically according to a tree structure. This tree structure can mirror that of your company at least in the case of employees, contractors, and agents. The hierarchical tree structure enables common roles to be easily and logically assigned to related groups of people. Thus, you can define one role for all employees in the HR department, another for those in marketing, and yet another for those in IT. Then you could assign more specific roles within each of these department roles—for example, with managers having different roles (particularly in terms of content access) from those of, say, interns working in that department. As with any similar hierarchical scheme, roles can inherit properties from roles above them, obviously with mechanisms to modify and restrict some of the inherited properties. The bottom line is that hierarchical roles simplify and expedite the process of portal personalization and administration.

Gadgets (a term popularized by portal specialist Plumtree Software) can in many ways be thought of as being a type of portlet or Web part, with the one crucial difference being that Plumtree assumes, from the start, that a gadget is a portal component operating on a separate computer. With today's highly networked, IP-connected IT systems, this distinction seems somewhat inconsequential, but, nonetheless, it is an integral part of Plumtree's concept of a gadget. Gadgets are used to integrate external application resources and plug in external content feeds (e.g., news, stock tickers). In this context, external application resources could also include collaborative tools such as e-mail, calendar, and corporate directories.

The full and formal name of a gadget is "gadget Web services." The phrase "Web services" in this instance, however, predates the current usage of this term and as such does not just refer to the nascent genre of modular, self-defining, self-advertising Web applications. Nonetheless, it should be noted that the gadget approach is indeed well suited for effectively integrating Web services into the Plumtree corporate portal framework. According

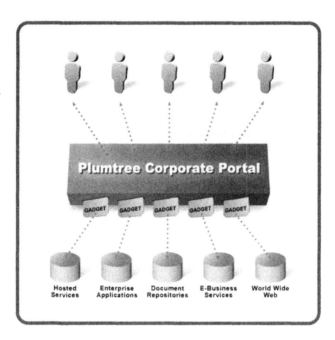

Figure 3.8
Plumtree Software's concept of gadget Web services as a means of integrating external applications and content with a corporate portal.

to Plumtree, gadgets are graphical "Web services" for portal users. Portal users interact directly with gadgets through a gadget-specific user interface. As with portlets and Web parts, multiple gadgets can be assembled within one portal view to provide personalized content and services to users. Figure 3.8 depicts Plumtree's high-level view of gadgets vis-à-vis a corporate portal.

Breadcrumbs, an apt name coined by PeopleSoft, describes a very useful portal feature that most of you probably have already seen and even used without ever realizing that there was a name for it; some portal servers will help you automate this capability. Breadcrumbs refers to the hierarchical, category-by-category navigational list that appears at the top of a portal "window" as you drill down through a list of links looking for a particular item. It is a useful but often ignored feature in the design of portals. A portal server that can automate the creation of this trail will at least ensure that you can easily offer it, where appropriate, if you decide your users will find it useful. (See Figure 3.9.)

3.3   A corporate portal relative to the rest of IT

A corporate portal is not meant to be a replacement for other existing IT systems or applications. Its express purpose is to serve as a Web-enabled focal point to existing and future IT systems and applications. It aggregates,

Figure 3.9   *The concept of a breadcrumb trail category-by-category navigational list, demonstrated here using a Web page from Oracle—although the term was coined by PeopleSoft. Source: Plumtree Software.*

synthesizes, structures, and personalizes information and services available from in-house systems, out-sourced operations, or external entities. It thus augments and complements existing IT infrastructures as opposed to being the latest panacea for IT systems or corporate applications.

A portal is nothing more or nothing less than yet another software application. It provides standard interfaces to diverse data sources and other applications and enables complex data integration spanning multiple, disparate sources. It is best thought of as an incisive and versatile data and application integrator replete with powerful presentation services. The corporate portal architectures discussed previously should have made this clear by their emphasis on data management services and external data-access mechanisms.

Portals do include certain mandatory built-in functionality such as search and collaboration. However, as portlets and Web parts have demonstrated, many a portal server quite correctly relies on separate, best-of-breed applications (e.g., Lotus Notes, Microsoft Outlook, Alta Vista) to deliver these key functions rather than trying to reinvent the wheel. This reinforces the concept of a portal being an application integrator.

A portal, however, is not an application server. Application servers provide a service-rich execution environment for running guest applications. Portals per se do not provide such execution environments. Instead, portals—in particular, the Java-based portals—run on application servers. Portal servers will specify the application servers they will work with, or, to be more precise, have been tested with. Some will even include a bundled-in application server to promote out-of-the-box installability.

To begin with, a corporate portal will leverage existing corporate applications and off-the-shelf applications. Some scripting or programming may be required to modify or extend the user interfaces of some of these applications to fit into the portal paradigm. JSPs, ASPs, Microsoft's COM objects, and JavaBeans are all proven and popular technologies that can be used to this end depending on your preferences. However, as a portal grows and evolves it is likely to spawn the demand for new portal-centric applications, whether it be for e-business, employee productivity, or e-commerce. Some of these will be developed as Web services; others will not. C, C++, Visual BASIC, or Java will continue to be the popular methodologies for developing both types of applications. Though developed explicitly for portal use, these Web services or applications will still be external to the portal. Thus, the concept of portals being application integrators is the vital bottom line to keep in mind when thinking about portals and applications, regardless of whether the applications already exist or are to be developed in the future.

A portal is also not an alternative to a Web server. A portal will rely on one or more external Web servers for all of its Web transactions consistent with the model of leveraging proven best-of-breed solutions rather than trying to reinvent the wheel. As in the case of application servers, but more rarely, portal servers may come with a bundled-in but separate Web server to expedite deployment. The reason that most portal servers do not bother to include a Web server is because it is assumed that a customer opting for a portal solution is already bound to have a Web presence implemented via a Web server.

3.3.1   Standalone dedicated platform or a shared system?

The physical separation of the portal from the Web servers and the other IT systems will depend primarily on the intended platform for the portal. Figure 1.4 showed a detailed framework for portal deployment with extensive use of firewalls to isolate the portal from IT systems and the networks via a DMZ. This framework, with its DMZ, assumes that the portal software (i.e., portal server) will be deployed by itself on its own server platform (e.g., mid-size UNIX server, multiprocessor Windows 2000 server). If an application server is a prerequisite for the portal, then you will obviously have to run one on this server just for the portal. The Web server(s) as well as any necessary application servers for running corporate applications will be deployed on other servers. In many cases this standalone portal approach is the optimum in terms of security, scalability, portal resilience, and manageability. "Standalone" in this context does not preclude the use of clustered or parallel portal servers to eliminate single points of failure as well as to bolster scalability and performance. What is important is that these systems are dedicated to running the portal.

The standalone portal approach is unlikely ever to be an issue if you intend to deploy your portal on one or more WinTel or LINUX servers, since the cost of the appropriate hardware systems to host it will be relatively easy to justify—particularly given the cost saving that can be realized, thanks to the portal. There are obviously caveats to this, and justification could start getting harder once you start going beyond three or four relatively powerful portal-specific servers. The cost-saving arguments could also be persuasively used to acquire a few medium-sized UNIX servers. However, the current trends when it comes to UNIX servers and even LINUX may start complicating the possibilities of deploying and maintaining standalone, dedicated portal servers—at least in terms of physical systems.

Mainframe-like, high-end UNIX servers, with lots of powerful, upgradable processors, multisystem clustering, and even logical partitioning, are now in vogue. Sun's Sun Fire 15K and IBM's "Regatta" p690 are good examples of such systems. The Sun Fire 15K can have up to 106 UltraSPARC III processors and support up to 18 logical, self-contained partitions, each running its own copy of Sun Solaris UNIX OS—with a minimum of four processors allocated per partition. IBM's p690, although offering only up to 32 processors, is even more powerful than the Sun Fire 15K according to the latest benchmarks, thanks to the processors in this instance being IBM's latest 1.3-GHz POWER4 microprocessors—currently the fastest processors on the market. A p690 can be logically divided into 16 partitions, with each partition powered by one or more processors, running either IBM AIX UNIX OS or a 64-bit LINUX OS. Both of these systems can be clustered.

Although these rather expensive UNIX servers are indubitably targeted at the high end of this market, they demonstrate where UNIX servers are going, with Sun, IBM, Compaq, and HP (premerger) also offering increasingly brawny mid-range systems. The issue here is that if yours is a relatively big UNIX shop, then some of these larger systems may indeed be the economically optimum way to address your ever-increasing workload demands—rather than continuing to use banks of smaller UNIX servers. The portal-related workload, which will continue to grow as user base and the services offered increase, will of course exacerbate the demand for more processing, forcing you to evaluate larger, readily partitionable, and upgradable systems as the strategic and cost-effective way forward rather than adding smaller machines.

IBM's ardent advocacy of LINUX can also have an impact on how and where you deploy a LINUX-based portal server (e.g., BEA's WebLogic Portal). IBM now supports LINUX on all of its hardware platforms, including mainframes and AS/400s (now known as iSeries). There is even a new LINUX-specific mainframe known as the z800 Model 0LF. If you have mainframes within your company, they might actually prove to be a very cost-compelling platform for running high-volume LINUX workloads, especially if you have relatively new mainframes or plan to upgrade to a new mainframe. There are many hardware and software options for running LINUX server images on a mainframe.

It is now possible to run thousands—possibly even tens of thousands—of UNIX server images on a single mainframe! In April 2000, IBM announced that it had tested 14,400 LINUX server images on a single 1999 mainframe using IBM's proven VM OS as the means for providing the server image virtualization. Even though you may not require this many LINUX servers to run your corporate portal, it is sobering to realize that around the same time that IBM made its claim, Web search Goliath, Google, was using a LINUX server farm consisting of 8,000 servers to handle requests for upward of 100 million searches a day. The bottom line is that if you are considering LINUX for your portal and also happen to have mainframes within your shop, you may be forced to consider the mainframe as an attractive LINUX platform for hosting your portal.

If you end up using a midsize or large UNIX server or LINUX on a mainframe as your preferred platform for your portal, then physical separation of the portal is not going to be feasible. Logical separation will nonetheless be possible. One option would be to run the portal server in a dedicated partition with its own complement of dedicated processors. This should isolate the portal from performance hits due to changing workloads within the rest of the machine and should also ensure that the portal will not be impacted if there are problems with some of the other software. It would also be possible to use software firewalls to keep the portal isolated from other applications. The key here is to make sure that security is not compromised in any way. So even if physical separation is not possible, use DMZ concepts (shown in Figure 1.4) to guarantee that public Internet access to the portal does not mean that unscrupulous individuals can use this access to hack into the rest of the IT infrastructure.

3.4 Integrating data-center resources

If your company relies on IBM (or compatible) mainframes, IBM AS/400s (now iSeries), other minicomputers, or UNIX servers for some or all of its IT needs, then it is imperative that your portal have suitable access to the mission-critical applications and data located on these so-called data-center machines. Since at least 70 percent of corporate data still resides on these systems, there is no shortage of solutions for effectively linking corporate portals with data centers, as noted in sections 2.2 and 3.1. Though there are upwards of 150 solutions from close to 100 vendors, these solutions can be divided into three main categories.

Two of these categories—thin-client and host publishing—are geared for channeling existing interactive data-center access via the portal. The other category, best generalized as relating to host integration, is geared toward the development of new portal-centric applications or Web services that wish to leverage data-center resources. The data center and application adapters available with most portal servers fall into this third category, since they require some level of scripting or programming to ensure that they have an appropriate portal-compatible user interface. Table 3.1 summarizes the key characteristics of these three portal to data center access techniques.

At this juncture it should be noted that there is likely to be some data-center access that is best done outside of the corporate portal, despite the desire to route all corporate IT access through it. Data-entry operators are invariably the most cited example when it comes to this "bypass-the-Web altogether" approach. The reason for this is not hard to find. Going through a corporate portal can be an unnecessary distraction and represent overhead for certain classes of users. Data entry operators are normally compensated by the volume of transactions they complete in a day. They want the fastest, most efficient, and least intrusive means of getting this done.

Any kind of intermediary processing, even host-to-HTML conversion, between them and their target host application could slow them down. In addition, portal or Web access, with its plethora of alluring content, could

Table 3.1 *Portal to Data Center Access Techniques*

	Thin-Client	Host Publishing	Host Integration
Category	Host application access via portal	Host application access via portal	Develop new portal-centric apps or Web services
Available from	Host access vendors	Host access vendors	Host access vendors and portal server vendors
Examples	IBM's Host On-Demand, Seagull's WinJa, WRQ's Reflection for the Web	NetManage On-Web, IBM's Host Publisher, Hummingbird e-Gateway	NetManage On-Web, IBM's Host Publisher, BEA's Java Adapter for mainframes
Characteristics	Host emulator in Java or ActiveX	Host-to-HTML/WML/XML converter	Programmatic connections to the host via Java-Beans COM or APIs
Executes on	Client	Server	Server
Primary output	Client-system specific (e.g., Windows on desktop)	HTML, WML, or XML	Depends on application or Web service, but in this case portal oriented
Web browser disposition	Invoked via a Web browser; output could be within browser	Browser-centric data displayed within browser in HTML	Depends on application or Web service, but normally browser centric
User interface modernization	Yes	Yes	Yes
Best suited for	Employees, partners	General public, mobile employees, partners	General public, employees, partners
Primary advantages	Continues terminal emulation paradigm Minimizes installation, maintenance, and upgrade costs	Zero footprint No host access software at the client Easily adaptable for tight integration with portals	Enables host application logic to be reused Totally extensible and permits synthesis of data from multiple sources
Key disadvantages	Requires software on client systems Difficult to ensure seamless portal integration	Still essentially a terminal emulation scheme Not meant for combining functions from multiple applications	Requires some development effort Requires the continuing presence of host application
Best use vis-à-vis portal	Tactical, short-term stopgap	Mid-term, portal integration with host data embellished with new HTML-formatted content	Strategic long term, especially for developing new Web services

be an irresistible temptation that detracts from the task at hand of maximizing transaction volumes—hence the understandable reluctance of some companies and government agencies to provide all their PC/workstation users with Internet access. Portal access falls into this same category of concern. There are likely to be certain users who are best served with a direct, client-to-host terminal emulation scheme with no user interface modernization or any attempt at portal integration.

3.4.1   Host publishing and host integration

Thin-client–based terminal emulation, at best, is a tactical, stop-gap solution when it comes to data-center access via a corporate portal. Though thin-client will work and work well, it will always be a somewhat incongruous solution vis-à-vis the overall portal paradigm. There are a number of reasons for this. For a start, a thin-client relies on having host access–specific software on the client system—albeit software that can be invoked from a browser via a Web page link or button. Although this software can be dynamically downloaded from a Web server and cached (to obviate the need for repeated downloads until a new version of the software is installed on the server), it still is counter to the concept of just requiring a standard Web browser to deal with a corporate portal.

The need for client-side software also makes this approach unsuitable for general, Internet-based public-access scenarios, since there will be an appreciable delay while the software is being downloaded and installed on the user's system. With today's understandable concerns about viruses, many users will be uncomfortable with the idea of having large amounts of software dynamically installed on their system. Thus, thin-client is not appropriate for b2c portal applications. The primary use of thin-client will thus be restricted to b2e scenarios. Figure 3.10 illustrates the architecture of a contemporary two-tier, client-to-host, thin-client solution.

Host publishing, as shown in Figure 2.6, is a more appropriate technology for realizing portal-based host access, given that it works via dynamic, bidirectional host-to-HTML, host-to-XML, or host-to-WML conversion. Thus, it dovetails nicely with the portal paradigm. This server-side approach, whose roots go back to 1996, was called "publishing" because it enables host data to be published on a Web page—now a portal view. Furthermore, the output of a host publishing solution can be easily plugged in to a portal view, given that the output can be in HTML or XML form. Thus, host publishing can very effectively and strikingly be used with ASP or JSP technology, with these scripting and data integration schemes augmenting the host data and modernizing the user interface.

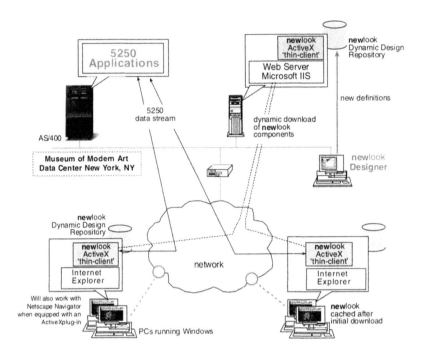

Figure 3.10   *The overall architecture of a thin-client terminal-emulation scheme, in this case showing looksoftware's newlook ActiveX emulator, with its powerful user modernization capability, as used at New York City's Museum of Modern Art. The rejuvenated AS/400 user interface shown in Figure 2.7 is made possible through this thin-client"configuration.*

Some of the leading host publishing systems will even allow you to alter the screen input/output sequence of a host application by letting you skip some screens entirely or combine I/O fields from different screens into a new consolidated view. You could even combine screen data from multiple applications, although at this juncture it is best to start looking at host integration techniques. Some host publishing schemes, such as IBM's Web-Sphere Host Publisher and NetManage OnWeb, can do both publishing and integration. They thus provide an attractive migration path. You can start by using publishing to portal-enable all the requisite data-center applications. Then you can look at host integration as a means to reuse the functionality of some of these applications to develop new portal applications or Web services.

From a portal-integration perspective, host publishing is a highly compelling and satisfactory solution for short- to medium-term data-center integration. It is also a very convenient and powerful way to generate XML representations of host screen data on the fly, without manual intervention.

However, this XML capability is not offered by all host publishing schemes. The downside of host publishing is that in the end it is still a screen-oriented, terminal-emulation scheme—albeit now using XML schemes at the front end rather than terminal-specific data streams. It does not have a role per se when it comes to enabling the business logic of existing host applications to be reused to build new applications other than its ability to generate XML renditions of host screen data. This is where host integration comes in Host integration enables the proven and valuable business logic found within existing mission-critical applications to be profitably reused when building new portal-specific applications or Web services. This ability to freely reuse existing business logic slashes development costs, compresses testing schedules, and enhances the resilience of the new application by minimizing the amount of unproven code included within it. Host integration obviates the need to reinvent the wheel when it comes to developing future portal applications and Web services. Thanks to host integration you will not have to develop a new customer lookup routine when you have already had one for the past 20 years on one of your mission-critical mainframe applications. You can just isolate and reuse that functionality within the new application being developed.

Host integration, however, does not allow you to just extract the necessary execution logic from the original application and then embed that "code" within the new application. This would not be practical for a variety of reasons, key among them being programming language incompatibility. Instead, host integration works by allowing the new application or Web service to make run-time calls to the original application, which then executes the transaction on behalf of the new application. This type of business logic reuse, is referred to as run-time transaction reuse since the new application, in essence, is making use of a transaction being executed by another application. The original host application becomes a subordinate task that is running on a different platform and passing pertinent data back to the new application.

The software interfaces necessary to realize run-time transaction reuse are normally defined in terms of JavaBeans (or EJBs), Microsoft COM, or sometimes even CORBA. The necessary objects to make run-time transaction reuse possible are created by the host integration solution, which provides a visual host transaction capture tool. This is typically a "design tool" that runs on a PC. A programmer will use this design tool to first access the appropriate host application and then navigate through the application to the desired transaction. The design tool will automatically record the necessary steps to access the application and navigate through the application to

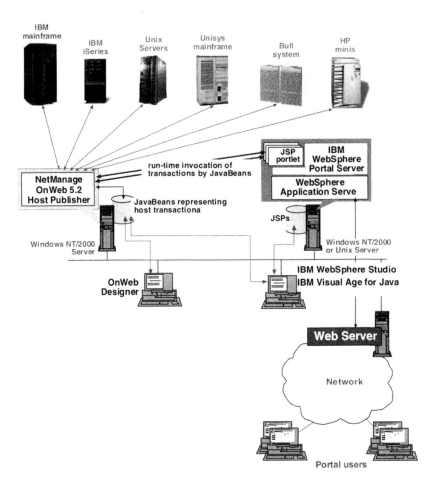

Figure 3.11
*Example of portal-
specific host
integration using
JavaBeans and JSP
portlets, in this
instance using
NetManage's
OnWeb to create
the JavaBeans, and
IBM's WebSphere
Portal Server to
run the JavaBean-
bearing JSPs and
invoke the necessary
host transactions
via OnWeb at run
time.*

the requisite transaction. The programmer will then capture the desired transaction and through it the underlying business logic by identifying the necessary input and output fields corresponding to that transaction. The design tool, yet again, will record what these input/output fields are and how they can be reached. The programmer will then request the design tool to automatically generate a reusable entity, say as a JavaBean or COM object.

Once this object has been created it can be readily embedded into new applications, Web services, or even JSP/ASP scripts. The object will contain all the necessary logic to invoke the application and the necessary transaction in real time on behalf of the new "application." Figure 3.11 shows how host integration, with its run-time transaction reuse approach, can be used to include host transactions within JSP portlets being used to realize a portal.

3.5   Putting portals on a platform

The platform you select for your portal will inevitably dictate many of its eventual operational characteristics. At a minimum, performance, scalability (i.e., the number of concurrently active users that can be realistically supported), resilience, and upgradability will in the end be contingent on your choice of platform. Ironically, and somewhat unfortunately, the choice for portal platforms, at least at present, is limited if you intend to use a portal server. The gating factor here happens to be the operating systems supported by the portal servers. Though many of the leading portal servers are Java based and hence theoretically platform neutral, the most commonly supported operating systems are:

- Windows 2000

- Windows NT

- IBM AIX

- Sun Solaris

- Red Hat LINUX

Although it is indeed possible to find portal servers that will support other flavors of UNIX, such as HP-UX and Compaq Tru64, the OS choices still boil down to Windows NT/2000, UNIX, and LINUX. Many may consider this range of OSs to be more than adequate and not notice anything incongruous. If yours is, however, an IBM shop, you may be surprised to see the absence of mainframe OSs (e.g., OS/390, z/OS) or OS/400, given that IBM has gone to great lengths since 1998 to make these compelling and powerful J2EE-compliant Java platforms. This is highlighted by the fact that Java application servers, a prerequisite for Java-based portal servers, are available on mainframes and AS/400s. The real issue here is not technical; it has to do with testing and support.

Java's proud claim of "write once, run anywhere" is meritorious given that Java execution environments are now readily available on all pertinent platforms, whether from the platform vendor or from third parties. However, as Java developers will quickly add, this supposed platform independence is realized only via a "write once, test on all platforms, and then make modifications" process. This is the rub. Java, in the end, still has some inevitable platform dependencies and idiosyncrasies. If you have both Apple Macs and Windows clients, you will already know this—to your cost. A Java applet that works immaculately on Windows may not work as well on a Mac. This is so much the case that there are still many Java applet–based client-side solutions that are supported only on Windows because the vendors of these applets do not have the resources to test and support the applets on Mac, UNIX, and LINUX clients. The same issue applies to portal servers.

A mainframe may not be your first choice as a portal platform given the perceived complexity of any type of mainframe deployment. If yours is a mainframe shop, however, you probably appreciate that in the long term a mainframe, especially with Parallel Sysplex, is unsurpassable when it comes to capacity, scalability, and, above all, "near zero downtime" reliability. This is the reason that some large companies use mainframes as powerful and ultrareliable Web servers. If yours is already a mainframe shop and you plan to have a high-volume portal, then a mainframe could be an ideal portal platform. Today's "on-the-fly" capacity-upgrade-on-demand features, whereby you can just pay for additional processing capacity when you need to handle peak loads, make this option even more attractive from a portal perspective. Currently, however, there are only two ways whereby you can leverage a mainframe as a portal platform. One approach, which is indeed attractive and highly viable, is to use LINUX, as discussed previously. The other is to opt for a customized solution.

3.5.1 Windows NT/2000 or UNIX?

With Windows NT/2000, UNIX, and LINUX being the three readily available options, the portal platform decision is going to hinge on a choice between Windows NT and UNIX. In most instances this will end up being more of a philosophical and emotional decision as opposed to a technical one—with few people still being able to agree on which of these popular OSs is better suited for enterprise use. If you already use UNIX for some of your mission-critical applications, in particular your Web servers, then you are likely to opt for a UNIX/LINUX approach. If, on the other hand, you currently do not have any UNIX servers in your company, then the chances are that you are going to favor an NT/2000 approach, at least to begin with.

Security and scalability, two pivotal issues when it comes to portals, should, however, be given considerable thought. The recent spate of successful and highly damaging attacks by hackers and virus creators on NT-family servers have severely damaged the credibility of NT when it comes to security, despite Microsoft's efforts to continually come up with fixes for the various security flaws and exposures. This is the case to the extent that respected consulting and analysts firms have put out advisories recommending clients not to use NT servers in situations where they can be accessed over the Internet (e.g., as the basis for a Web server). A corporate portal server, to be effective, needs an Internet interface. Consequently, security is a pivotal issue that has to be considered and weighed if you want to opt for an NT approach.

The other contentious issue is that of scalability. This, fortunately, will be an issue only if you plan to have a high-traffic, high-volume portal that will regularly be servicing a few thousand concurrent users. If your portal is likely to be supporting 4,000 or more concurrent users in the near future, then you really need to do some diligent homework, testing, and reference checking before you decide to go for an NT approach. Though Windows 2000 is much more scalable than NT 4.0, there are many who will still insist that UNIX will give you better and more predictable scalability when you are dealing with high-traffic volumes and lots of users. There is also the issue of hardware.

Performance and scalability are not just OS issues. The underlying hardware plays a big role in this too. UNIX servers, along with mainframes, have always endeavored to push the performance envelope with RISC, parallel processings, and now clustering. If your company is already using medium sized to large UNIX servers or mainframes to handle its current user loads, then the chances are that you will start with a UNIX server for your portal. Scalability issues are talked about further in the following chapter.

Another pertinent consideration when selecting a portal platform is your current in-house expertise and experience base. If yours is predominantly an NT server shop, then bringing in a UNIX server may just complicate things and delay your deployment options. On the other hand, if you want to migrate toward UNIX/LINUX, a portal certainly can be the killer application to justify this transition. Another option is to consider outsourcing the installation, deployment, and initial maintenance of a UNIX server. In the long term, however, it is important that you have in-house resources to look after, manage, and maintain and upgrade your UNIX server(s), given the mission-critical and pivotal nature of a corporate portal.

You always have the options of changing horses in midstream. Though not optimum it is not a show stopper, given that the same portal servers will work both on NT and UNIX. So if you want, you can indeed start with an NT implementation to cut your teeth on the intricacies of managing portals—using a platform you know and already have lots of experience with. Down the road, as your user base and transaction volumes grow, you can think about moving to a UNIX implementation.

3.5.2 Java or decaf?

In much the same way as the debate between Windows NT and UNIX, Java versus decaf is another "religious"—as opposed to overtly technical—conundrum. Unfortunately, as with NT, this too revolves around one's feelings about Microsoft, although it should be immediately noted that Windows NT/2000 is a proven, popular, and practical platform for Java. So at least the issue is not whether you can successfully run a Java-based portal server on a Windows NT server.

The issue is whether your partialities lie with Java or Microsoft .NET. It is another spin on the old "open" versus proprietary debate, except that now Microsoft, rather than IBM, is the purveyor of proprietary, platform-specific solutions. The Java camp, in the context of portals, is packed with most of the super-heavyweights, including IBM, Sun/Netscape (i.e., iPlanet), Oracle, BEA, and PeopleSoft. Others, like SAP, support both J2EE and .NET. Microsoft, in turn, offers its own portal server—SharePoint.

Given that Java has been around since 1995, most corporations by now have a well-honed view of Java. If yours is already a committed Java shop, the portal decision is a no-brainer. There are lots of powerful and proven Java-based portal servers on the market. Evaluate some from names that you are comfortable with, and off you go. If your company is already committed to .NET, your options are also cast in stone. You will not have as many options from big names as you would with Java, but there are enough .NET-oriented portal servers to ensure that you have a choice. If you are still on the fence, then it is time to start doing some serious thinking.

Some may claim, justifiably, that Java has not lived up to its once exalted expectations, but there is no denying that Java is very popular, has enviable backing, market traction, and lots of momentum. On the other hand, Microsoft totally dominates corporate desktops and departmental servers. Much depends on your company's philosophy, vision, and aspirations. Whether you like it or not, Java carries with it a connotation and aura of "big company." On the other hand, despite Windows being the desktop of choice for the Fortune 500, saying that you are Microsoft-centric all the way projects an impression of "smallness." There are always exceptions, but this "big" versus "small" perception is something that you should ponder. If you envisage that your corporate portal will be the next big thing to hit your company, as it most likely will, then give some serious thought to Java. Remember, going with Java does not mean that you can't use a Microsoft platform.

Web services, fortunately, are also not a gating factor when it comes to deciding between Java and .NET. Both schemes set out to promote the development and deployment of Web services. Yet again, this is an issue as to what you and your company are comfortable with. Java versus .NET, vis-à-vis Web services, will be discussed further in Chapter 8. For the time being the only thing to note is that the Java camp, with all of its big players, has invested heavily in making Web services a reality and as such has considerable momentum. Equally, .NET continues to gain attention and followers. The key thing here, however, is that Web services is unlikely to be the deciding factor between Java and .NET. There is much more at stake vis-à-vis this decision than what makes the best platform for developing and deploying Web services.

3.6   Q&A—A time to recap and reflect

Q: Is there a single, fixed architecture for implementing corporate portals?

A: No. There is no industry standard per se when it comes to an architecture for corporate portals, although it is fair to note that all credible portals have to offer a minimum and common set of core functionality. However, the exact mechanism for delivering this core functionality set will differ between various portal servers.

Q: What is the core set of functionality that needs to be provided by a portal server?

A: The basic set of functionality needed to implement a successful corporate portal includes a Web interface; presentation services for user interface management; data management services; external data access mechanisms; security, authentication, and personalization; portal development tools; and portal administration and management tools. Data management in this context will encompass content management, search, collaboration, and workflow management functionality. Content management, in turn, will address content publishing, content structuring, content syndication, content aggregation, content delivery, content directory, and content categorization. In addition, a portal will also typically include powerful directory functions and a rules engine for enforcing various rules-based services.

Q: What are some examples of rules-based services?

A: Rules, as well as roles, can be used to facilitate portal personalization. Rules directories with appropriate rule-enforcing engines can also be used for content delivery and subscription management, content categorization, and workflow management. In the case of content delivery and subscription management, rules can be used to customize and update any push-based data as well as the auto-alert triggers. Rules-based alerting also can be extended to cover workflow processing—for example, a department manager getting automatically notified when an employee requests vacation time using a portal-based Web service. Rules can also be effectively used for categorizing content, with a key advantage being that global changes to the categorization taxonomies can be accomplished simply by updating the relevant rules.

Q: What is a portlet?

A: A portlet is a content channel or an application "window." It is, in essence, the active visible component that end users see within their portal view. It is the portal equivalent of an application window on a Windows desktop.

Q: Why is the concept of a portlet (or equivalent) so important?

A: For a start, portlets provide modularization and function isolation. Each portal application will be associated with a specific portlet. Thus, each portal application can be developed, maintained, and updated independently. The other big thing with portlets is the availability of extensive, prebuilt portlet libraries, which include portlets from the portal server provider as well as from third parties.

Q: What are some of the equivalents to portlets?

A: Microsoft's Web parts vis-à-vis digital dashboards, SAP's iView, People-Soft's pagelets, and Plumtree's gadgets are all concepts similar to portlets.

Q: What are ASPs and JSPs?

A: ASPs stand for Microsoft's active server pages. ASPs are a powerful and popular server-side scripting mechanism that was introduced with Microsoft's IIS Web Server 3.0 around 1997. JSP, for JavaServer Pages, is the Java equivalent of ASPs. Both ASPs and JSPs set out to simplify the creation and maintenance of Web pages with dynamically generated content.

Q: What options are available for integrating traditional data-center host systems with portals?

A: There are, in the main, three techniques: thin-client terminal emulation, host publishing, and host integration. The first two of these techniques are Web-oriented methodologies for terminal emulation–based host access. Host integration, on the other hand, enables the proven business logic of existing host applications to be reused within new portal applications or Web services.

Q: What are the popular platforms for deploying portal servers?

A: Although many of the leading portal servers are Java based, they are not platform independent. The operating systems most commonly supported by portal servers are Windows 2000, Windows NT, IBM AIX, Sun Solaris, and Red Hat LINUX. This OS support, in essence, dictates the hardware platforms that can be employed. Windows NT and UNIX servers are thus the primary choices today, although it should not be forgotten that IBM mainframes can be a very attractive platform for deploying large numbers of LINUX server images.

Q: Are Web services supported by .NET platforms?

A: As a new genre of Web applications, Web services are indeed supported by Microsoft's .NET as well as by Java initiatives. The Web services enabling protocols, such as XML, SOAP, WSDL, and UDDI, are readily available with .NET or with Java application servers. With the Java camp having lots of followers with deep pockets, it is possible that Web services could get more of a boost and momentum from the Java world than from .NET. But other than that and the perennial Microsoft-related issues pertaining to security, scalability, and robustness, there are no technical impediments that dictate that Web services will be better on Java than on .NET.

4

Security, Scalability, and Speed

If a "7-11" is open 24 hours a day, 365 days a year,
why are there locks on the door?

—Nick Featherman

Security, scalability, synchrony, and speed are the vital "four Ss" for maintaining a successful corporate portal—with synchrony in this context referring to the art and science of keeping portal content up-to-date, accurate, coordinated, and linked. The need for robust, fail-safe security measures to safeguard portal resources and the other IT systems accessible from the portal is obvious and inescapable. Despite the billions of dollars spent to bolster Internet security during the past few years, nobody as yet feels safe or invincible. The widespread denial-of-service attacks in 2000, instigated through various packet-flooding schemes, are still vivid in the minds of all those who were impacted. Reports of new e-mail–borne viruses and worms are unceasing and always disquieting. IT departments are now in a constant state of high alert, nervously awaiting news of the next attack.

Though security is paramount, corporations can no longer afford to be totally cut off and isolated from the Internet because of fears of potential attacks. For a start, there is too much to lose. The advantages of the Internet—information access, near zero-cost bandwidth, unprecedented global reach, universal e-mail—are unique, manifold, and far-reaching. Furthermore, the currently ongoing development of Web services is going to make the business-related functionality available on the Web even greater and more incisive.

Ten years ago companies could not function without fax machines. Business partners and customers always wanted to fax documents or receive information in the form of faxes. Although the Internet and e-mail changed some of these habits, faxes are still heavily used when it comes to purchase-order transmittals, invoice distribution, and order placement. Down the road, five years from now, Web services will be like faxes. Partners, customers, and prospects are going to be saying "get your order-processing application to hook up to our purchase order–issuing Web service." In much the same way that you could not tell people that you did not have a fax machine, you will not be able to tell people that you are cut off from the Web because you are afraid of viruses and attacks—unless, of course, your company's business plan is to forgo doing business and become progressively less competitive.

In addition, and somewhat ironically, one can justifiably argue that from an overall corporate IT security standpoint, it is actually better to have an open and active interface to the Internet than to be cut off from it altogether. The rationale behind this claim is very simple: It is an inescapable fact that companies as a whole as well as individuals within them have valid reasons for wanting information, in electronic form, from the outside world.

It might be as simple as a Word file containing a report that your 11-year-old daughter is doing for school that you want to format at work using the full-blown PageMaker package you have on your work PC and then print on the department's high-resolution laser printer. Or it might be a whole new parts catalog, with ten of thousands of entries, being sent over by a supplier. Today, these as well as most other data imports into a company will be realized using e-mail attachments, FTP, or some form of VPNs. Because of the concerns about Internet-related security, all companies with Internet interfaces now have firewalls, automatic e-mail scanning checkers, file-quarantine areas, and stringent procedures for handling files emanating from the Internet.

If a company does not permit data transfer across the Internet, then employees, always resourceful to a fault in such matters, will resort to other means to bring in data. It could be diskettes, ZIP drives, or, given the ready availability of CD-RW drives, CD-ROMs. In the case of partners and suppliers it could be in the form of tapes. Viruses, Trojan Horses, or malicious applications can be easily transported on any of these media. And this is the rub. Compared with the safeguards now available to detect and intercept attacks transmitted via the Internet, the measures and policies in place for handling attacks from non-Internet-related data transfers are invariably patchy and primitive.

Though never in the same class as security when it comes to concern, diligence, and heartburn, the speed and scalability of a corporate portal is nonetheless a pivotal and pressing issue. A sluggish, unresponsive corporate portal is bad for business, plain and simple. One could, slightly tongue-in-cheek, even say that it is better not to have a portal at all than to have one that is so slow and erratic that it drives users to distraction.

A sluggish, temperamental corporate portal will force users away. Prospects and customers are likely to defect to competition, particularly in fields such as online investing, personal travel reservation, mail order, and home banking. People are on increasingly tighter schedules, and time is precious. They will not hang around, twiddling their thumbs, waiting forever for a response if they can flip over to an alternate portal and get what they want without the wait. Once they defect it will be hard to lure them back. While suppliers and partners cannot be as fickle, they too are not going to be overly amused. Employees are captive, but slow portal performance is guaranteed to impact overall productivity and cause frustration; as a result, the portal is blamed for delayed work or missed opportunities. You could imagine hearing: I only had 12 minutes to check my e-mail, before I boarded the plane, to see if they had called about the bid. The portal was jammed. I couldn't even open the e-mail window!

The speed and scalability of a portal, though different issues, go hand-in-hand, since they can both be significantly influenced by choice of platform and system resource availability. Speed, in this instance, relates to the response times experienced by portal users. Response times need to be crisp and consistent. This can be a challenge when users are accessing the portal through the Internet. There could be many variables that are way outside your control and purview that can impact response times in terms of both consistency and crispness. There can be bandwidth issues, localized congestion, slowdown at an ISP due to server malfunctions, or even resource contention with other applications on a user's desktop. Realistically speaking, all that you can do is speed things up as much as possible at your end so as to compensate for potential slowdowns between the portal and the end user.

Scalability, in the true sense, relates to the ability of a system, in this case a portal, to smoothly adapt to increasing workloads whether as the result of additional users, an increase in traffic volumes, or the execution of more complex transactions. Thus, scalability has to do with accommodating growth. However, some think of scalability in a different way. They see it as the system's ability to handle a large number of users (or workload). There is obviously a correlation here. A system that can adroitly handle a large numbers of users without noticeable degradation in performance is also likely to be able to handle growth. Keep in mind, though, that the laws of physics and computing dictate that any given system configuration will always have a workload ceiling.

The goal when it comes to scalability is to make sure that you can easily get around a workload ceiling by adding additional resources (e.g., more processors or memory), upgrading the system, or migrating to a system clustering scheme with load-balancing. The keyword in the preceding sentence, just in case you missed it, was "easily." Scalability falls into the category of a "nice-to-have" problem. You will have to start tackling scalability only when your portal grows and becomes increasingly popular and more mission critical. Hence, having to justify the need for more systems resources is not going to be a stumbling block. But what you need to make sure of from the get-go is that you can continue to grow your portal, within its existing framework, without quickly running out of options because of system limitations. So when it comes to scalability the key issue is that of "ease of expansion" as opposed to the "cost of expansion."

Synchrony of portal content, the last of the big "four Ss," will be dealt with in Chapter 5 within the overall context of management. This is the right place to discuss this vital issue, since proactive content management is imperative to the success of a portal. There is no point having a secure, speedy, and scalable portal if the portal's content is insipid, out of-date, or incomplete. Poor content, just like poor performance, will alienate users.

4.1   Trying to put locks on corporate portals

If you think about it from a security-specific perspective, the challenges of trying to maintain a secure Internet-accessible corporate portal has many parallels to enforcing security within a large department store. Precluding unauthorized access to corporate assets via the portal is akin to preventing shoplifting, while safeguarding against viruses is the equivalent of making sure that no malicious packages are secreted within the store. If your portal plans to accept payment for goods or services via credit cards or electronic checks, then the issues of minimizing credit-card fraud or "bad" checks become familiar to store managers. Despite all of these tribulations, a department store or even a bank with a vault full of valuables, if it intends to stay in business, has to keep its door wide open during business hours—barring none (with the possible exception of previously convicted "trouble-makers"). The same holds true for corporate portals that intend to offer b2c and e-commerce functionality.

Firewalls are the equivalent of door locks in the case of corporate portals. However, just as with door locks on a department store, you cannot use firewalls in such a way that they keep out the general public. Firewalls are extremely proficient and powerful at restricting access to all but a set of preapproved IP addresses or users coming from specific, authorized ISPs. This so-called packet filtering, unfortunately, is of no use when it comes to a corporate portal that offers public access, since all IP addresses, irrespective of where they are coming from in terms of ISPs, need to be granted access. The only exception is barring the addresses of known habitual offenders (though they are likely to continually use new addresses) and possibly those of "unscrupulous" competitors.

An open, public-access portal is obviously an irresistible and inviting intelligence-gathering mechanism for your competitors. This is a fact of life in today's Web-centric society. Hopefully, it works both ways. Just as your competitors will roam around your portal, gathering information as to what your company is up to, folks in your company can regularly check out the portals of your competitors to keep close tabs on them. Depending on the competitive dynamics (e.g., a competitor plagiarizing content or borrowing ideas), you could use firewalls to filter out all packets bearing IP addresses corresponding to those used by the competitors in question. However, as you can appreciate, this is really more of a gesture than a real deterrent, since determined competitors will use other addresses (e.g., home computers, hotel connections, wireless services) to get around your roadblock.

Corporate portal security cannot be enforced simply by using judiciously positioned and configured firewalls, although it is still imperative to deploy firewalls in so-called application layer, proxy mode to enforce a DMZ around your corporate portal. Figure 4.1, which is a simplified version of the full-blown configuration shown in Figure 1.4 in Chapter 1, illustrates the concept of creating a DMZ around a corporate portal; the modes of operation for firewalls, such as application layer firewalls, are discussed in the following text.

In addition to firewalls and the oft-discussed issue of authentication (e.g., two-factor authentication), some of the other key topics that pertain to corporate portal security include:

- Digital certificates

- Public key infrastructure (PKI)

- Secure sockets layer (SSL)

- Intrusion detection

- IP Security (IPSec)

- Lightweight directory access protocol (LDAP) directories

- Virtual private networks (VPNs) that provide security (i.e., encryption) and "tunneling" across the Internet so that Internet bandwidth can be securely used by employees and partners for accessing corporate IT resources, including the corporate portal

- Single sign-on

All of these topics are discussed in this chapter. These are underlying security-facilitating methodologies that you need to know about, but do not have to worry about per se. Although a corporate portal will invariably end up exploiting many of these methodologies, much of the heavy lifting related to these methods will be performed automatically and transparently through joint efforts by the portal server, application server, and Web server. In addition, you will invariably have the option of either getting auxiliary security enforcing products from the likes of RSA, VeriSign, and IBM/ Tivoli, or get on-the-fly, real-time, outsourced security validation of portal users from a service such as the VeriSign Authentication Service Bureau. For example RSA's ClearTrust offering includes facilities for enforcing and managing two-factor authentication, digital certificates, and single sign-on.

Figure 4.1
Though firewalls alone do not provide anything close to adequate security for a corporate portal, it is imperative that firewalls be used to create a DMZ around the portal server so that there is no direct connection between the Internet and the other non-portal IT systems.

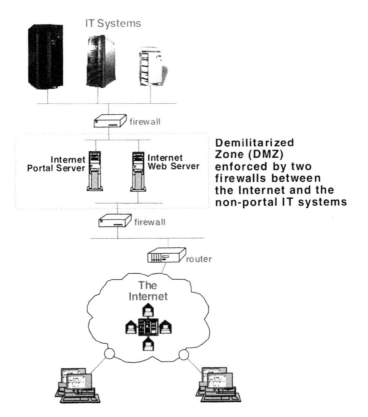

Thus, the goal of the following sections is to give you adequate background so that you can ask the right questions about security of your development team and server software vendors.

Viruses may appear to be conspicuous by their absence in the foregoing list. There is, however, a good reason for this. Viruses, especially e-mail–borne viruses, are really not a portal-specific problem. Implementing a corporate portal is unlikely to affect a corporation's vulnerability to viruses one way or another. For a start, e-mail–borne viruses, now the most prevalent form of virus propagation, occur whether a corporation has a portal or not. The only issue here is whether you permit e-mail exchanges in and out of your company. If you do, then you are vulnerable. Even if you restrict e-mail to your intranet, you can never be immune, since employees can inadvertently introduce an e-mail virus onto their machines—and hence to the e-mail system—by bringing in an infected diskette or CD-ROM.

While e-mail capability is routinely offered by corporate portals as a part of their overall arsenal of collaborative tools, distribution of viruses via e-mail is still really an e-mail issue rather than a portal issue. In most cases portals will typically leverage a company's existing e-mail infrastructure for the collaborative services it offers, as opposed to implementing a portal-specific e-mail scheme. Hence, measures for the detection and deflection of e-mail–borne viruses have to be continually performed independent of the presence of a portal. Though some may rightly argue that the presence of a portal will make it easier for hackers to determine valid e-mail addresses that pertain to the company, shying away from portals for this reason is akin to ending corporate marketing activities, because that too could provide hackers with hints as to the company's e-mail address and URL.

The other concern when it comes to viruses is that of a hacker using the portal as a means through which to infiltrate the company's IT infrastructure in order to plant a virus on a server. This is a valid concern, although it falls into the category of preventing unauthorized access to the portal and the resources accessible through it. The danger of this can be thwarted through the use of DMZs, authentication, and personalization (e.g., rigorously controlling who has write access).

4.1.1   Digital certificates

Digital certificates are an electronic credential (in the form of a small file) issued by a trustworthy organization such as a large company (e.g., IBM, Microsoft) or a security-specific entity such as VeriSign. Figure 4.2 shows a page from VeriSign's portal, providing an introduction to one of its public

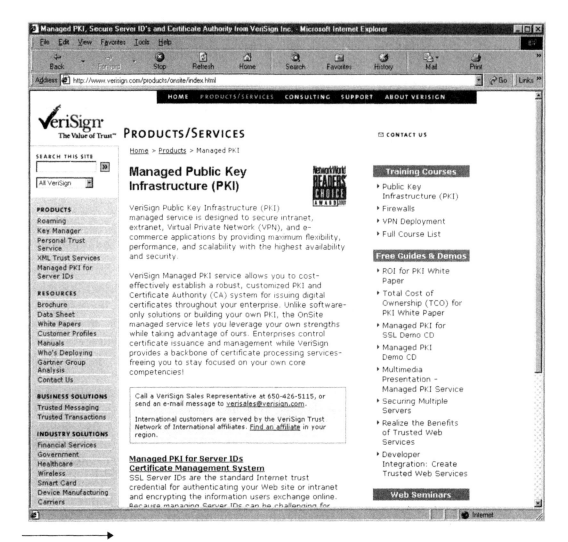

Figure 4.2   *One of the many VeriSign public key Infrastructure–based digital certificate offerings.*

key infrastructure–based digital certificate programs. The digital certificate (DC) vouches for an individual's or business's identity and authority to conduct secure transactions over the Web. DCs are, in essence, the Internet equivalent of a travel passport. They are a universally accepted means of establishing one's identity and thus gaining entry to a protected resource. DCs are meant to replace traditional user IDs and passwords, which are not as secure or trustworthy.

The issuing organization of a DC is called a certificate authority (CA)—VeriSign is an example of an existing and well-known CA. Refer to www.pki-page.org for an extensive list of CAs around the world as well as products that can be used to set up a CA. A CA can issue a DC to individual users, a server, or an application. If your company currently does not have any DCs, you may want to contact a CA and begin the process of acquiring a valid DC.

The acceptance of a DC as a valid credential is totally contingent on the recipient's trust in the CA. Thus, just having a DC is not enough. You need to have confidence in the CA that issued it, especially since there are no uniform requirements, at least at present, as to what information a CA checks before issuing a DC. Some public Internet CAs may ask users only for their names and e-mail addresses in order to issue a DC. This is clearly inadequate.

Fortunately, DCs today are closely tied in with PKI. CAs that support the PKI Exchange (PKIX) standards typically insist that the requester's identity information be further validated by a registration authority (RA) before a DC can be issued. RAs are an integral part of a public key infrastructure. There are proven PKI-specific products (e.g., RSA's Keon and IBM's Tivoli Trust Authority) that can be used by companies so that they can act as RAs. These systems allow companies to set up centralized or distributed electronic "enrollment centers" that validate user requests for DCs on behalf of the CA. Figure 4.3 shows a section from RSA's portal introducing the PKI capabilities offered by Keon.

The key thing to bear in mind is that a DC, in the end, is only as good as the CA that issued it. Therefore, all DCs are not necessarily equal. If you are going to accept DCs, as you will invariably have to, given their widespread use as a base-level security measure, then you will have to check which CAs meet your security criteria. For example, you may not want to accept DCs from unknown CAs. Typically, you will be able to use your rules-enforcing engine to accept and reject DCs based on a list of acceptable CAs. You will, of course, have the option to extend and modify this CA list if, for example, you discover that a CA that you have been hitherto rejecting has since changed its policies and is now compatible with your criteria.

Digital certificates leverage public key cryptography. Public key cryptography relies on the use of a pair of associated keys for encryption and decryption known as "public" and "private" keys. There is a mathematical relationship between these two keys that guarantees that anything encrypted using one key can be cleanly decrypted using the other key. Which key is made "public" and which is kept "private" is totally arbitrary. With public key cryptography, one can freely distribute the "public" key without in any way compromising or revealing the nature of the "private" key. The public

Figure 4.3   *RSA's Keon, one of several products on the market that enables companies to act as CAs and possibly even as RAs.*

key can even be stored in a public directory or a Web page. The "private" key, true to its name, must, however, be kept guarded and secret.

The "public" and "private" keys work only in tandem. That, so to speak, is key. In other words, a document encrypted using the public key can be decrypted only using the private key. The document cannot be decrypted using the openly available public key, since this would nullify the whole point of encryption. The same applies the other way around. A document encrypted using the private key can be decrypted only using the public key.

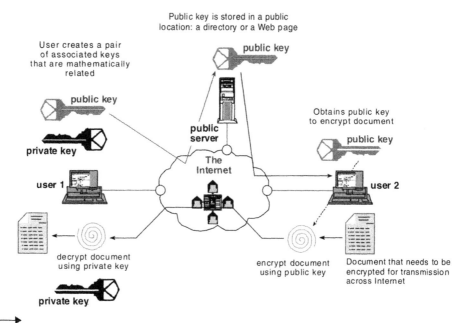

Figure 4.4   *The overall dual-key concept of public key cryptography.*

This too make sense, since the private key is kept secret and as such should not be available for use by other parties. Figure 4.4 provides an overview of how public key cryptography works, and Table 4.1 summarizes which keys are used for which operations. A DC will include the certificate holder's public key.

Digital certificates are defined by the X.509 standard. An X.509 certificate is typically a small file that contains:

- The DC holder's "distinguished name" (DN)—the identifying information for the certificate holder, which, depending on the identification criteria employed by the issuing CA, can include common name

Table 4.1   *Summary of which Keys are Used for Specific Operations*

Operation	Key Used
Send an encrypted document	Receiver's public key
Send an encrypted digital signature	Sender's private key
Decrypt a received encrypted document	Receiver's private key
Authenticate received digital signature	Sender's public key

of the certificate holder, holder's organization (i.e., company name), any organizational units, street address, fully qualified domain name (i.e., company URL), an IP address, and an e-mail address

- The certificate-issuing CA's distinguished name, which will include the same set of information as that of the holder's DN

- The certificate holder's public key

- The CA's digital signature—a "hashed" (i.e., encoded) code that in turn is encrypted using the "private" key of the CA and is then used as the seal of authenticity for the DC. (A digital signature, not to be confused with a digital certificate, is the equivalent of a tamper-detection seal on a pharmaceutical product.)

- A validity period (i.e., shelf life) for the DC

- A unique serial number for the DC

Figure 4.5 shows some of the DC details available from a Web browser (in this instance Microsoft Internet Explorer) about a certificate used to establish a secure connection.

Today, there are several different types of DCs, each for a specific security scenario. Some of the main types of DCs include:

1. CA certificates, which digitally validate the identity of the CA, containing its identifying information as well as its public key. A CA certificate can be signed (i.e., further validated) by another

Figure 4.5
Actual screen shot of a Web browser's "Properties" window, showing the details of a currently active digital certificate.

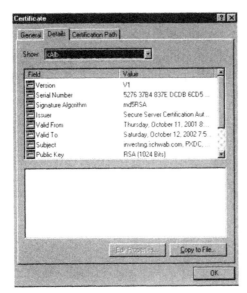

CA (e.g., VeriSign) or be self-signed if the CA does not require additional validation. A self-signed certificate is referred to as a "trusted root" for obvious reasons.

2.   Server certificates to validate a server's identity and provide information as to who owns them. They will contain the public key of the server's owner.

3.   Client or user certificates, which validate the client's identity and contain the client's "public" key. Authentication of server and client certificates can be used as the basis for encrypted, client/server communications per the SSL protocol.

4.   Object-signing certificates that are used as the basis for digital signatures, which vouch for the integrity of the accompanying object as well as the originator of that object.

4.1.2   Public key infrastructure

Public key infrastructure (PKI), as indicated by the inclusion of the term "infrastructure" in its name, provides an incisive framework for facilitating secure—but at the same time accessible and easy to use—public key encryption and digital signatures. The term "public," however, can be deceptive. PKI is not a centralized, public service for distributing and managing keys. The "public" in this context refers to the public key in the public-private key combination. Today, PKIs are typically implemented on a corporate basis using PKI-facilitating products from a variety of vendors, including IBM, VeriSign, and Entrust. IBM now even includes a comprehensive PKI on its flagship z/OS operating system for mainframes.

PKI sets out to hide the intricacies involved in providing a robust public key encryption system so as not to intimidate users. In the true spirit of an infrastructure sustaining a utility, similar to that of the electric power grid or the cable TV network, PKI is a nonintrusive, transparent service. You can use PKI without actually knowing or caring that it is there, what it does, or how it does it.

There is a three-way, symbiotic relationship between PKI, digital certificates, and digital signatures. The current use of digital certificates for Internet applications is contingent on PKI. Without PKI, DCs would not be as convenient to use or administer. PKI, per se, consists of four primary components:

1.   CAs, which issue and validate digital certificates as discussed previously

2.   One or more registration authorities (RAs), which work with the CA to verify a requester's identity prior to the issuance of a digital certificate

3.   One or more public directories (typically based on LDAP), where digital certificates, which will contain the public keys of their owners, can be stored

4.   A comprehensive and foolproof certificate management system

As an infrastructure scheme, PKI is expected to cater to key backup and recovery. Users typically have to enter a password to access their public key encryption keys. Users forget their passwords or may leave the company. If there is no way to recover encryption/decryption keys in such instances, valuable company information, which previously has been encrypted, may be forever lost. Thus, it is essential to have a secure and reliable way, whereby a designated and fully validated security administrator can recover encryption key pairs through the PKI system. Since such recovery will be possible only if the key pairs are properly backed up, it is assumed that the CA will automatically keep a backup of keys that have been issued.

In this context of backup and recovery, it is, however, important to note that recovery is required only for the key used for encryption/decryption. Keys used for digital signatures are not expected to be backed up or to be recoverable. The reason is that having duplicate (i.e., backed up) and thus recoverable "signing keys" undermines the overall integrity of a PKI. This has to do with something called "nonrepudiation."

Repudiate means to disown or reject an action. Thus, the process whereby a person denies involvement in a transaction is known as repudiation. Disowning a hotel charge made to a credit card via the "signature-on-file" scheme favored by North American hotels is an example of a repudiated transaction. Nonrepudiation precludes a person from being able to disown participation in a transaction. In the digital world this means ensuring the sanctity of digital signatures. A prerequisite for this is the inability of users to deny using their digital signature—hence the undesirability of having back-ups of signing keys.

If there are no backups and the user has sole and secure custody of the signing keys, then the latitudes for repudiating a digital signature are considerably reduced. However, just as in the nondigital world with pen and ink–based signatures, there will still occur situations in which users will try to repudiate digital signature–backed transactions. At this point, other electronic logs and traces will have to be used to enforce nonrepudiation.

The loss of a signing key, unlike that of an encryption key, is not catastrophic to business; the user will just have to obtain new keys to use with future signatures. The desirability of keeping backups of encryption keys but not those of signing keys means that users should not be allowed to use the same keys for both purposes, because this will again mean that there will be more than one copy of the signing keys. Thus, a PKI must support two key pairs per user: one pair for encryption and the other for digital signatures.

Then there is the issue of the longevity of key pairs. Just as with passwords, to maximize security key pairs should be periodically updated. A PKI can enforce this based on key expiration thresholds. However, since users may need to go back and decrypt documents encrypted with older keys, the PKI also needs to maintain a history whereby prior keys can be securely recovered. Yet again, this would not apply to signing keys. The PKI should destroy the old signing key pair each time a new pair is assigned.

Another issue pertaining to PKI and DCs relates to certificate revocation. In the event of a security compromise, DCs may have to be immediately revoked in advance of their built-in expiry setting. This may happen, for example, if a private key corresponding to the public key published in a DC gets into the hands of an unauthorized individual. Another instance would be when a user leaves a company. To handle certificate revocation, a PKI must maintain a scalable mechanism to publish the status of all certificates, active or revoked. Application software validating a DC will first make sure that it has not been revoked.

The final topic related to PKI has to do with cross-certification, given the current absence of a global PKI scheme. Cross-certification is also referred to as PKI networking. Cross-certification permits multiple, autonomous CAs to work cooperatively so that they have a mutual trust relationship. One scenario for this might be that of CAs for trading partners having the ability to validate DCs issued by the other CAs. Another scenario might be that of a large multinational company that decides to implement CAs on a geographic basis for scalability and management purposes. Yet again, today's leading PKI solutions are typically able to address all such requirements.

4.1.3   Secure sockets layer (SSL)

SSL, a client/server–based security mechanism developed by Web browser pioneer Netscape Communications around 1996, is the current basis for most of today's secure transactions across the Web. SSL is so widely used that it appears to be ubiquitous. It is supported by all popular commercial Web browsers and Web servers (e.g., Microsoft's Internet Information Server (IIS), the "open software" Apache Software Foundation's Apache HTTP Server, IBM's HTTP Server, etc.). In the context of Web servers it is used between a browser and the Web server. But it can also be used in other scenarios, such as host access. In such cases, SSL is used between a host gateway (e.g., a "tn"-server in the case of mainframe or AS/400 access) and a host access client. The key here is that SSL only works in client/server mode.

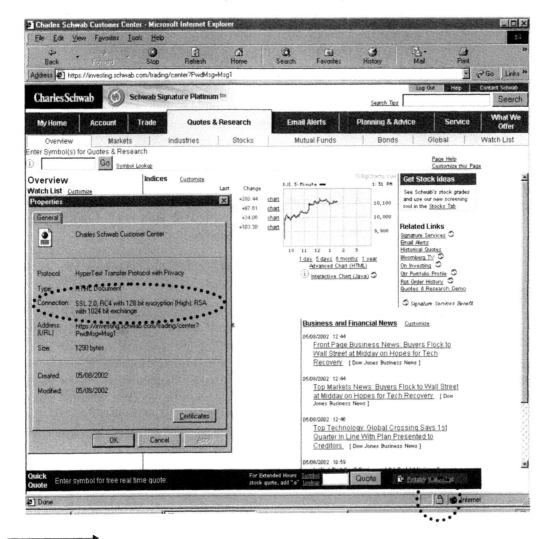

Figure 4.6   *The locked padlock indicating a secure SSL connection, along with a superimposed browser's "Properties" window showing that SSL 2.0 with an RSA encryption algorithm is being used for this secure connection with the Charles Schwab portal.*

The little locked padlock icon that gets displayed at the bottom of a Web browser window whenever a secure transaction is being performed (e.g., credit-card purchase or online stock trading) indicates that the security in force has been supplied via SSL technology. Figure 4.6 shows an example of the locked padlock icon indicating that SSL security is in force.

Whenever the locked padlock icon is on display, the address field at the top of the browser showing the URL invoked is likely to display "https:// www. etc. etc.," rather than "http://www. etc. etc." The "s" following the HTTP denotes SSL and in this case HTTP with SSL, or HTTP over SSL. HTTPS transactions are usually conducted across port number 443, while HTTP typically uses port 80. SSL, consequently, is not something new or rare. It is a scheme that most people have already encountered and have successfully used even without realizing that they were doing so.

SSL is a transport layer (i.e., layer 4) protocol. As such it provides authentication, integrity, and data privacy for applications running above the TCP layer (i.e., layer 3). SSL supports digital certificates. Given its client/server orientation, SSL uses digital certificates to authenticate the server and the client, although client authentication may in some cases be optional. This authentication process, which is achieved via what is referred to as an "SSL handshake," typically requires a user ID/password exchange— with the user ID and password being conveyed in encrypted mode using a public key. Following this authentication process, the SSL protocol sets about negotiating a common encryption scheme acceptable both to the client and the server. SSL per se does not do end-to-end data encryption.

Providing end-to-end, client-to-server encryption was never a goal of the SSL protocol. There are well-established industry standards (e.g., 56-bit DES and 168-bit triple DES) and commercial ciphers (e.g., RSA) for enforcing end-to-end security. What SSL does is negotiate an encryption scheme acceptable both to the server and the client (e.g., triple DES) and then invoke this mutually accepted encryption scheme for encrypting the data flowing between the client and the server. Thus, the security services provided by SSL can be summarized as follows:

- Server authentication via digital certificates

- Optional client authentication with digital certificates

- Acceptable encryption scheme negotiation between the server and the client

- Invoking the accepted encryption scheme to ensure that the data flowing between the client and the server are indeed encrypted and tamperproof on an end-to-end basis

The latest version of SSL is called transport layer security (TLS). The two terms will get used interchangeably in the future, with SSL most likely getting used more often even when TLS is being referred to, given its current familiarity. Figure 4.7 provides a high-level schematic of how a secure SSL connection is established between a Web server and a browser user.

A firewall in the context of a corporate portal enforces an access control policy between the outside world (i.e., the Internet) and the internal network associated with the portal. Most people think of firewalls as a means of blocking unauthorized and unknown traffic. However, the oft-stated issue when it comes to firewalls and portals is that the open access required to make a successful portal precludes the ability to use a firewall in this traf-

Figure 4.7
High-level view of the process involved in setting up a secure SSL connection between a Web server and a Web browser user. This process is the same for secure SSL connections between other client/server pairs (e.g., client-to-portal or PC-to-host).

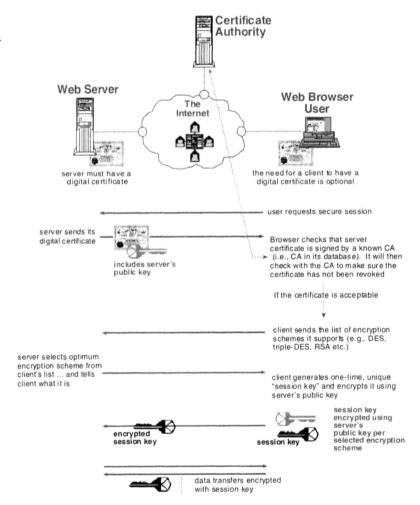

fic-blocking mode. Instead, in the case of portals, firewalls need to permit traffic to enter and serve only as observant gatekeepers monitoring and logging that traffic and preventing outsiders from being able see the actual IP addresses of the internal corporate network.

In keeping with the DMZ concept shown in Figure 4.1, it is assumed that you will be using more than one firewall around your portal; hence, the reference to them in the plural. In addition, because one firewall by itself will invariably be a vulnerable single point of failure, it is best to use two or more firewalls, at each interface, to achieve load-balancing and failover protection.

So when it comes to corporate portals, firewalls serve as security "choke points" through which all inbound and outbound traffic must flow. This choke point concept, coupled with the DMZ approach discussed earlier, ensures that you can immediately cut off traffic coming into the portal, in the event of an emergency, by "unplugging" the firewalls. This choke point concept also makes sure that there is a single, central, uncircumventable point whereby all traffic in and out of the portal can be logged.

In essence there are two basic types of firewalls: (1) network layer or packet-filtering firewalls and (2) application layer firewalls A network layer firewall, often referred to as packet filters since that is their function, is the simplest type of firewall. It is also the least useful in the context of portals. These simple firewalls make their permit or restrict decisions based on the source and destination addressing information as well as the port numbers specified in headers of individual IP packets. They compare addressing and port information against prespecified security policy definitions and either pass the packet along if it is approved or discard it unceremoniously if it is not approved.

In general, this type of packet filtering is primarily restricted to two criteria. The first is that of only permitting access based on the known IP address of the connecting computer. This approach is ideal for restricting access to known users such as company employees or selected partners. This scheme can also be extended to permit or deny access based on the ISP from which the packet originated. This blocking scheme has been very successfully employed to block traffic from ISPs that used to take a rather cavalier attitude about discouraging their clients from "spamming."

The second filtering criterion that can be used relates to the Internet "service" being sought by the packet, which typically has a correlation with port numbers. With this approach, you could block Telnet (i.e., host logon) access while permitting unrestricted traversal of e-mail traffic. This type of "service"-based filtering might appear, at first sight, to be applicable for portal scenarios. In reality, this is rarely the case, since today's consolidated corporate portals offer so many different services.

Though you can certainly buy very fast packet-filtering firewalls, this type of filtering function is now typically performed by routers, with Cisco routers noted for their prowess in this department. Since a corporate portal requires little, if any, packet filtering, it is best to use a router to do what little filtering you may need (e.g., block known troublemakers or competitors) rather than incurring the unnecessary cost of specialized, standalone packet filters. Packet-filter firewalls do not hide the IP infrastructure of the internal network from the outside world. That is a big security exposure. Application layer firewalls do provide this protection. Simple packet-filter firewalls, given that speed of filtering is their overriding goal, also do not offer packet-logging capabilities.

Application layer firewalls, per their name, are application "aware." This means that in marked contrast to packet filters that work just by checking addressing information in the packet header, application layer firewalls understand the nature of the data contained in the packets. This understanding is derived though the use of proxy servers within the firewall. These proxy servers act as minisurrogates for the production applications to which the traffic is destined. Thus, for example, you can have a mail server proxy or a Web server proxy on the firewall that intercepts and examines the traffic that wishes to go through to your corporate e-mail server and Web server.

A key function that can be performed by application layer firewalls is that of address translation or, to be more precise, network address translation (NAT). As with a packet filter, an application-level firewall first starts by checking addressing information against the predefined policies. Packets that fail this test are immediately discarded. However, packets that pass the test are not immediately forwarded. Instead, the packet is totally disassembled and the original addressing information and packet header are stripped away from the "data" content—albeit only after this addressing information has been logged. It then puts the "data" into a new packet that contains the firewall's addressing information as that of the packet originator.

This address-substitution function ensures that users outside the corporate network do not see the actual IP addresses used by the corporate network. This precludes them from using the actual IP addresses to try to log on to certain machines. The firewall thus acts as a true gateway between the internal network and the outside world. Application level firewalls are thus a mandatory prerequisite around your corporate portal, in essence forming the "sentinels" that create your DMZ.

The advantages of an application level firewall can be summarized as follows:

- It hides and protects the IP infrastructure information of the internal network from the outside world.

- It provides the same degree of packet filtering possible with a simple network layer firewall.

- Its application proxy approach safeguards against application-specific attacks.

- It provides comprehensive traffic logs and statistics.

Figure 4.8 illustrates the network-separating functions of an application level firewall. Obviously, there is going to be a cost associated with obtaining these application level firewall advantages. For a start, application level firewalls are slower than simple packet filters, since they do considerably more work, thereby slowing down network performance. In addition, the application proxies, as you could imagine, are somewhat complex to set up and maintain. There could also be rare situations in which your firewall vendor may not have a proxy for an application you intend to use. Despite these challenges, you have no choice when it comes to firewalls of this type;

Figure 4.8
The network-isolating functions of an application-level firewall, which is also sometimes referred to as a "dual-homed" gateway, given its role of having a leg in each camp, so to speak.

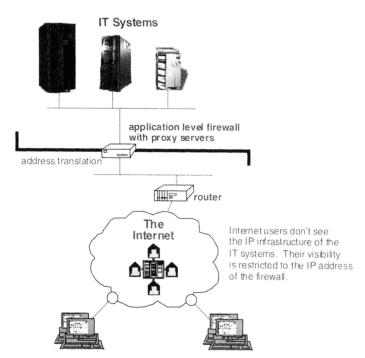

they must be your first line of defense between the Internet and your corporate portal.

4.1.4   Intrusion detection systems (IDS)

IDS, a rapidly burgeoning technology sphere in the context of Internet security, augments and complements firewalls. IDS protects against attacks that may originate from within the company (e.g., from a disgruntled employee) or attacks that use the availability of end-to-end encryption, à la SSL, to get malicious packets past application level firewalls. It can also guard against legitimate users inadvertently misusing system resources. A sad fact of current corporate life is that the danger of attacks on corporate systems from within is actually greater than that of attacks from the outside. Hence, IDS is taking center stage when it comes to IT security measures.

Using IDS is akin to installing an electronic burglar alarm for your IT systems. Its goal is to continually and closely monitor the systems to quickly detect any unauthorized access or misuse of the IT systems, including the corporate portal. In some instances, in addition to generating the necessary alarms to warn operators of potential attacks, the IDS may even be able to automatically intercept and thwart damaging attacks.

There are many IDS systems now readily available on the market, with Cisco and IBM, of late, making concerted efforts to provide decisive leadership in this arena. For example, the new Cisco IDS 4250 is specifically designed for gigabit-range high-bandwidth scenarios. Refer to http://www.cerias.purdue.edu/coast/ids/ for an extensive list of links pertaining to IDS.

On the whole, IDS systems rely on two types of detection schemes: (1) *anomaly* detection and (2) *misuse* detection. Anomaly detection works by the IDS continually monitoring users and the systems for behavior that deviates from what is deemed to be normal use. Such behavior is detected by compiling logs of normal system-usage profiles and checking ongoing activity against those of prior activity. Just some of the parameters that are checked for anomalies include average CPU load, number of new network connections per minute, number of active processes per user, and average disk access rates. It should, however, be noted that detecting anomalies is not an exact science, given all the possible variables involved. Some anomalous behavior may go undetected until it is too late.

Misuse detection, on the other hand, works by looking for behavior that matches a known attack scenario (e.g., a known method for secreting a virus or planting a Trojan Horse), known intrusion techniques, or known system vulnerabilities (e.g., NT server weaknesses). Since misuse intrusions are thus clearly defined, attacks on known vulnerabilities of a system can be detected by watching for certain actions being performed on certain objects (e.g., system boot records or master directories). High-performance pattern-matching technology, in some cases boosted by specialized hardware chips, is used for this, with data on incoming packets being compared with known sequences.

Today it is possible to get IDS solutions for host systems and for networks. Since each performs a specialized set of tasks, they complement each other rather than being competitive. IDS is a valuable and incisive security safeguard for corporate portals. Just as with an application level firewall, DCs, and SSL, IDS falls into the category of a mandatory security feature. While a host IDS will closely monitor the portal per se, it is best to also have a network IDS to try to intercept attacks before they reach the portal. In practice the IDS will work in tandem with the application level firewall.

4.1.5   IP security (IPSec)

IPSec is a framework of open standards developed by the Internet Engineering Task Force (IETF) to ensure the secure exchange of packets at the IP layer (i.e., the network layer). The advantage of providing such security at the network layer is that all applications using that network can benefit from the security on a uniform and consistent basis. In contrast, higher-level security schemes such as SSL are application specific. Thus, for example, separate SSL implementations will be used between a Web server and a browser, as well as between that same browser user and a host system even if all the encrypted packets are traversing the same network between the end user and the data center.

IPSec provides for data confidentiality, integrity, and authenticity vis-à-vis IP networks. It has been heavily and very successfully used since around 1998 to implement VPNs across the Internet. Thus, its credentials and capabilities are now beyond reproach. Support for IPSec is also readily found within popular routers (e.g., Cisco) and host IP stacks (e.g., UNIX, Windows, mainframes). Consequently, the role of IPSec, when it comes to Internet security, is destined to grow and become more pervasive, which is why it is being discussed here.

You may want to investigate the options of using IPSec as an underlying security scheme for some or all of your b2b and b2e applications. Another thing about IPSec is that it can be used in conjunction with other security schemes in a layered, hierarchical fashion. Thus, if you really want to go overboard on security for some applications, you can use IPSec at the network layer and then have SSL at the application layer. IPSec also does not have to be installed on an end-to-end basis. You can use IPSec between routers only on certain legs of an end-to-end network path. Thus, IPSec is a powerful and flexible security-enforcing mechanism to have in your arsenal when planning safeguards for your corporate portal.

IPSec relies on digital certificates and public key encryption. Today PKI can be effectively used to manage the encryption keys to be used by IPSec. In the early days of IPSec, it relied on a protocol known as Internet security association and key management protocol/Oakley (ISAKMP/Oakley) for its key management. This mechanism was also known as Internet key exchange (IKE). IPSec supports two encryption modes: (1) transport-mode encryption and (2) tunnel-mode encryption.

In the case of transport-mode encryption, IPSec encrypts only the data portion (i.e., the payload) of each IP packet. It does not encrypt the original IP header, which means that addressing information is not protected. This can be a vulnerability if a hacker is scanning traffic either to obtain IP addresses of IT systems or to detect corporate traffic patterns (e.g., a marked increase in traffic between two companies that might signal a potential acquisition of one of those companies by the other). The advantage of not encrypting the header is that intermediate routers can process the header to provide services such as quality-of-service (QoS)–based priority forwarding.

Tunnel-mode encryption, which is more secure, encrypts both the header and the payload. However, since the original header with its addressing information is now not available for routing purposes, a new header has to be appended to the encrypted IP packet. The new header will specify an IPSec "proxy"—typically a router—as its destination. This proxy will decrypt the entire packet and forward it to the final destination end point.

IPSec per se consists of multiple interrelated protocols, as follows:

1.   Authentication header (AH)

2.   Encapsulation security payload (ESP)

3.   IP payload compression (IPComp)

4.   Optional IKE (now being superseded by PKI)

The authentication header, when attached to an IP packet, vouches for the integrity and authenticity of the data, including certain fixed fields in the "outer" IP header, by appending a strong cryptographic checksum to the packet. If the recipient can recreate the checksum using a secret key known only to the sender and the recipient, then the recipient can be sure that the packet did originate from the expected sender (as opposed to an impersonator) and that its contents were not tampered with in transit.

AH, by itself, however, does not provide data confidentiality by encrypting the data. For that you use encapsulating security payload. IPComp is a means to compress packets before they are encrypted by ESP. IPComp, however, can be used without ESP, if all you want is packet compression. In addition, AH and ESP can be used independently or in tandem. As with SSL, IPSec does not specify its own encryption algorithms. Instead, it works with industry standard (e.g., triple DES) or popular commercial (e.g., RSA) algorithms.

4.1.6   Single sign-on and LDAP directories

Single sign-on (SSO) is, in effect, your attestation that you have utmost confidence and trust in your portal's security and authentication measures. SSO is not a new concept and has been offered in various ways, particularly on mainframes, in the past. What is new and significant when it comes to corporate portals is that SSO has been further empowered with digital certificates. The premise of SSO, as stated by its name, is the elimination of the need to individually log on to separate applications or to be repeatedly authenticated when trying to access "protected" information. SSO thus fits in well with the whole corporate portal paradigm of strong authentication and personalization.

SSO is a double-edged sword, although one side, thanks to DCs and authentication schemes such as two-factor authentication, is now getting significantly blunter. The downside of SSO is that once you get in you have unrestricted access to all applications and resources—albeit constrained by the personalization rules in play. This is where the trust in the authentication systems implemented to control initial portal access comes in, especially when fortified with digital certificates. If you trust your authentication system, as you should, since it is pivotal to the whole concept of portal security, then you might as well offer SSO, since it greatly simplifies things for the user.

The obvious risk is that if somebody compromises your authentication mechanism (e.g., by putting a gun to a user's head), then that perpetrator can do a lot of unhindered damage. But as ever, the risks have to be weighed against the overall advantages. SSO does not have to be universal. It does not have to apply to the most sensitive of resources or applications. Thus, there are always compromises, with "compromise" always being the key word when it come to portal security.

The upside of SSO is that it makes the portal experience that much pleasanter and more productive. There is also the credible argument that SSO actually enhances security by eliminating the risk of password detection. Already, most corporate users are inundated with passwords they are expected to remember. They need one to unlock their PCs and another to log on to the LAN server. Then there are all of the application-specific user IDs and passwords. If the user also surfs the Internet and subscribes to various personalized services, that will add another set of user IDs and passwords. Given that most people can't keep track of all of these credentials by memorizing them, they write them down. And that is the risk. Security can be easily compromised if an unauthorized person gains access to this scribbled list of user IDs and passwords (e.g., stealing a briefcase).

SSO obviously is an answer to this problem of password protection. Rather than expecting a user to remember and maintain a large list of passwords, you institute a strong authentication scheme, where the user only has to remember one password—albeit one that will need to be periodically changed. A user has a better chance of remembering just one password without having to write it down somewhere. This in the end is the ultimate justification for SSO. All of today's major portal servers offer SSO as a part of the overall security suite. If you plan to implement a solid authentication scheme, as you must, then you might as well provide SSO.

LDAP and SSO are not really related, and one can always have one without the other. LDAP, a lean-and-mean version of the OSI X.500 directory standard, is rapidly becoming the preferred and accepted standard for accessing directory information. It will soon be the de facto standard for directory access. Since user IDs and passwords can be stored in LDAP directories, LDAP can be used as a mechanism for authentication. However, this type of authentication is not as strong as using digital certificates and two-factor authentication. Still, LDAP's role is by no means restricted to maintaining authentication directories, nor is its role restricted to corporate portals.

LDAP is a powerful, extensible, and generalized directory mechanism that can be used to realize any type of directory (e.g., a rules directory) required by a portal. LDAP will also work in distributed mode with information stored across multiple, dispersed directories. It can even be used to store keys within a PKI scheme. All of the major portal servers offer LDAP directory support in one form or another. Directories are imperative to the operation of portals. Rather than using any proprietary schemes, opt for LDAP directories wherever possible. Given the strategic importance of LDAP, support for LDAP could be a prudent, high-priority evaluation criterion for your portal server. If a portal server on your short list does not support LDAP, it might be worth getting a credible explanation from the vendor as to the justification for this omission.

4.2   Capacity planning for a corporate portal

The speed and, down the road, the scalability of a corporate portal is going to be contingent on the workload it has to perform and the anticipated growth of that workload. In this context, workload will be a factor in determining the number of concurrent users accessing the portal and the types of transactions being performed by those users. Capacity planning is the inexact science of trying to predict what these workloads are going to be at pre-specified milestones in the future.

In reality, capacity planning, though never simple, gets easier the more empirical data you have regarding past trends. To this end it is gratifying to know that there is no shortage of useful products on the market that can provide you with a plethora of information about Web server or portal server usage, traffic patterns, user profiles, and statistics. Some of the better known of these include WebTrends Intelligence Suite, IBM's WebSphere Site Analyzer, Web-Stat, Sane Solutions's NetTracker, WebSideStory's Hit-Box, 123LogAnalyzer, Sawmill (at sawmill.net), Statomatic, and Omniture SiteCatalyst (once MyComputer.com's SuperStats).

The problem, however, is that if you currently do not have a portal then you are unlikely to have the necessary data to help you when it comes to capacity planning. If you already have one or more portals (e.g., b2e) you are in slightly better shape on this front, though you are still going to have to do a lot of estimating and extrapolation. Usage statistics from your Web site can, at best, serve as a preliminary baseline as to the bare minimum resources you will need.

The work done by a static-content Web server is going to be considerably less than that performed by a full-function, corporate portal sustaining interactive transactions. In addition, there is the whole issue of public access over the Internet if you plan to offer b2c functionality. This is the biggest and most challenging variable when it comes to determining acceptable capacity for your initial corporate portal implementation. You could be a victim of the unforeseen popularity of your portal with the public. The issue here, as you can imagine, is that the Internet user population is measured in tens of millions as opposed to tens of thousands.

Within the industry, the incident that for obvious reasons is often cited to illustrate the server-choking effects of a sudden influx of public interest is that of Victoria Secret's first fashion show Web-cast. The bottom line is that the Internet is a huge target audience, and if you set out to lure that audience to your site, you need to be prepared to handle potentially large volumes of users and traffic. As mentioned earlier, this could be a nice problem to have—assuming, of course, that most of these portal visitors fall within your anticipated demographics and are furthering your business goals.

4.2.1   Some guidelines for determining initial capacity

Assuming that you are indeed planning to implement a consolidated portal offering b2e, b2c, and b2b functionality, at least some of the potential user volumes can be easily identified and quantified. For a start you will know the exact number of employees, agents, and partners who will have access to the portal. If this set of users is geographically dispersed, you can factor in applicable time zone variances that will stagger some of the online activity. Then there are the usage patterns.

Prior statistics of IT usage will definitely help, especially given that these users will now be accessing these IT resources through the portal. But this, unfortunately, will enable you to establish only a "minimum" portal-usage figure for this in-house user crowd. The portal will offer many of these users additional capabilities; thus, their active "online" time will increase. Then you need to factor in e-mail, collaborative efforts, and Internet access.

Users who previously spent only 50 percent of their workday actively using the current IT systems might end up using the portal for significantly longer periods. Since the goal of the portal is to be the single focal point for all information, applications, and services, it might be best to assume that most users will spend considerable time using the new portal. The one good thing here is that at least you can estimate with some certainty what the in-house usage requirements are going to be by taking the overall employee base and then factoring in time-zone variances and average connect times for various categories of user (e.g., salespeople, data entry, administrative, HR, marketing, and others).

You can also do the same type of usage pattern estimation for partners, distributors, and agents, given that you know how many you are going to start off with and who they are. Time-zone variations will play more of a role, because some of these players are likely to be scattered across the globe. If users in this group currently have some type of remote-access capability into your IT systems, then you can obtain some detailed and pertinent statistics about usage and traffic patterns, especially if you have a remote-access system that loves to generate reports. As with in-house users, these usage patterns are going to change. Ideally, you are going to provide these "associates" with increasingly more enticing and incisive content, applications, and services. This may not be on day one, but it is best to factor in some of this extra workload for the future.

The portal server and application vendors will be able to provide you with some guidelines as to resource requirements, particularly when it comes to memory and disk storage. Processor-related parameters will, however, invariably be couched in terms of number of "active" users for a particular type of system configuration (e.g., 1,500 concurrent users on a dual 1.2-GHz Pentium III system with 1 GB of memory). Such claims are rarely very specific about the performance metric (i.e., what type of response times the 1,500 concurrent users were enjoying). You will have to drill into this. Ask for references. Talk to others using the product. Document their experiences. Get as much details about their exact system configuration, particularly about other tasks running on the same machine. This obviously is key.

Vendor claims of users per system (e.g., for a database system), for obvious reasons tend to focus on dedicated systems. Unless we are talking about the portal server itself and the vendor figures are for a representative portal running all of the basic functions, any figures based on dedicated systems will have to be factored to take into account other active tasks. On the other hand, you may end up using multiple systems, with some systems dedicated for high-profile, high-volume services such as the Web server, database server, and "tn" server. As ever, there are lots of permutations and possibilities. The good news is that there is no need for you to ever get boxed in, so to speak.

Now comes the big variable: the amount of potential traffic over the Internet from customers, prospects, competitors, prospective "associates" (e.g., new distributors), investors, industry analysts doing research, journalists, and window shoppers. Since the b2c portion of the corporate portal is targeted at eventually handling much of your current call-center workload, you can use current call-center statistics to provide some guidance as to potential volumes. However, as you can appreciate, portal usage patterns will not exactly mirror those of a call center. For a start, unless you run out of capacity very quickly, you are not going to be putting users on hold. Consequently, the portal will handle more current customer calls than a call center, given that you are not constrained by needing one operator per customer. But since a portal is open 24/7, user access may be more staggered. So there will be some give and take here.

The ultimate issues are those of popularity, growth, and scalability. Increasing customer and "associate" reach via the Internet is one of the primary objectives of having a corporate portal. Thus, it is disingenuous to bemoan that trying to estimate potential Internet interest is a problem. All that you can really do is come up with some good estimates based on as much advice as you can get from knowledgeable parties—in particular, vendors, consultants, and contractors with prior, hands-on experience. You will not be the first or last to underestimate the capacity for a portal. All those agonizingly slow portals you no doubt have encountered attest to this. Whatever numbers you finally come up with should include a healthy chunk of overcapacity to handle unanticipated interest. This capacity will not go to waste. Portal usage will continue to increase—hence the need for scalability.

4.3   Factors that influence speed

The platform you select for deploying your portal (e.g., UNIX, Windows, or LINUX on the appropriate hardware) will define an immutable performance envelope for your system—for a given hardware configuration. However, the overall performance of your portal, in terms of response times seen by users, is going to be influenced by a variety of other factors, including some that will be out of your control. For a start, one of the most important factors that will influence portal performance will be the capacity of your Internet (and possibly intranet) connection(s). There will be little point in having a powerful, multiprocessor UNIX server hosting your portal if your connection to the Internet is through ISDN.

Ensuring adequate Internet bandwidth—or, to be more precise, overall network bandwidth—needs to be your first objective. Remember that a portal will increase your overall network traffic, including traffic to and from the Internet, whether due to b2b, remote b2e access, or b2c. Consequently your current Internet connection(s) may not suffice unless the current connections are grossly underutilized. Similar considerations will apply to in-house LAN infrastructures. Ethernet LANs at 10 Mbps may no longer be adequate, and this may be the time to start thinking about 100 Mbps or even gigabit infrastructures.

Having "fast" Internet connection(s), with multiple connections offering link failure protection may, however, still only be half the battle in terms of getting good Internet throughput. Your ISP could be a bottleneck! You may need to do some rigorous round-trip testing to make sure that your current ISP configuration meets your needs. If not, you may have to change

ISPs or even consider getting a direct connection to an Internet network access point (NAP); that will shorten your path into Internet "backbone," bypassing ISPs. You can find lists of geographically local NAPs via Internet searches. Many of the major telecommunications providers around the world offer NAP capability.

In addition to connection capacity and ISP capability, your network "throughput" will be "gated" by a variety of other factors. Key among these are:

- Firewall throughput

- Router/switch performance

- Speed of IDS scanning

- Encryption/decryption overhead

- Compression/decompression delays

Hardware-assist functions are available within routers and some hosts to expedite encryption and compression functions. You might want to investigate these. In some cases, hardware-assisted encryption/decryption may not deliver the dramatic increases in throughput you may expect. You may want to study performance figures available from vendors and do a classic price-versus-performance determination. However, it is also worth noting that hardware-assisted encryption technology keeps on making major strides. Thus, this decision may need to be reviewed periodically. It is also possible to get application-specific integrated circuit (ASIC)–based hardware solutions for firewalls and IDS.

4.3.1   System issues

After the network connection, the platform per se is the next challenge. But as with the network, this again is a multifaceted issue. A fast system can be hamstrung by slow or congested disk I/O. So you have to continually look at the whole rather than individual components. A major decision here is whether you opt for "wintel" servers or UNIX servers—with LINUX giving you the option to chose either PC, UNIX, or even mainframe hardware. Though there are always exceptions, UNIX systems, in general, offer you more clout and capacity than "wintel" approaches. UNIX may also have the edge when it comes to reliability and resilience.

The ability to have multiple processors per system and clustering are two other key factors that should be considered in terms of ensuring platform "power." All three potential hardware platforms (i.e., PC, UNIX, and mainframe) support multiprocessor servers and clustering, with UNIX systems and mainframes offering more capability on these fronts than PC systems. UNIX servers from the likes of IBM and Sun now easily support 30 to 100 RISC processors running at gigabit clock rates. They also offer clustering and partitioning approaching those pioneered in the mainframe world with IBM's unparalleled Parallel Sysplex "fail-safe" clustering.

Having multiple processors can definitely expedite workload processing, though it is well known that adding more processors to a system does not result in a linear increase in processing capacity. Thus, having two processors is not going to give you twice as much processing power. Instead, the increase is likely to be in the 1.6 to 1.7 range. There are also diminishing returns as the number of processors involved starts to increase, albeit only once you start getting well into the double digits or possibly even triple digits. This is where clustering comes in. Rather than continuing to add processors to the same system, you can start to cluster systems, each with multiple processors. Clustering also has the irrefutable advantage of providing redundancy to cope with single system failures.

Load-balancing is another pivotal technology when it comes to corporate portal performance. Load-balancing addresses not just performance but also scalability. By now, most companies have had some exposure to load-balancing, since it has been widely used in the context of Web servers, application servers, backbone routers, and host systems. Portal servers—or, to be more precise, the application servers that host them—excel at load-balancing, especially if we are talking about the Java-based solutions. They offer both vertical and horizontal load-balancing (sometimes also known as "cloning"). Vertical load-balancing deals with multiple instances of a software server implemented on the same machine, whereas horizontal load-balancing deals with software server implementations distributed across multiple machines (or partitions).

Today, you have multiple options for realizing load-balancing. You could get load-balancing functionality from a network device, an application server, or possibly even from the portal server. Exactly what approach you opt for will depend on the overall system architecture that you pursue. What is important, however, is that you ensure that you have adequate flexibility and options when it comes to load-balancing your portal software as well as all of the auxiliary support functions used by the server (e.g., HTTP server, database servers, "tn" servers).

Caching and server mirroring are the last key issues that need to be addressed here; mirrored servers are discussed in detail in Chapter 5. Caching is routinely used to speed up Web server responses. The concept of Web content caching is intuitive and is essentially the Web equivalent of the caching mechanisms that are now invariably used, to great effect, in contemporary computers, irrespective of their type, to accelerate instruction processing and data retrieval. With computer caching, regularly or recently used groups of instructions and data are maintained, temporarily, within high-speed memory so that they can be quickly accessed to satisfy subsequent references without the delay of having to again retrieve the instructions or data from a slower, high-volume storage medium (e.g., disk).

Web caching extends this concept to apply to heavily used Web content. Oft-requested Web content is maintained in high-speed memory on a device close to the end users making the request. This eliminates Web server–related delays and reduces the number of requests that have to be processed by the server. As with load-balancing, a variety of hardware and software–related solutions are now available for Web caching. In the case of a portal, caching will be restricted to static content such as news items, company information, product descriptions, and the like. Variable and interactive content obviously cannot be cached. Once you have defined a short list of portal server vendors, you should ask them what their recommendations are for caching, since effective caching is highly implementation dependent. Some may even discourage caching, citing the dynamic nature of portal content.

There are also "edge server" offerings from the likes of IBM and Akami that should be considered in the context of load balancing and content caching. Edge servers are designed to be deployed at local and remote network boundaries, away from data centers, server farms, and portal servers. Their role is to provide specialized local services on behalf of back-end servers—in this instance, the portal servers—to improve Web application response times, availability, and scalability. Their forte is intelligent load-balancing that dynamically directs user requests to the most suitable (e.g., least busy) server, content caching (including JSP and servlet caching), powerful rules-based request forwarding based on differentiated quality of service, and content filtering and blocking.

4.4   Planning for scalability

Portal performance and scalability, though separate issues, are influenced by many common factors. The platform issue, obviously, is paramount. Though Microsoft and Windows NT fans will argue this vehemently, many in the IT community claim that UNIX systems are inherently more "scalable." In the context of portals, the UNIX/LINUX versus NT issue is likely to be decided in the light of factors other than scalability (e.g., in-house expertise, other existing IT servers). One note of comfort here is that many, but not all, of the popular portal servers support both NT and UNIX systems. Hence, you have at least the option of changing platforms down the road if and when scalability becomes a major issue.

As with performance, scalability may not be restricted to system expandability. Scalability could be constrained by Internet connection capacity, firewall throughput, or disk storage bottlenecks. So scalability has to be looked at from a holistic standpoint. Increasing memory, increasing the number of processors per system, and clustering are all powerful and proven ways to increase system capacity—assuming, of course, that there are no "hard-wired" limitations in any of the software that precludes continued growth.

Though software-imposed user or workload limitations are unlikely in today's portal-related software, this is an important issue that should be addressed with the various vendors. Operating system limits involving "threads" and processes should no longer be an issue, even though all seasoned IT professionals can probably recall such limitations being commonplace with some server software not that long ago.

A scalability-facilitating capability, originally pioneered on mainframes by IBM but now becoming available on UNIX systems, is the concept of "capacity on demand." Capacity on demand (CoD) enables you to acquire (or lease) a "base" system that can satisfy your current, nonpeak workloads at an attractive price. This base system, however, is configured with additional resources (i.e., processors, memory, and I/O "paths") that can be dynamically invoked on the fly and used as needed.

The use of these additional resources is automatically logged, and the user is billed for their use at a later date. That is the beauty of CoD. It allows you to have additional capacity on tap without having to pay for it when you are not using it. It can be used to handle peak loads or future growth. It is, in effect, a valuable scalability-related insurance policy. If you are going with a UNIX solution, CoD is something you must investigate. Sun and IBM now both offer this capability on mid-range and high-end UNIX systems.

Load-balancing is the other perennial standby when it comes to addressing scalability, with mirror sites (discussed in Chapter 5) taking the concept of distributed servers to the next plateau. As with performance, the good news is that you are unlikely to hit a brick wall when it comes to scalability. The public Internet portals and the heavily trafficked corporate portals (e.g., Microsoft, Amazon, IBM, CNN) attest to the fact that it is indeed possible to implement sophisticated portals that can adroitly handle increasing workloads.

4.5   Q&A—A time to recap and reflect

Q: What are the vital "four Ss" for maintaining a successful corporate portal?

A: Security, scalability, synchrony, and speed; synchrony in this sense refers to the art and science of keeping portal content up-to-date, accurate, coordinated, and linked. Portal speed and scalability, though separate issues, go hand in hand, since they are both influenced by many common factors. Portal speed in this context refers to the response times experienced by end users, while scalability relates to the ability of the portal to grow to accommodate increasing user populations and workloads.

Q: Why aren't firewalls alone effective in providing adequate protection for a corporate portal?

A: A firewall's strong point is that of successfully restricting access to internal IT systems to all but a set of preapproved users. This works well with a b2e or b2b portal, where the authorized user population is known. On the other hand, the potential user population of a b2c portal is variable and unknown. Thus, a firewall cannot be employed as a gatekeeper, since the portal, like a brick-and-mortar department store, needs to be open for the public—at worst, barring only known offenders. Though firewalls cannot be used in gatekeeper mode, it is, nonetheless, imperative that you use application-level "proxy" firewalls around your portals so that the internal IP addressing structure of your IT system is not visible to the outside world.

Q: What is a digital certificate?

A: A digital certificate is an electronic credential (in the form of a small file) issued by a trusted organization (called a certificate authority) that vouches for an individual's or business's identity and authority to conduct secure transactions over the Web. Digital certificates leverage public key cryptography.

Q: What is a public key cryptography?

A: Public key cryptography relies on the use of a pair of associated keys for encryption and decryption—known as "public" and "private" keys—where there is a mathematical relationship between these two keys that guarantees that anything encrypted using one key can be cleanly decrypted using the other key. With public key cryptography, one can freely distribute the public key without in any way compromising or revealing the nature of the private key. The public key can even be stored in a public directory or a Web page. The private key must, however, be kept guarded and secret. The public and private keys work only in tandem. A document encrypted using the public key can be decrypted only using the private key.

Q: What is public key infrastructure (PKI)?

A: PKI provides an incisive framework for facilitating secure but at the same time easy-to-use public key encryption and digital signatures. The term "public" is deceptive, since PKI, at least at present, is not a centralized, public service for distributing and managing keys. Today, PKIs are typically implemented on a corporate basis, using PKI-facilitating products from a variety of vendors, including IBM, VeriSign, and Entrust.

Q: How does SSL differ from IPSec?

A: SSL and IPSec both offer data confidentiality via encryption, with both relying on industry standard or popular commercial encryption algorithms for this purpose rather than using their own encryption methodology. IPSec is a network layer security scheme, whereas SSL is an application-specific scheme that is implemented at the transport layer. The original IP header of IP packets can be encrypted with IPSec, while SSL addresses only data (i.e., payload) encryption. IPSec also offers optional data compression, while SSL does not.

Q: Are platform type and platform configuration the key factors that will dictate the speed of a portal?

A: While important, these are not the only major factors that can influence portal performance. Network throughput and disk storage performance can be equally—if not more—critical. A portal implemented on a very fast system will still deliver poor response times to Internet users if the Internet connection between the portal and the Internet does not have adequate bandwidth to handle all the traffic. Performance can also be hampered by firewall throughput, encryption/decryption overhead, intrusion detection system delays, and network congestion.

Q: What are some of the system-related techniques I can use to boost portal performance?

A: Provided there are no I/O bottlenecks, processing power and memory availability can eventually become gating factors. Thus, it should be easy to add more processors and memory to the system. However, adding more processors does not provide a linear increase in processing capability, and there are markedly diminishing returns when the number of processors starts to approach large double digits. This is where clustering, load-balancing, and mirror sites come in.

Q: Will Web caching make a noticeable difference to corporate portal performance?

A: Caching has been very effective at boosting Web server performance. For caching to be effective, however, the content it is dealing with needs to be static. If the content is rapidly changing, caching is not effective, because it can't use previously cached content. This is the challenge of trying to use caching with portals. Although a portal will definitely contain static content, many of its functions will be dynamic and interactive. Caching will not be of any help in expediting these dynamic and interactive functions.

Q: What is "capacity on demand?"

A: CoD, a capability now available on mid-range and high-end UNIX servers, is a very powerful and useful scalability-facilitating feature. It enables you to acquire (or lease) a "base" system that can satisfy your current, non-peak workloads at an attractive price. This base system, however, is configured with additional resources (i.e., processors, memory, and I/O "paths") that can be dynamically invoked on the fly and used. The use of this additional resource is automatically logged, and the user is billed for such use at a later date. CoD thus allows you to have additional capacity on tap without having to pay for it when you are not using it.

Managing and Monitoring Corporate Portals

A danger foreseen is half avoided.

—Thomas Fuller

Managing a corporate portal is not easy. To assume otherwise would indicate exuberant optimism. This is not to say that portal server vendors have not gone to great lengths to try to make this task as easy as possible. The issue is not the lack of appropriate management tools or shortcomings within the tools. The issue, plain and simple, is that the scope of things that need to be managed in order to sustain a successful corporate portal is wide and diverse. The things that need to be carefully and constantly managed include content, users, security, personalization, performance, system resources, and network connections. Portal management thus stretches total system management to new extremes with content management being one of the most critical and portal-specific challenges.

Content synchrony, as mentioned in the previous chapter, is one of the vital "four Ss" of a successful corporate portal, with synchrony referring to the need to keep portal content up-to-date, accurate, coordinated, and linked. The HTTP 404 "page cannot be found" error message tends to gall users, and utmost effort and care should be expended to ensure that portal users never encounter this inexcusable lapse in portal content management. Content management, at a minimum, needs to address creation, approval, versioning, collaboration, syndication, publishing, control, and personalization in the context of portal content. It needs to be thorough and uncompromising but at the same time flexible and "light." This is a difficult but essential compromise.

Since portal content, especially when it pertains to announcements, product/service data, or corporate "capabilities" is now considered by the public to be gospel, it is imperative that this type of portal information be accurate, up-to-date, and, above all, approved by the relevant executives. To meet these requirements you need to have a nimble content creation, revisioning, and approval mechanism that leverages collaborative tools. If you fail to do this, the portal becomes a bottleneck that starts to negatively impact major corporate processes and goals. For example, not being able to get all of the necessary content on the portal in time should not become the reason that you have to delay an important product announcement that the company had been working toward for the past six months.

Unfortunately, this is not a hypothetical scenario. Many companies, especially big ones, have had this happen to them in the past. It has happened so often that many portal managers, having been chastised, now establish announcement schedules by working back from the time it would take them to get the necessary content ready for the Web. This, though prudent and pragmatic, is not right. The portal is supposed to be a business-enhancing tool—not an impediment. With this in mind, our goal is to implement a content-management system that is powerful and all-encompassing without being cumbersome and complicated.

Given the importance of content management, all portal server solutions provide some level of functionality to facilitate content management. Some, including Microsoft's SharePoint Portal Server 2001, PeopleSoft's PeopleSoft 8, CA's CleverPath with its Enterprise Content Manager, IBM's Portals with Content Manager, Epicentric Foundation Server, and BroadVision InfoExchange with One-to-One Content, have gone to great lengths to offer extensive capabilities on this front.

In addition, most portal servers will allow you to use supplementary third-party content-management products. Some of the offerings you may want to look at as possible adjuncts to your portal server include Microsoft's Content Management Server, Interwoven's Team Site, FatWire Update-Engine 6, Vignette V6 Content Suite, Documentum 4I, iLevel Insite Server, EM3 iOn, Merant PVCS Content Manager, and Empolis sigmalink. Figure 5.1 shows Merant PVCS's highly visual graphical view for managing the portal site architecture and page relationships independently of page design and layout.

The bottom line is that it is highly unlikely that you will have to concoct a proprietary in-house scheme to handle your content-management needs. Instead, you should have no problem finding a powerful and proven off-the-shelf solution that will adequately address your need and is also extensible enough to keep up with your needs as they evolve in the future. There are even some outsourcing options (e.g., CrownPeak), although this is not a

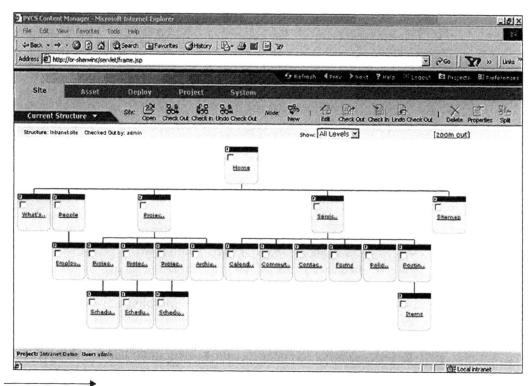

Figure 5.1 *Merant PVCS's highly visual graphical view for managing the portal site architecture and page relationships independently of page design and layout.*

function that you typically think of as being a good candidate for outsourcing. This, however, may depend on your in-house situation. If resources are tight, you could consider outsourcing as a way to augment your in-house capabilities.

At this juncture some of you may be wondering why so much emphasis is being placed on content management, especially if you already have lots of experience maintaining a Web site that also requires content management. The key differences between content management for a home page Web site and for a corporate portal relate to the larger total volume of data in the case of a portal as well as a greater diversity in the types of data involved. A Web site, in general, deals with HTML-formatted documents and possibly some PDF documents. On the other hand, a typical corporate portal will include structured and unstructured documents (e.g., Microsoft Word files and plain-text files), application data, HTML-formatted documents, databases, scanned images, facsimiles, computer output, directories, multimedia files, and XML documents.

The growing strategic significance of XML adds a new dimension to content management. For a start, content-management systems should be able to provide means whereby "nondevelopers" not familiar with the intricacies of XML will still be able to easily create documents with some level of XML-based descriptors and structuring. Rather than expecting the document author to define and insert the necessary XML tags and declarations, these schemes enable the author to just concentrate on the intrinsic structure (e.g., title, headers, tables, diagrams) and content of the document using contemporary word processor–like techniques.

This type of automated XML "generator" is similar to Microsoft FrontPage or MacroMedia DreamWeaver in the context of HTML. These user-friendly HTML tools allow you to compose sophisticated and vivid Web pages using visual, drag-and-drop, graphical techniques without having to know anything about HTML. The HTML is generated automatically by the editor based on the graphical layout created by the user. The XML generators set out to emulate this type of "technical transparency" when it comes to XML. Corel's XMetaL (once SoftQuad) is a good example of such a product. XMetaL 3 is a comprehensive XML document creation and editing system, replete with support for XML schema, embedded ActiveX, extensive corporate specific customization, and even collaboration.

XMetaL 3 can be used as a plug-in with the content-management solutions from Documentum, Interwoven, Vignette, and Empolis described previously. As with automated HTML generators, the XML "code" generated by the likes of XMetaL is fully editable and extensible. So you are in no way boxed in. The auto-generators give you a jump-start in creating XML documents and eliminate a lot of effort, time, and frustration from the process. Thus, they will certainly reduce XML development–related cost and expedite the time taken to generate valid, error-free XML documents. For conventional XML editors that require you to know XML, look at products such as Microsoft's no-charge XML Notepad and XML Spy.

In addition to providing tools to facilitate XML document creation, content-management systems are also exploiting XML to provide data templates with customized XML-based entry fields. Users can populate these templates and create documents (e.g., product description, company announcements, manufacturing reports) without any knowledge of XML or even awareness that XML is being used within the documents they are creating. (See Figure 5.2.) The beauty of this approach is that documents produced this way are automatically XML-structured and can be easily manipulated, regardless of their page layout or design. The data in them can be readily formatted in multiple ways to suit different audiences, and the

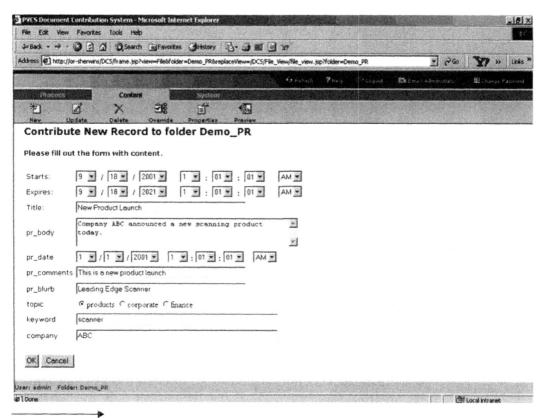

Figure 5.2   *Example of "nontechnical" users creating structured data using XML-based templates, again using Merant PVCS Content Manager as the source.*

data can be reused and repurposed in many ways to meet the needs of different applications.

Though content management is the primary portal-specific management issue, it is still only one facet of the overall portal-management challenge. A busy corporate portal is the epitome of a mission-critical system. Once your portal is in full swing and serving as the focal point for all corporate data, applications, and services, you cannot afford to have it malfunction or go down for any protracted periods of time. Since it is a focal point, it can also become a single point of failure. The financially punishing implications of mission-critical application failures (e.g., travel reservation systems, credit-card authorizing systems, online trading systems) are well known.

A corporate portal, ironically, can exacerbate this even further. In addition to becoming a high-profile, mission-critical application in its own right, multiple other mission-critical applications running on other IT systems would be "front-ended" by the portal. If the portal goes down, the primary access means for these other applications will also be disrupted, compounding the seriousness of the problem. Thus, providing resilience and reliability through clustering, mirror sites, anticipator management, and whatever "self-healing" technology is available (e.g., IBM's Project eLiza on the new UNIX servers) is of paramount importance.

5.1   Content management

The overall content-management process can be broken down into five separate and somewhat intuitive functions or phases, as follows:

1.   Content collection

2.   Content creation

3.   Content control

4.   Content delivery

5.   Content surveillance

Content collection addresses pulling together your existing content and data irrespective of its format and source. Obviously you want to minimize the need to recreate or reformat this information. Any content that is already available via your existing Web server or intranet portal should be in a form (e.g., HTML, .pdf, download for a desktop application such as Microsoft PowerPoint) that you could immediately use with the new portal—at least on an interim basis to expedite time to market. In the case of application-specific data all you probably would have to do is provide access to the application via the portal, typically using a host publishing or host integration methodology, as discussed in Chapter 3. This could also be the case for some database-access scenarios. All you will need to do is to ensure that the database system can be invoked via the portal.

This is also a good time and place to start thinking about XML, especially if there is already a corporate mandate (or even a desire) for XML compatibility down the road. Trying to hand-code the XML conversion is not going to be feasible from a cost or time standpoint unless you really are looking only at a handful of documents or files. Fortunately, there are tools that can automate the XML conversion. These are called "N converters," where the "N" refers to non-XML as in non-XML-to-XML converters. There are also "S converters," which allow you to translate an existing XML document into a different XML structure. The following Web site, part of the "Free XML Tools" initiative, is a good place to start when looking for such converters: www.garshol.priv.no/download/xmltools-/cat_ix.html. N converters typically rely on rule-based schemes to control the nature of the XML output. N converters are currently available for converting text, word processing documents, databases, and HTML into XML.

If you currently do not have a business-process management (BPM) or a business-process integration (BPI) system in place, this might be a good time to evaluate the advantages of implementing such a system for three reasons:

1.   It will provide you with a solid framework and methodology to map out how your existing business processes work and how they are interrelated, especially in the context of working out who owns, uses, and updates the current content and data files that you are trying to bring into the portal.

2.   It will be a useful discipline and control mechanism, going forward, as you start to develop new portal-oriented business processes.

3.   The advent of XML and Web services gives business-process integration a whole new impetus by facilitating disparate process integration using XML as a means of universal data interchange.

Business-process management, though arcane at best, is not a new Internet-related technology per se. It has been around in one form or another since the PC-inspired business-process reengineering mania that started to sweep through the business world starting in the late 1980s and resulted in considerable much-needed streamlining, rationalization, and optimization in the ways companies did business. BPM enables companies to create, model, map, and manage business processes that span diverse applications, platforms, departments, and even enterprises in the case of b2b. With BPM you can have a consistent and clear picture of all the processes (including applications and data sources) involved in executing a given business task (e.g., complete order-fulfilling process from accepting the order to shipping the product).

Well-known and proven BPM solutions are available from a wide variety of vendors, including most of the big ones. Start by researching the offerings available from the likes of Microsoft (i.e., BizTalk Server), IBM (i.e., WebSphere Business Integrator), BEA (i.e., WebLogic Integration), Oracle, Sybase, iPlanet, Tibco, Metaserver, and Jacada. BPM solutions typically consist of a visual process modeling and mapping tool, as shown in Figure 5.3, along with other tools and services to analyze, define, monitor, and

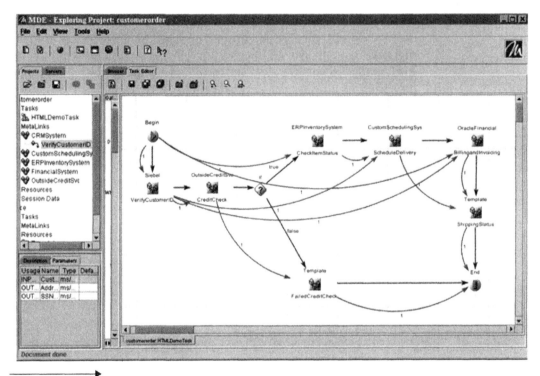

Figure 5.3   *Example from Metaserver of a graphical map showing the processes involved in fulfilling a customer order.*

administer processes. Some solutions include development tools that will enable you to integrate processes using mechanisms such as XML.

5.1.1   Content creation and control

A corporate portal will need fresh content on a continual basis, even if it's just periodically updated company, industry, and market news. Portal users—especially employees, agents, partners, and "associates"—will look at the portal as a constant source of stimulating (and hopefully inspiring) information. This is an implicit promise of a corporate portal. Though the "internal" users are a captive audience, a corporate portal is a very powerful and immensely cost-effective means to motivate this base, bolster morale, propagate company values, keep them "engaged" in the company goals, and ensure that they feel truly empowered when it comes to company information. Fresh and compelling content is also key to attracting external users and making sure that they will come back on a regular basis. The bottom line is that pumping pertinent new content into the portal is an ongoing and demanding task.

A portal, to be successful, will need content from a variety of internal people and sources as well as external data feeds, including syndicated content. Many of the internal people from whom you will need regular and quick turnaround content updates (e.g., people in marketing, HR, or investor relations) may not be conversant with HTML or XML. Although you would ideally like content to be delivered in as close to publishable form as possible, it would be impractical and even detrimental to expect these content creators to become Web publishing experts. It could delay the content acquisition process and impact productivity. In addition, if the content is not going to be in an acceptable XML-structured form, then it might actually be advantageous to receive it in a native format, which can be converted into different forms later on.

To avoid setting limitations on the content providers, the content-management system has to be capable of readily accepting content in many different forms and formats spanning all of the widely used tools and editors. It should definitely be able to work with the popular desktop productivity applications (e.g., Microsoft Office, WordPerfect Office, Lotus SmartSuite), HTML generators (e.g., Microsoft FrontPage and MacroMedia Dream-Weaver), and ODBC-based relational databases. However, going forward, costs could be reduced and efficiency improved if at least some of the regularly updated portal-oriented content (e.g., news, job postings, product updates) could be created and maintained in a portal-friendly—ideally, XML—form. As mentioned earlier, content-management systems are already addressing this with template-based schemes. The other option is to promote the use of automatic XML generators such as XMetaL.

Although portal servers and some content-management systems will permit authorized users to publish content updates in real time to either a staging or live production portal system, this is a capability that you may want to severely restrict. To ensure the fidelity of portal content you have to maintain stringent and fail-safe controls on the content that appears on your portal. To do this you need a flexible library system, a helpful version-tracking mechanism, and an electronic content-approval process. A good content-management system will include all these features.

The version-tracking mechanism will obviously go hand in glove with the library system. The primary goal of a version-tracking system is to make sure that no one can, inadvertently or otherwise, overwrite or modify another user's modification. There will be an indelible sequential history of all changes made to the document so that people can always go back to a specific version without fear that it might not contain all of the previously made changes (or suggestions). Version-tracking systems, by necessity, work on a document "check-out" basis.

Once a document is registered with the system, a person can edit it only by first checking it out of the system. You could impose check-out rules to streamline this process and minimize potential conflict. This would eliminate the possibility of several people making changes to the document at the same time. For example, you could impose serial updates by specifying that a document can be checked out only by one user at any given time. Such serialization, though simplifying the update coordination and consolidation process, will obviously slow down the document update and approval cycle. You might even lose momentum and motivation if key people can't get to the document in time and then get distracted by other projects or priorities.

Version-tracking systems can handle parallel updates when multiple people are working on checked-out versions of the same base document. This is key to collaborative document review, update, and approval. If such parallel updates are permitted, the version-tracking mechanism will typically inform the other currently active "updaters" each time a copy of the base document is checked out or checked in by yet another user. The user checking out or checking in a document will also be notified of the other users who are currently working on the same base copy. This way everybody can have an idea, assuming of course that they care, of who else is currently involved in the process.

Some, when notified as to who else is working on the document, may decide that it would be prudent to wait until specific reviewers have finished with the document so as to avoid duplication and frustration. The bottom line is that the version-tracking system has to be flexible and cater to all possible review/update scenarios without ever losing or corrupting an update. In addition to the reviews and updates you need to have a formal and well-documented approval cycle before a document is finally ready for publication. If you need to publish the content in multiple languages, this would be an appropriate juncture to perform the translations, since the translated content should also be reviewed and approved to avoid any faux pas.

Content-management systems will provide automated, workflow-oriented, approval routes for content. Once you have a document that incorporates all of the modifications agreed on by the reviewers, the CM system can launch this document along a specific approval route. Again, you can use a rules-based methodology to determine the approval route used for the particular type of content—with you having the flexibility to have as many different approval routes as you need. You will also have the option of specifying the approval criteria for each approval route. In essence you have four major content approval schemes:

1. Serial approval scheme (more than likely mimicking the hierarchical reporting structure of the company), whereby all members of the route have to sequentially approve the document

2. Parallel approval scheme, with all members having to approve the document (but not in a sequential manner as above)

3. Parallel approval scheme, with majority approval

4. Parallel approval scheme, with one "overriding vote" approval

Figure 5.4 graphically illustrates the various approval schemes that you could use; bear in mind, however, that you are not restricted to choosing and sticking with just one scheme. Just as you can have different approval routes for different types of content, you can also have different approval schemes per route or based on the nature of the content.

Serial Approval

first approver   last approver

Parallel Approval Schemes

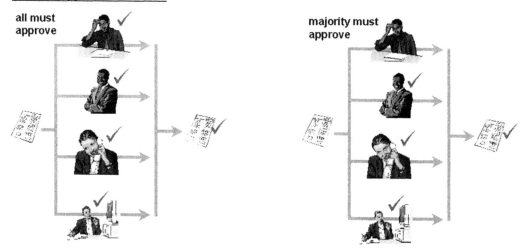

all must approve

majority must approve

Figure 5.4   *Three of the available (and most popular) content-approval schemes possible with a content-management system.*

5.1.2   Content categorization, publication, and surveillance

Once you have approved content, it needs to be properly categorized and indexed according to the portal's taxonomy, as discussed in section 3.1, so as to ensure that the search and personalization functions have necessary visibility to this new content. Without this, the new content could get "lost" and not be seen by all of the intended target audience. This categorization process typically includes adding metadata tags to describe the key elements of the content being described. Most content management systems will provide you with "wizards" that will help you create these metadata tags.

At this juncture, you finally have publishable content, in some form or another. It may already be in HTML, if the reviewers or approvers wanted to see it in final form. Preferably, it could be in XML with an appropriate XSL for formatting and displaying the data. It might still be in native form. It is now a question as to how you intend to publish it, and this to a large extent will depend on your underlying portal server. You may have a portlet mechanism that directly accepts HTML or XML. You may still have to create a JSP or equivalent to get all of the interactive features you need for that portlet. Some servers may give you a template-based approach for assimilating new content.

This is where your portal page designers and portal "maestros" really start earning their keep. Though the CM system and the portal server will provide you with means to publish content, you still need to ensure look-and-feel consistency and add the required pizzazz and vibrancy. This cannot be automated, and it is this corporation-specific personalization that will set the tone for your portal. In time you will want your portal to have its own unique trademark "personality" that is instantly recognizable to its user community.

Most portal servers will allow you to dynamically update content in real time. This is a powerful and useful capability that you may want to use judiciously. You could establish guidelines as to which portal views or individual portlets might be "hot-swapped" in real time and which might not. Some portlets (e.g., stock ticker, Webcam, syndicated external news channels) and portal views by their very nature are going to be displaying live, "unstaged" data. You may want this option for any portlets displaying news. Other than that, you may want to first stage all new portal views and portlets and try them out in a test environment before making them live.

The need for staging and testing will, with luck, be an issue that will crystallize during the portal planning and initial implementation phase. You and your team may discover that you really would like the luxury of being able to test new content for a few hours before making it live to catch any "bugs" before the calls to the help desk and e-mail complaints start to flood in. In some instances, such as a new announcement, you will have no choice but to stage the new content until the time that it can be officially released. Portal servers usually provide a mechanism whereby you can have specific time-based activation of content.

The staging and testing period gives you and your team a chance not just to make sure that the new content is on target but also to ascertain that all of the links, buttons, dialog boxes, and logon scripts off the new portlets and page views work as they are supposed to. The portal server (and possibly some of the content-development tools and the CM system) may provide some rudimentary tests to validate the links and buttons of a new portlet or page view when it is being published. But such automated tests are unlikely to be adequate, and they do not check dialogs, transactions, and logons. This should be done by hand before the content is made live to avoid embarrassment and frustration. The bottom line is that you have to continually remind your team that your corporate portal is mission critical and that you cannot really afford to have any glitches caused by lassitude.

5.2   Keeping on top of usage patterns and statistics

Accurate, incisive, and pertinent usage patterns and usage statistics, with cumulative totals and trends, are imperative to the successful operation of a corporate portal for many reasons. Key among these are the following:

1.   Providing management with solid data to justify the portal-related costs

2.   Facilitating capacity-planning decisions

3.   Helping the marketing division to ascertain the success ratios of various advertising and marketing initiatives, including the impact of announcements and product launches

4.   Gathering vital demographic profiles relative to the general public visiting the portal to add to the corporate market intelligence pool

5.   Delivering leads to sales and partners

6.   Checking that the performance of the portal, especially in terms of its ability to handle large numbers of concurrent users, is within predetermined levels

7.   Ascertaining the search engines and referrer sites (in particular partners and distributors) that are directing traffic to the portal

8.   Determining the relative popularity of different content, services, and applications so that action can be taken if actual usage patterns do not reflect the company's expectations

9.   Double-checking content and Web link integrity, since many systems will provide statistics of "page access failures"

10. Keeping tabs on and informing the appropriate personnel of competitors, journalists, industry analysts, and financial analysts visiting the portal, based on analysis of known domain names

11. Providing management and marketing with impressive portal usage statistics they can use in corporate promotion material (e.g.: We are getting 6,000 hits a day on our new corporate portal and we expect this to increase by ...)

12. Serving as a supplementary intrusion-detection system (possibly with real-time altering) to identify and highlight anomalous usage patterns

As mentioned in section 4.3, there are plenty of proven, well-known, and feature-packed usage-analysis and reporting tools on the market, including outsourced solutions (e.g., Web-Stat). Some of the better known of these tools are also listed in section 4.3. The portal server vendors will also indubitably have their own recommendations as to tools that they have had experience with. The bottom line is that you need to have at least one or possibly several usage-analysis tools in order to stay on top of your ongoing portal operation. Not having the right tool would be akin to undertaking a long, cross-country trip in a car with no fuel gauge, trip odometer, or speedometer.

In addition to having the right tools, you also need to institute a strict, infallible regime for collecting, reviewing, reporting, archiving, and forwarding this portal usage statistic. In many ways this information is as key an indicator of a company's health and vigor as its stock price and sales numbers. It can actually be a "leading indicator" presaging the fortunes of the company. An unexpected and inexplicable drop in portal usage, spanning a few days, should be brought to the urgent attention of senior management. The same is also true of high volumes of sustained activity.

If you have around-the-clock monitoring of your system and network management systems, you may want to consider adding real-time monitoring of portal usage to the list of managed entities so that trained and experienced operators can quickly detect any unexpected trends. The analysis tool that you select may facilitate such real-time monitoring by providing certain threshold-based alarms. Real-time monitoring, however, is not a substitute for collecting, analyzing, and plotting all the usage data on a periodic (i.e., daily or weekly) basis.

5.3   Enhancing reliability, resilience, and availability

Just as with other mission-critical corporate applications, a corporate portal needs to have "uptime" figures that ideally approach or exceed 99.9 percent of the planned and scheduled uptime. While mission-critical applications running on IBM mainframes with their unparalleled high-availability characteristics can now boast uptimes in the 99.999 percent range, this level of nonstop operation is still not the norm for Web-related applications. This is primarily because the nonmainframe systems used for Web applications still do not have the highly evolved hardware and software features (e.g., Parallel Sysplex, "MVS" operating system)—and in some instances the operational discipline—that make high availability in the 99.99 percent range a possibility.

Downtime of 20 hours a year with 24/7 operation is still essentially the norm for UNIX systems. This does not sound bad at all until you realize that the single-year downtime for mainframe-based mission-critical applications can be less than 30 minutes! To be fair, Sun and IBM are now feverishly working to add mainframe-type reliability and resilience capabilities to their new mid-range and high-end UNIX servers. In fact, this has been a resounding theme of recent UNIX server announcements (e.g., Sun's Sun Fire 15K in September 2001 and IBM's p690 a month later) from these two vendors, who are in fierce competition for marker leadership when it comes to industrial-strength enterprise UNIX servers. Dynamic, firmware-enforced logical partitioning, à la mainframes, is set to become a standard feature on large UNIX servers, further enhancing the on-the-fly, hot-swap, dynamic system resource reconfiguration and failover capabilities already available on those systems.

Logical partitioning by itself is a powerful, indefatigable, and relatively low-cost resilience-boosting feature. With logical partitioning, system resources (e.g., processors, memory, I/O cards) can be cleanly assigned (and, if necessary, dynamically allocated and reallocated) to autonomous system images, each running its own copy of the operating system and application software. What is key here is that each partition runs its own set of software, including the operating system. This ensures protection against processor, memory, I/O adapter, operating system, or application failure, since each partition is a minisystem in its own right, typically with multiple processors per partition.

In essence, partitioning allows you to have virtual (and dynamic) clustering on the same machine. Thus, with a load-balancing scheme you can have multiple copies of your portal and Web server running on separate partitions, each with its own complement of dedicated hardware resources but interacting with the same pool of users and disk storage. That way if you have a problem on one partition, only the work being done on that partition is impacted.

Applications running in the other partitions will continue to work unaffected, oblivious to the fact that there has been a failure in another partition. Users from the affected partition can be transferred across to the active partitions. Partitioning thus provides redundancy and resilience within the same system—albeit through the use of multiple copies of software and load- balancing. Figure 5.5 illustrates how logical partitioning can be used to enhance corporate portal resilience in the context of UNIX servers.

Figure 5.5
Using logical partitioning on a high-end UNIX server to enhance corporate portal resilience.

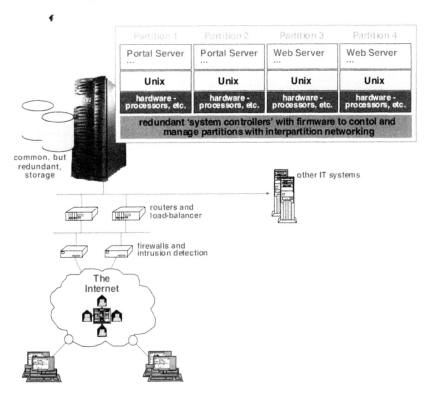

When evaluating partitioning and clustering in the context of UNIX and LINUX, do not forget that mainframes are also an option. Partitioning and clustering with high-speed interpartition communication is their forte—not to mention inherent, rock-solid "can't remember the last time our mainframe crashed" reliability. Today there are multiple options for running LINUX server images on mainframes, including the option of dedicated native-mode LINUX partitions, known as Integrated Facility for LINUX (ILF) and even a LINUX-specific, aggressively priced mainframe known as the z800 Model 0LF. If you already have mainframes or want a high-end, eminently scalable, high-availability LINUX server, you should also add mainframes to your list of potential server platforms.

In general, the factors that can influence and enhance system resilience and uptime, vis-à-vis a corporate portal, are as follows:

1. Overall, innate platform stability and resilience (in one way or another the issue boils down to the perennial UNIX/LINUX versus Windows NT debate)

2. Hardware redundancy (e.g., multiple processors, redundant power, redundant cooling) as well as hot-swap capabilities

3. System startup and ongoing diagnostics and fault-bypass schemes, such as memory scrubbing and redundant array of independent disks (RAID) storage

4. Logical partitioning

5. Clustering

6. Self-healing, self-managing capabilities

5.3.1 Bolstering memory and storage reliability

Memory scrubbing is a process whereby the contents of memory are read, checked for single-bit errors, and, if necessary, corrected during periods when the system processors are idle. This ensures that any accumulated errors within memory are identified and corrected using standard error-checking and correction (ECC) technology. If the errors discovered exceed preset thresholds, the memory management system will take the failing chips offline (i.e., deallocate them) and substitute spare chips in their place. Nascent self-healing technology such as "Chipkill" memory is now taking memory protection to even greater heights.

RAID storage, which is increasingly becoming a preferred means for providing enterprise storage, relies on using multiple disk drives to create a single logical disk. RAID can improve disk-storage reliability, resilience, and performance and can provide protection against disk failures. RAID solutions, however, come in several different flavors with some (e.g., RAID-0) oriented primarily toward performance rather than resilience. Although RAID could be implemented using software, the norm is to rely on special RAID-specific disk controllers for implementation.

A concept called "striping" is one of the underlying principles of RAID. A stripe is an adjacent (i.e., contiguous) sequence of disk blocks. A stripe could be a single disk block, or it could be made up of a large number (i.e., thousands) of disk blocks. The RAID controllers and drivers split up their constituent disk partitions into stripes and perform all of their operations in the context of these stripes. The primary difference between the various RAID flavors, known as RAID levels, is how the stripes are organized and how data are stored in them. Of the RAID levels that offer redundancy, RAID-1 and RAID-5 are the most widely used.

RAID-0 is a pure "striping" scheme, which has no redundancy; the data are written across multiple, interleaved disk drives. RAID-0, which is used to boost performance, actually decreases disk storage reliability, because the failure of one of the underlying disk drives will disable the whole RAID drive. On the other hand, RAID-1 is a mirroring scheme that offers significant protection against disk failures. With RAID-1 mirroring, every drive or drive array has another spare drive of the same capacity associated with it. Every block of data that is written to the primary drive is also written to the corresponding mirror drive.

Thus, the mirror always has an exact copy of the data on the primary drive. RAID-1 systems, in addition to offering automatic data backup, can also improve data-read performance by permitting data-read operations to be split across the two mirrored drives. It does not, however, improve data-write performance, since the data have to be written to both drives in real time. Given that data access (i.e., data read) is going to be more prevalent in a typical corporate portal, especially if it includes a large b2c component, RAID-1 offers a good compromise between resilience and performance.

Another relatively popular alternative for portal applications that will give you the best of all worlds is to use both RAID-0 and RAID-1 in tandem. This RAID-1+0 scheme is called a "layered" approach, since one RAID technique is layered on top of another. RAID-1+0 combines the straight "striping" of RAID-0 with the data mirroring of RAID-1. Thus, you still end up with a corresponding mirror array for every primary array, but having RAID-0 gives you the added performance. RAID-2, -3, and -4 are no longer deemed strategic; RAID-5, however, is.

RAID-5, like RAID-0, is a "striping" scheme but with the powerful data-protection capability of having parity checks (i.e., where parity is a kind of checksum). If any one of the disks should fail, the data on the remaining disks can be used to reconstruct the data that were on the failed disk. For every byte written across a striped set of disks, an extra byte—the so-called parity byte—is written to another disk. You need a minimum of three physical disks to create a RAID-5 striped set. Most RAID-5 systems today support hot-swappable disks, so that one of the drives can be changed while the system is running without interrupting data I/O operations. Though having parity is a powerful and appealing data-protection feature, creating and writing the parity does slow down performance.

Storage area networks (SANs) provide another topical and valuable disk storage option for corporate portal scenarios. An SAN is a dedicated, high-volume, disk-storage solution built around a high-speed network in which the network is typically built using the industry-standard Fiber Channel technology, which can operate in the 1-Gbps to 2-Gbps range over copper or optical cabling over relatively long distances. The storage capability on an SAN is typically made up of one or more storage systems, where each storage system could be a RAID system, a tape system, a tape library, a CD-ROM library, or JBODs (i.e., just a bunch of disks).

SANs offer scalability and redundancy. SANs can work with a variety of networking schemes, including IP. SANs represent an easy and cost-effective way to realize data redundancy via data mirroring with SAN drives acting as the secondary storage. SAN solutions are now readily available from a variety of high-profile vendors, including most of the big server vendors. The chances are that you probably are already using RAID or SAN in some form within your company or have at least evaluated them for future use. If you are not already using RAID or SAN, the corporate portal represents an ideal opportunity to try these strategic resilience-enhancing storage solutions.

5.3.2   Self-managing and self-healing technology

Self-managing and self-healing technology to promote high availability is now a major initiative across all server lines, driven by IBM's grandiose, far-reaching blueprint for self-managing systems known as Project eLiza. IBM is not alone, however. As with logical partitioning, Sun is making a concerted attempt to try to match IBM in the high-availability stakes when it comes to the enterprise UNIX server market. The goal of self-managing technology is to create automated, heuristic processes that will simplify some of the complexity inherent in running today's sophisticated IT systems, with corporate portals being a good example of such a sophisticated, complex, and multidimensional system. IBM is referring to such self-managing systems as representing "autonomic computing."

The term "autonomic" relates to the human body's capability to manage a variety of complex tasks, ranging from fighting infection to regulating its internal temperature despite physical exertion and fluctuation in outside temperature, automatically and without any conscious effort by the owner of that body. Such involuntary but crucial body functions are known as autonomic functions, and the part of the body's nervous system responsible for controlling functions not consciously directed by a person is known as the "autonomic nervous system." IBM's intent is to provide similar fully automated, "subconscious" intervention for computer systems so that they can detect, recover, and heal from a variety of ailments without human intervention and without impacting system operation.

IBM's patented Chipkill memory, found in mainframes and the high-end UNIX servers as well as in IBM's Netfinity (i.e., WinTel) servers, is a good example of Project eLiza–derived self-detecting, self-healing technology. IBM claims that Chipkill virtually eliminates memory-based system failures—with this being one of the most frequent causes of system downtime. Chipkill, which can detect multiple bit errors and correct most of them transparently, is credited with being 100 times more effective than ECC technology on its own. A part of this technology is based on the concept of "bit scattering."

With bit scattering, the memory chips are organized such that the failure of any specific memory module affects only a single bit within an ECC "word." This allows for error correction and nondisruptive recovery even when there is a complete chip failure. (Note some parallels with the RAID technology discussed earlier.) With Chipkill, if a memory error does occur, the memory subsystem is designed so as to automatically and gracefully take the inoperative memory chip offline while the server keeps running. Fault anticipation is another major plank in self-managing technology. Memory scrubbing, found on high-end Sun and IBM UNIX servers, is an example of this. A somewhat comparable, automatic component–deallocating system that applies to processors, as opposed to memory, is referred to by IBM as "Repeat-Gard."

With "Repeat-Gard" extensive and continuous tests are done on the processor and associated circuitry while the system is running, and any intermittent errors found are logged. When the system is next booted, this log is checked to see whether the errors previously found exceed preset thresholds. If the thresholds have been exceeded, "Repeat-Gard" will automatically deallocate the suspect processors (given that contemporary servers have multiple processors). If spare processors are available, it will automatically substitute them until the original processors are replaced.

The concept of "blind-swap" as it applies to PCI adapters is another example of what vendors are doing to continually increase high availability. Blind-swap is an on-the-fly, totally nondisruptive hardware insertion-and-removal capability that takes hot-swappablity to the next higher plateau. With "blind-swap," PCI adapters can be inserted or removed, at will, without the I/O drawer containing the PCI slots having to be moved to a special service position.

The bottom line is that server vendors are working feverishly to provide availability- and resilience-enhancing features to nonmainframe systems so that new Web-centric mission-critical applications can also enjoy uptime in the 99.99 percent range. Check out the various high-availability and self-healing features being offered on UNIX servers, including mainframes if LINUX is in the equation. Intel servers, however, are not offering as many of these features as UNIX, and mainframes are unlikely to be left behind in this area for too long. So the good news is that ensuring high uptime for corporate portals is going to get progressively easier and affordable.

5.4   Mirrored portals

The concept of data mirroring for data redundancy and backup was discussed in the context of RAID and SAN storage solutions. With both RAID and SAN, the mirrored drives do not have to be in close proximity to the primary drives; this immediately gives you the possibility for distance mirroring. Distance mirroring is a quick and convenient means for implementing both remote archiving and disaster recovery scenarios. Following the events of 9/11, disaster recovery has been elevated to a whole new level of significance and priority. Since the corporate portal will become the focal point for future corporate data access, providing a sound disaster-recovery scenario for it as a whole, as well as the data associated with it, is obviously of paramount interest.

Going forward, your IT disaster-recovery plans may need to start from the perspective of the portal and then fan out to the various IT systems accessed through it, since the portal will have become the familiar mechanism through which most users now interact with the other systems. The bottom line is that if a disaster should befall your primary IT site, you need to be able to quickly recreate a backup corporate portal system and have users automatically directed to the new site. Given the amount of dynamic and transactional data associated with a typical corporate portal, implementing such a disaster-recovery backup scheme is not a trivial undertaking. The good news is that it is eminently doable and the large system vendors are offering various solutions of differing sophistication to facilitate such implementations.

A mirrored portal would be the ultimate in terms of an immediate takeover, hot backup scenario. A mirrored portal stretches the concept of clustering and load-balancing to embrace physically distant clusters. Rather than having the servers in close proximity to each other, sharing a common pool of storage (which in turn could be mirrored for redundancy), a mirrored portal scheme assumes that the servers are a considerable distance apart. The reason for the geographic separation is twofold. One is to provide adequate separation in the event of a major disaster. The second is to geographically relate load-balancing, with the primary site and the mirror site dividing up the user population based on their proximity to one or other of the sites.

The events of 9/11, though hopefully never to be repeated, provided some valuable lessons vis-à-vis disaster recovery. Having backup sites near the primary site (e.g., within the same city) was not prudent. People at the backup site may have had to leave the building, and there were travel restrictions for days afterward that made it difficult to get people to some of the backup sites. Ironically, in this instance the ban on air travel added a new twist when it came to distant backup sites. At least the people at the distant sites were not curtailed by safety- or travel-related issues. The problem was getting key people from the primary site to the backup site, especially if they had to carry data backups on tapes or disks.

Many a company was forced to hire trucks and minivans to transport people and data to the backup sites. All in all, 9/11 was a rude wake-up call vis-à-vis corporate disaster-recovery preparedness. Mirrored sites, not just from a portal standpoint but also covering the other IT systems, though indubitably a costly and complex proposition, would have delivered near-transparent backup and recovery. Thus, there has been a new and urgent interest in mirrored site technology.

The concept of geographically distributed mirrored Web servers and FTP servers is not new. The goal here, particularly when it came to downloads, was to give users the option of selecting a geographically closer server to minimize the transit delays over the Internet. This is obviously of relevance only if you are dealing with a large, widely dispersed user audience. To make this type of mirroring meaningful and worthwhile, the mirror sites should be at least a few thousand miles apart.

If you plan to have a large portal with an active worldwide user base, then the rationale and justification for mirror sites can be based on two factors: disaster recovery and load-balancing. Rather than load-balancing across multiple servers at the primary site, you would now load-balance across multiple, dispersed sites, with each site in turn possibly having multiple severs sharing the load. The challenge, of course, is to obtain the necessary data and transaction synchronization between the two sites. This, however, immediately raises the issue of what you intend to "replicate" at the mirror site, given that a portal, per se, is a transaction system in its own right with its own complement of data but is also a front end to the other IT systems and the applications running on them.

Consequently, portal mirroring really has to be looked at from a holistic standpoint. More than likely, particularly given the cost involved, implementing portal mirroring is a decision that would need to be discussed and decided at the highest management levels. If you want a true, immediate cut-over disaster recovery scenario, you have no choice but to mirror the complete IT infrastructure, with the portal being just one of the components. Since management will want details of what can be achieved, the degree of protection, and the costs involved, start by looking at some of the options. Remember that with a mirror site, as opposed to just a backup site, you are striving to get double duty out of the mirror by also using it as a geographically dispersed load-balancing system.

For data replication begin by looking at such solutions as Sun's StorEdge, Compaq's StorageWorks Virtual Array, and IBM's Geographic Remote Mirror (GeoRM) for AIX (i.e., UNIX/LINUX). For an automatic site takeover capability look at GeoRM's "big brother"—the High Availability Geographic Cluster (HAEGO). HAEGO is a UNIX implementation of an extremely innovative, impregnable, transaction and data–synchronizing, instantaneous takeover system that IBM developed for mainframe environments in the mid-1980s. It was called the extended recovery facility (XRF).

XRF could provide recovery where, at worst, users would lose just the last item they typed in. In some cases there would be nothing lost. In the event of a failure to the primary site, users who were using that system would be able to continue working, with no data or keystrokes lost, after a momentary "hiccup." XRF or HAEGO was thus targeted at recovery rather than mirroring, although these schemes could be adapted to serve as an underlying basis for a mirrored operation. Since the exact level of mirroring possible and how it can be achieved will vary significantly, based on the platforms involved, you will have to talk to the various vendors and disaster-recovery specialists to determine the optimum architecture for your specific configuration.

The bottom line is that a mirrored portal site can give you both load balancing and the ultimate in instant recovery in one integrated package. The requisite technology and the expertise is available and proven. The pivotal issue, however, is that of cost and operational complexity on one hand versus the benefits of no-downtime disaster recovery on the other. Your company must already have disaster-recovery objectives, plans, and budgets. Now the portal needs to be factored into these plans, with mirrored portals becoming one of the possible options.

5.5   Managing and monitoring corporate portals

Managing and monitoring a portal, as mentioned at the start of this chapter, is not easy. Still, there is nothing magical or mystical about it either. Ultimately, it is a complex, high-visibility, transaction-oriented, mission-critical application, hopefully with a high volume of users. Thus, the overall management requirements for a corporate portal do not differ greatly from those for any other high-volume, transaction-oriented, mission-critical application with a fast-changing user population. Obviously there are portal-specific management and monitoring functions. These include the following:

- User administration with user ID allocation, user group definition, directory setup, and personalization

- Portal security administration and monitoring, including intrusion-detection system configuration, PKI administration, and digital certificate surveillance

- Content management, including administration of all portal-specific databases

- Administration and customization of collaborative tools

- Portal usage and performance tracking, including monitoring of system usage consumption and load-balancing utilization

- Rules-engine maintenance and fine-tuning

- Search-engine maintenance

The portal server and the auxiliary security, content-management, and usage-tracking products will provide you with the management tools for these functions. Today, they will invariably be browser based and "point-

and-click" oriented. The browser-based aspect will ensure that authorized operators will be able to perform these management and monitoring functions from anywhere in the network—even using wireless PDAs, handheld computers, or intelligent phones in many instances. Thus, operators will not have to be "tied" to a specific console or be confined to the data center. In emergencies, senior operators could even proactively intervene from home or from the golf course.

In addition to the portal-specific, software-oriented management tasks, the hardware and operating system hosting this software will need to be managed. The hardware could be a UNIX server, an Intel server, or a mainframe, and the OS is likely to be either UNIX, LINUX, or Windows NT. The requirements and disciplines for managing such platforms are well known, and you probably already have pertinent in-house expertise and experience. If not, you will either need to train existing operators on how to run these platforms in mission-critical mode or recruit a few experienced operators. Contractors are another option. Since uptime is of the essence, it is also important that you obtain the necessary maintenance contracts from the hardware and software vendors to provide you with the real-time coverage you need.

A healthy and responsive network infrastructure is key to the success of the portal. While you may have to upgrade certain network components to meet the traffic demands imposed by the portal (e.g., upgrading the Internet connection[s], beefing up the firewalls), the portal, in the end, is just another user of the overall corporate network. You already have a methodology in place for managing, sustaining, and nurturing this network. Although the impact of the portal needs to be factored in (particularly in terms of increased traffic), the portal per se will not change the way the network has to be managed.

If you already maintain a mission-critical network, then you would continue with the existing management products, procedures, and processes to ensure that the added demands made on the network by the portal do not degrade its reliability. If your network is not as resilient as you would like, this would be a good time to determine what it would take to fix it so that it can meet mission-critical criteria. This might require the upgrading of older, unreliable or inadequate capacity equipment. In some cases you may have to upgrade the software or firmware. You may also need new management tools.

The other IT systems accessed via the portal will each have its own specific management regime independent of the portal. The connections and sessions from the portal to these systems will require management, but these should not be viewed as being any different from the connections and sessions that would be required even if the portal were not there. Thus, the presence of the portal is somewhat irrelevant. The various applications running on these IT systems will have their own management systems that offer user and connection management and monitoring. You will still continue to use these tools and manage these applications more or less the same as they were being managed prior to installing the portal. The only difference the portal is likely to have made is to increase user volume.

The final, rather important issue in this context pertains to who will be managing and monitoring the portal. Some of the portal-specific functions (e.g., content management) will require specific and specialized skill sets. Others, such as security and user administration, may be best handled by those currently handling network administration and security—albeit after some hands-on training. Exactly who this will be will depend on the size of your current IT operation and the budget available for the portal. If you already have 24/7 operator coverage of your IT systems, you should definitely plan to extend this existing coverage through the introduction of additional personnel to embrace the non-content-related aspects of maintaining the portal. If you currently do not have 24/7 coverage, this may be something you want to consider. It all depends on how mission critical the portal is going to be.

5.6   Q&A—A time to recap and reflect

Q: What is involved in managing a corporate portal?

A: A portal needs to be managed as a total system—albeit within the context of your overall IT and networking infrastructure. This means that there will be portal-specific management functions in addition to all the other management tasks that need to be performed around the portal to sustain the other IT assets, the corporate network, and the Internet connections. Portal-specific management functions include user administration, personalization, security surveillance, content management, collaborative tool maintenance, usage monitoring, rules-engine upkeep, and search-engine upkeep.

Q: Why is content management so pivotal?

A: Content, along with speed and security, is what makes or breaks a corporate portal when it comes to non-b2e users. Fresh and vibrant content, in addition to being bait, is a vital, and relatively inexpensive corporate "advertising" mechanism to promote corporate vision, solutions, and values. However, you cannot just throw content on to the portal. Portal content is viewed by many as the corporation's "official line." Thus, it has to be accurate, up-to-date, error free, complete, and approved. However, this process of getting new content on to the portal cannot be allowed to become a burden and a bottleneck. Content management sets out to simplify and automate all of the many tasks associated with creating, reviewing, approving, syndicating, publishing, and controlling content.

Q: What types of services are offered by content-management systems?

A: There are six major categories of services offered by CM systems—namely, content collection, content creation, content control, content categorization, content delivery, and content surveillance. Content collection deals with assimilating your existing data, including content syndication, whereas content control deals with version control, review cycles, and approval mechanisms. Content categorization ensures that search engines and portal personalization will correctly recognize any new content, and content surveillance ensures that all the links, buttons, dialog boxes, and logon scripts on new portlets or page views are active and accurate.

Q: Does XML help when it comes to content management?

A: Yes, it most certainly does. XML provides you with a strategic and industry-standard way to maintain content in a format-, application-, and platform-independent manner. XML-structured content can be reused and repurposed in multiple ways for different applications. XML can thus be a great asset to content management vis-à-vis portals.

Q: Are there tools to automate and facilitate production of XML-structured documents?

A: Yes. There are many different types of tools. There are so-called N-converters that will use rules-based conversion methods to convert text, word processing documents, databases, and HTML documents into XML-structured documents. Then there are XML generators such as Corel's XMetaL that enable you to create documents using normal word processing conventions but then automatically generate XML equivalents of those documents using predefined conventions or templates. In addition, there are template-based data-creation schemes whereby the data entered into templates are automatically represented in XML.

Q: Why is it so imperative to carefully monitor and track portal usage?

A: Portal usage patterns and statistics, collected using tools from the likes of WebTrend, Sane, IBM, WebSideStory, and Sawmill, have many important uses. Key among these is to provide management with justification for the portal and, when the usage figures are impressive. enough bragging rights

along the lines of "our new portal is getting 1,000 hits an hour." These statistics also serve as an invaluable and irreplaceable source of data for capacity planning. They also enable the marketing departments to assess the
effectiveness of marketing campaigns and to determine which sites are referring leads to your portal. Trying to run a corporate portal without a good
usage-tracking mechanism would be akin to trying to fly a small plane, at
night, without a compass or altimeter. It could be done, but it could be haz-
ardous to your health.

*Q: Why is logical server partitioning so attractive in the context of corporate por-
tals?*

A: Logical server partitioning, if available on the server of your choice, is a
powerful, low-cost, and sure-fire way to enhance overall system resilience.
Partitioning provides protection against processor, memory, I/O adapter,
operating system, or application failures. In essence, it provides virtual clustering with load-balancing on the same machine.

*Q: What are some of the technologies available to boost memory and storage
resilience?*

A: Memory scrubbing and Chipkill technology set out to minimize system
downtime caused by memory failures. With memory scrubbing the contents of memory are read, checked for single-bit errors, and, if necessary,
corrected during periods when the system processors are idle. Chipkill can
detect multiple-bit errors and correct most them transparently. Chipkill
relies on a technique called "bit scattering," whereby the memory chips are
organized so that the failure of any specific memory module affects only a
single bit within an error-checked "word." This allows for error correction
and nondisruptive recovery even when there is a complete chip failure. On
the other hand, RAID and SAN technology significantly enhance the
redundancy and resiliency of system storage.

Q: What are self-managing and self-healing systems?

A: Self-managing and self-healing systems are computer systems that can
detect, recover from, and heal a variety of ailments without human intervention or impacting system operation. The goal is to simplify the complexity inherent in running today's sophisticated IT systems. Chipkill memory
technology, described previously, is an example of a self-healing technology.

Q: What are the advantages of a mirrored portal site?

A: Mirrored portal sites give you geography-oriented load-balancing and the
ultimate in nonstop disaster recovery in one integrated package. A mirrored
portal is a geographically dispersed server cluster that is working in load-bal-

ancing mode with the primary portal site. All of the data and transaction logs are continually duplicated across both sites. When both sites are active, they complement each other by sharing the work load—with network routers forwarding users to the nearest or least-busy site. In the event that one site goes down, the other site continues to work, unaffected, and can take over the displaced users.

6

Knowledge Management

Information is not knowledge.

—Albert Einstein

The express goal of contemporary knowledge management is to incisively address the above-quoted concern expressed by Albert Einstein. Today, more so than ever, it is imperative to distinguish knowledge from information, to separate the chaff from the wheat, so to speak. Thanks to computers, the Web, the media, and the incessant cell phones, society is awash in information. Professionals, in particular, are inundated with a relentless surfeit of information from all quarters. The problem is that this information overload can actually get in the way of gaining pertinent knowledge.

An expansive customer database is only information; it is not knowledge. Knowing what drove most of these people to become customers is, however, knowledge. Recognizing underlying demographic patterns within this customer base would also constitute knowledge. So would identifying definite purchasing patterns and schedules for the repeat customers. Therefore, just having access to tons of customer information, though gratifying, is not enough. You need to be able to slice it, dice it, and squeeze it to extract gainful knowledge. The same is true for all other forms of information as well.

A list of constantly updated stock prices on a PC screen, though useful, is still information. Knowing what is driving the market or a particular stock at a given juncture is knowledge. Knowledge is dynamic. The knowledge pertaining to the same pool of information can and should change over time. Ideally, the knowledge base should grow and become increasingly relevant. But knowledge does not necessarily always have to be progressive. yRecognizing that information that the company had been using to base some of its decisions on in the past is fundamentally flawed and useless is also a form of knowledge.

Corporate information (e.g., customer lists, product inventories, and manufacturing schedules) is a valuable corporate asset. Corporate knowledge is even more valuable. Information is power, and knowledge is absolute power as well as security. Consequently, the knowledge is likely to be even more restricted and guarded than the information it is based on. Thus, there will be a distinction between those who work with information (e.g., a telemarketer) as opposed to those who extract and leverage knowledge (e.g., a V.P. of marketing). This is important to keep in mind in the context of corporate portals. Knowledge "bases" and knowledge-management tools will more than likely be tightly controlled resources selectively accessible only by authenticated and authorized users. Figure 6.1 highlights the concept that from a corporate portal perspective, knowledge management is the apex of the information-management process.

Thanks in particular to increasingly sophisticated data mining technology, companies today are getting very good at knowledge extraction and exploitation. Direct-marketing companies, mail-order firms, and some e-retailers by necessity are continually pushing the limits of this technology. Today, nearly any public transaction that you make tends to leave some form of electronic trail. In this respect, credit-card transactions are just the

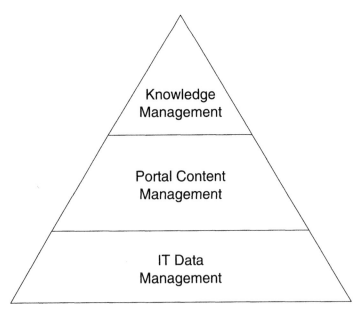

Figure 6.1   *Knowledge management is the apex of the overall corporate information-management challenge. This diagram was inspired by a concept promoted by ADAKOS GmbH relative to its knowledge-management solutions.*

tip of the iceberg. Video rental companies track your rentals, while super-markets and pharmacies, using the disingenuous "loyalty cards," track your buying habits. Then there are the frequent-flyer programs that can pinpoint your every stop on a trip, not to mention the information gathered through persistent warranty/registration schemes and hard-to-resist manufacturer's rebate programs. The bottom line is that one way or another, albeit at a cost, companies can obtain a vast amount of information about the general populace to supplement their in-house base of customer information. This information to support corporate decision making will be stored in a "data warehouse"—a continually expanding repository of raw data culled from many sources.

Data mining is what turns all of this diverse and disparate information into marketing gold. Data mining through complex and convoluted statistical analysis allows you to unearth correlations and patterns inherent in data. Let's assume that your company has a new performance-enhancing tennis racket ideally suited to give aging players a boost with their game. Your marketing manager wants to mount a very targeted " incentivized" (e.g., manufacturer's rebate) direct-mail campaign to potential buyers. Since there is a target age range here, you do not want a list of all tennis lovers. You want a list of known tennis players, possibly in a specific geography, who are over 50 years old and meet specified thresholds for spending habits—particularly on recreation-related items.

Today's data mining technology (or a data mining–services provider such as Acxiom) will enable you to home in on exactly this target market by extracting and correlating data from multiple data sources (e.g., purchase records, subscriptions to tennis magazines, public records, club member-ships). Figure 6.2 shows some of the knowledge management products and services offered by Acxiom, a long-term leader in this field. Figure 6.3 shows Amazon's invariably percipient product recommendation suggestions, which are based on the use of a cookie (for identification and personalization) coupled with collaborative filtering techniques to painstakingly track all activity performed on Amazon's Web site.

Data mining can improve the efficacy of company processes, eliminate low return on marketing and product expenditure, and contribute positively to the company's bottom line. When cleverly used, it can, at a minimum, ensure:

1.   Thorough, unambiguous understanding of customer demographics, behavior, and preferences

2.   Insight into purchasing rationales and triggers

3. Understanding of the optimum positioning for marketing messages and campaigns

4. Appreciation of the factors contributing to customer loyalty

5. A better grasp of competitive pressure and the impact of technology evolution

The ability to visualize data, typically consolidated from multiple sources, is an important factor when trying to gain insights into the patterns or relationships that may exist within the data. Contemporary knowledge-management solutions offer some powerful and graphic visualization tools

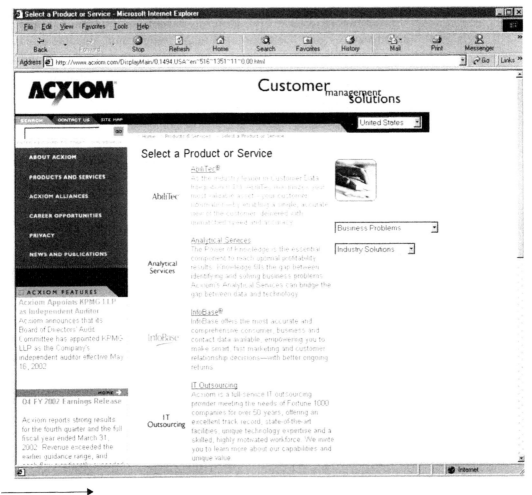

Figure 6.2   *Acxiom, one of many companies offering knowledge-management products or outsourced services.*

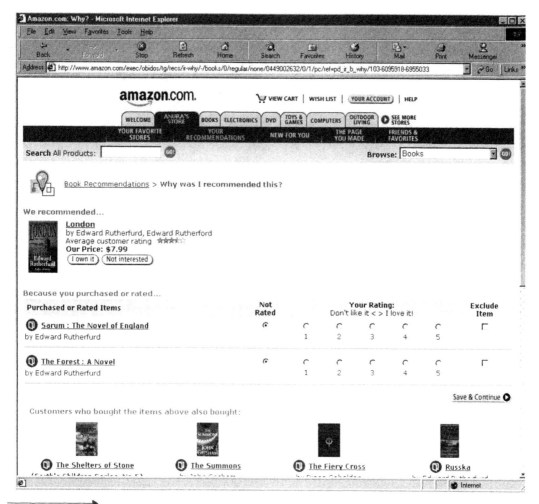

Figure 6.3 *Amazon's personalized product recommendations that attest to its efforts to collect and maintain pertinent knowledge about the interests and buying habits of its customers.*

to accommodate most requirements. The visualization tools typically work with many different types of data. Thus, such a solution will be a utility function vis-à-vis a corporate portal's knowledge-management functionality. Figure 6.4 shows a high-end visualization scheme now available for commercial applications, and Figure 6.5 illustrates the overall data mining process.

Knowledge management, data warehousing, data mining, business decision support (also called business intelligence), or online analytical processing (OLAP) are not new disciplines. Executive information systems (EISs)

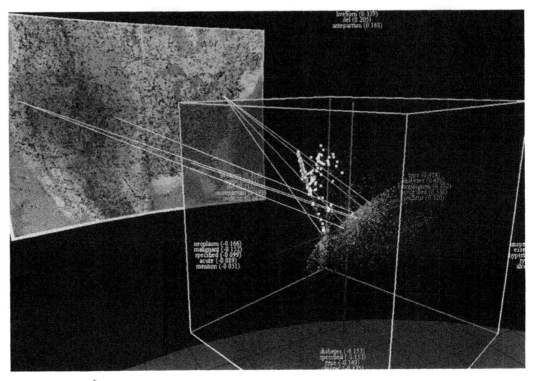

Figure 6.4 *High-end data-visualization technology, called STARLIGHT, now available for business intelligence applications from the Technology Commercialization Office of the Pacific Northwest National Laboratory's National Security Division at www.pnl.gov/nsd/commercial/starlight/.*

go back to the early 1970s when the first visual display units (VDUs) started to appear on a select number of desktops. Thus, knowledge management is in no way bound to the corporate portal or even to Web technology. Nonetheless, a corporate portal is increasingly becoming the ideal platform for implementing and delivering knowledge-management solutions. For a start it is the natural and logical focal point where all of the necessary data, users, and applications conveniently intersect.

Knowledge management moreover, as highlighted in Figure 6.1, is the apex of the whole information-management mandate assigned to a portal. Thus, knowledge management can be provided as a value-added extension to the content-management process by incorporating the relevant tools—albeit just to authorized users. The powerful authentication and personalization capabilities inherent in a portal provide a perfect, built-in, and infallible infrastructure for controlling this access. A portal is also ideally

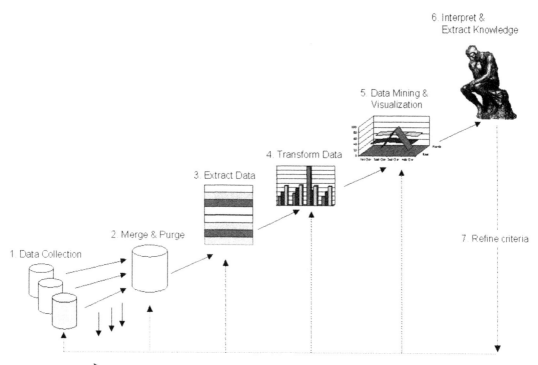

Figure 6.5   *The overall data mining and knowledge-extraction process based on a model proposed by the Automated Learning Group of the National Center for Supercomputing Applications (NCSA).*

equipped to deliver any and all necessary collaborative functions to facilitate team-based knowledge-gathering projects; knowledge sharing; and interactive, real-time knowledge refinement.

Delivering knowledge management via the portal, as opposed to via separate desktop applications installed on the PCs of selected executives, also fits in with the concept of users having consistent access to all the applications and services they need via the portal. It also ensures that you can also conveniently and securely share some knowledge-management functions with selected partners. Given all of these factors, knowledge management has been a key function associated with portals from the very early days of portals, as mentioned in Chapter 2. Business-intelligence (or decision-processing) portals were a popular type of second-generation b2e portal. Knowledge management was the basis for these types of portals. Now, with consolidated corporate portals, knowledge management has become one of the many value-added services available to select users.

Then there is an interesting flip side to knowledge management vis-à-vis corporate portals. Portal usage, especially by customers, partners, and prospects, can become an increasingly valuable source of data that can be profitably analyzed using data mining techniques to determine trends and preferences à la the Amazon model shown in Figure 4.3. The need to use portal usage analysis and reporting tools to continually keep tabs of the portal operation was discussed in Chapters 4 and 5. What can now be done is to feed the data obtained from these tracking packages into the knowledge-management system. There could be customer data patterns buried in here that might, when processed with the right data mining tools, help clarify previously collected customer behavior (e.g., why customers prefer a certain product or option over another).

XML and Web services will in time transform knowledge management and make it even more powerful and pertinent. The potential and promise of XML in this respect is hard to question. Despite the glut of information available today, most of this information is in proprietary form and is not self-defining. Knowledge-management tools have to support a variety of specific data types or formats in order to provide necessary data coverage. But there are always exceptions and omissions. Data that are not in a supported format cannot be analyzed and have to be ignored despite any potential significance.

Then there is the whole issue of data ambiguity and misrepresentation due to the lack of suitable qualification (e.g., the word "chip" found in an HTML-oriented Web document could be either a semiconductor, a person's name, a potato-based snack, or even a chocolate confection). XML, down the road, can obviously fix most of these problems and provide data uniformity and self-definition. Web services, on the other hand, are ideally suited to complement XML by providing increasingly specialized services on an "on-demand" subscription basis.

During the next few years vendors will, indubitably, start to offer knowledge-management functions—whether they be new visualization tools, data analysis methods, or data-merging options—in the form of Web services. This would essentially be a middle path between acquiring a knowledge-management product and outsourcing. Web services would typically be a way to add new capabilities to existing knowledge-management products—the equivalent of on-the-fly, Web-based plug-ins.

The possibilities are immense and exciting. It would be possible to subscribe to a particular service just for a specific marketing project. It would be possible to experiment with different technologies in a cost-effective manner, since subscribing to a Web service would be the equivalent of a short-term lease of a service. The bottom line is that knowledge management, today, is already very sophisticated and is guaranteed to deliver handsome dividends in corporate portal environments. Nonetheless, XML and Web services are poised to usher in a whole new and even more eloquent and capable generation of knowledge management.

6.1   Enterprise resource planning

In today's corporate culture, enterprise resource planning (ERP) applications will invariably form the underlying foundation on which knowledge-management systems will be built. Although ERP predates the popularization of the Web, Web technology, e-business, and portals have given ERP a whole new emphasis. The original goal of ERP applications was to obviate the need for corporate-specific, home-grown, and in-house–maintained applications. The ERP initiative, led by SAP, offered a comprehensive range of customizable, modular, off-the-shelf, feature-rich applications that addressed every facet of corporate business.

ERP applications were proven, ran on multiple platforms, and supported client/server architectures that could gainfully exploit the desktop processing capabilities of PCs and workstations. They offered lots of functionality and guaranteed interoperability between different applications. Rather than writing new applications or extending decades-old applications to address new business needs, corporations could buy or lease an ERP application that would meet their needs. There were plenty of tools and consultants to convert old data to work with the new applications, help with the overall deployment, and provide training. It was a compelling proposition.

ERP could minimize development costs, expedite time to market, reduce application upkeep costs, offer "future-proof" functionality guarantees, and be platform neutral. Corporations embraced ERP with gusto—though some did not realize the degree of cost savings they had been led to anticipate, because of unexpected hidden costs and complications during the data migration and application roll-out phases. Nonetheless, ERP is here to stay, and corporate portals will only serve to make ERP solutions even more attractive by heightening the demand for new application functionality to serve the fast-growing community of external users.

6.1.1   Supply chain management as an example

Rather than trying to reinvent the wheel in-house, corporations can turn to ERP applications to meet some of the e-business functionality that may be necessary to maximize the value of the portal. Supply chain management (SCM) is a good example of this. Web-based SCM has been an unmitigated success during the past few years, helping to dispel some of the post-dot-com skepticism leveled at e-business processes. Though SCM can be done outside the scope of the Web, the Web imbues SCM with universal, "zero-cost," high-speed connectivity, popular networking standards, device independence (e.g., wireless support), and standard-based security (e.g., SSL). Thanks to Web-based SCM, companies can:

- Dramatically increase the efficiency of internal and b2b processes to realize tangible gains in overall productivity

- Automate certain process (e.g., automatic inventory reordering, billing)

- Minimize the cost of surplus inventories

- Quickly react to and exploit price changes affecting supplies, components, and services

- Minimize the expenses associated with intercompany interactions by using the Web to convey necessary data (as opposed to faxes, couriers, and overnight deliveries)

- Easily open up their supply chain to a much wider audience of suppliers, manufacturers, logistics coordinators (e.g., shipping), and distributors around the world to obtain the most favorable competitive pricing and schedules

- Provide authorized suppliers and partners with secure, self-service functionality (ideally via a portal) to obviate the need for them to locate and interact with a company representative for routine queries and status updates

- Compress supply-cycle and thus time-to-market schedules

- Optimize manufacturing schedules well in advance, based on up-to-date accurate information on both supply and demand parameters to benefit from as many cost-saving factors as possible (e.g., fine-tuning shift scheduling, terminating surplus leased storage, renegotiating transport contracts)

XML, with its promise of facilitating standardization and interoperability, is, of course, a compelling proposition for making Web-based SCM even more pervasive and popular. Thus, as is to be expected, there is a tremendous amount of work being done to define XML "vocabularies" and standards for SCM. For example, there is the BASDA e-business XML (eBIS-XML) standard implemented by the Business and Accounting Software Developers Association (BASDA). Its goal is to permit orders and invoices to be automatically exchanged between disparate accounting applications.

In order to seed the market and encourage adoption of this standard, BASDA even promotes the concept of sending eBIS-XML, via e-mail, to suppliers and partners that may not have an accounting system that currently supports eBIS-XML. As with any XML-qualified document, humans will not have any problems reading the content of the document despite the distraction of all the \XML tags. Thus, they will be able to manually act on the e-BIS-XML-based order or invoice included in the e-mail.

Visit XML.org and www.oasis-open.org for information on other SCM-specific XLM initiatives such as ebXML, cXML, RosettaNet Partner Interface Processes (PIP), Microsoft's BizTalk framework, VISA XML invoice specification, and IBM's Trading Partner Agreement Markup Language (TPAML). In parallel with XML, Web services will also play a pivotal role over the coming years in terms of adding new functionality to SCM applications (e.g., instantaneous spot-pricing of commodities, currency calculations, competitive shipping quotes, on-the-fly credit ratings). Between XML and Web services, SCM, despite all of its success during the past few years, is ready to make another quantum leap in terms of interoperability, universal reach, and value-added functionality.

Though now a proud standard bearer for the viability of b2b e-business, SCM is but just one of the many applications that fall under the category of ERP. If anything, it is one of the newer types of ERP applications, given that the initial ERP applications focused on accounting, finance, and manufacturing processes. Today, the wide repertoire of ERP applications, available from a range of well-known vendors, includes:

- Human resource management

- Accounting and finance processing

- Manufacturing support

- Project management

- Product life-cycle management

- Customer relationship management (CRM)

- Supply chain management (SCM)

- Supplier relationship management

- Sales-force automation

- Business intelligence

Some of the key vendors of contemporary ERP applications include SAP, Oracle, IBM, Microsoft, BAAN, PeopleSoft, Ariba, Siebel, J.D. Edwards, and i2. Some of these (e.g., Siebel and Ariba) specialize in one or two of the ERP fields (e.g., CRM or SCM), whereas others such as SAP and Oracle offer a wider range of solutions, though it is fair to say that none can credibly claim that they cover the entire range of ERP possibilities. Figure 6.6, for example, shows BAAN's ERP repertoire with its holistic approach to the activities of a corporation relative to the ERP activities it addresses, and Figure 6.7 illustrates i2's value chain–management concept, which embraces supplier relationship management, SCM, and "demand-chain management" (which is essentially another spin on CRM). At this juncture it is also worth noting that some of large ERP vendors—in particular SAP, IBM, Oracle, PeopleSoft, and Microsoft—also offer corporate portal solutions to complement their ERP offerings.

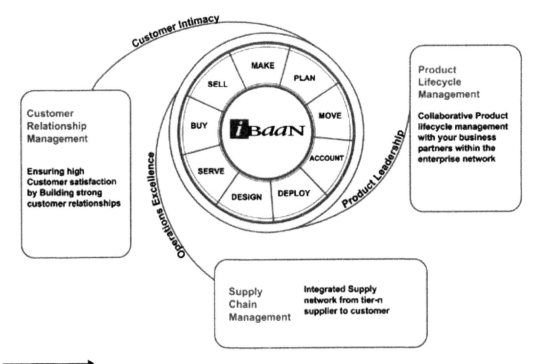

Figure 6.6   *BAAN's ERP repertoire, which synthesizes and revolves around CRM, SCM, and product life-cycle management—with a holistic approach that tries to address all aspects of a corporation's operations relative to these activities.*

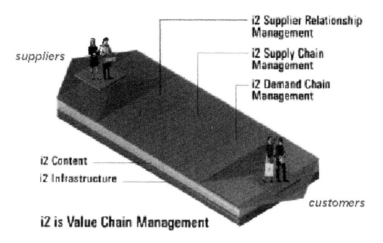

Figure 6.7   *i2's value chain management concept, which brings together supplier relationship management, SCM, and demand-chain management; the latter is essentially CRM in another guise.*

6.1.2   **ERP applications and corporate portals**

ERP applications and corporate portals intersect with and impinge on each other in multiple ways and at multiple levels. Each can exist without the other, though there is inescapable synergy—and e-business potential—when you bring them together, as shown in Figure 6.8. Since ERP applications per se are not a new venture by any stretch of the imagination, it is safe to say that all companies already have some type of corporate position and allegiance when it comes to ERP. If you currently do not have any ERP applications installed, then the corporate portal implementation plans should not in any way be delayed or jeopardized by trying to combine the two issues. ERP applications, despite their potential ROI down the road, are costly and by nature somewhat involved. It boils down to the adage

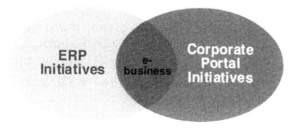

Figure 6.8   *Although synergy and e-business come about when you integrate ERP with corporate portals, corporate portal initiatives can proceed independent of ERP.*

about being very selective in the battles you want to fight, which rings particularly true in today's supercharged IT cultures.

If your company has to date resisted going with ERP applications, this is not the time to resurrect the issue, because the portal by itself is also an expensive and far-reaching proposition. Go ahead and implement the portal. Down the road, when the portal is humming and justifying its existence, inexorably, on a daily basis, you can raise the issue that certain ERP applications (e.g., SCM or CRM) could further enhance the value and usefulness of the portal. Until then, just provide the necessary interfaces to the in-house applications that are being used to realize the necessary IT functions.

The chances are, however, that it is unlikely that you will have to butt heads at this juncture trying to justify ERP. If your company is considering a contemporary XML-capable corporate portal, then it is likely that it has also seriously evaluated the potential merits of ERP solutions sometime during the past seven years, especially when looking for Y2K workarounds. If the company decided against ERP, it's best to let sleeping dogs lie for the time being, as mentioned previously. What is more likely, however, is that you already have some ERP applications. If so, that is indeed a good start.

If you already have one or more ERP applications, the first task vis-à-vis the portal is to ensure that authorized users—whether in-house, "mobile," agents, or partners—can securely access the applications via the portal. If the applications are already Web-enabled, then portal integration should be trivial. You could provide point-and-click access to the application via hot links in an appropriate portal-view page, controlled via the standard portal personalization rules.

If the applications are not currently Web-enabled, you essentially have two options. One is to "upgrade" an application by getting a Web interface module from the ERP vendor. The other is to implement a generic host publishing solution, as discussed in section 3.4.1, which will provide you with a global Web-enablement solution that will work with all ERP and other host applications. This latter approach is likely to represent the more strategic, lower-cost option, particularly if you have multiple applications that need to be Web-enabled. Even if you only need to Web-enable a few applications, implementing a generic solution that will work with any application provides "future-proofing" in the event you have to integrate other applications down the road.

Once you have portal-enabled ERP applications, the issue becomes who, if anyone, on the outside could benefit from having authorized access to one or more of these applications. The obvious candidates are partners, distributors, suppliers, agents, and other associates. But this is a line-of-business decision that might require senior management ratification, as opposed to a portal implementation–related issue. Then there is always the possibility that the applications, in their current form, though addressing some of the needs of this external audience, are not the total or appropriate solution. This again is a line-of-business decision.

A key issue could be that the applications, especially if they were acquired prior to the mid-1990s, were not designed to be extended for external b2b collaboration. For example, to achieve the level of external interaction desired you may have to upgrade to or acquire a new SCM, supplier relationship management, CRM, or project management application. Or you might need to leverage host integration technology, as also discussed in section 3.4.1, to cost effectively extend the application to meet the new requirements. Though it is a portal-inspired "opportunity," this is not a portal-specific issue.

All that the portal is doing in such scenarios is providing an open, secure, consistent, and convenient mechanism to facilitate e-business. In reality, the suitability of existing ERP applications to perform mission-critical e-business functionality needs to be thrashed out within the context of the corporation's overall e-business objectives and strategy rather than as a portal-related challenge. The portal is part of the solution. It is not the cause of the problem.

There is, however, another e-business–related scenario in which the portal may actually be the cause for precipitating certain ERP decisions. This refers to situations in which budgetary approval for a corporate portal was contingent on its delivering specific e-business–based cost savings (e.g., reduction in order, invoice, and account processing costs via SCM or reduction in call-center operations cost via a self-service CRM operation). In such situations having the right ERP applications to make the necessary e-business happen becomes a part of the overall corporate portal charter as well as a clearly measurable metric pertaining to the performance of the portal.

Though now a portal-related issue, sourcing, testing, and implementing the appropriate ERP applications will most likely require support and cooperation from other IT groups. The bottom line, in general, is that going forward there will be an inevitable overlap of corporate portal and ERP initiatives driven by the needs of e-business. Still, from a portal perspective ERP applications will be only one of the many services offered through the portal, while to those responsible for ERP the portal may be just the latest way to offer access to their applications.

6.2 Contemporary knowledge management

Knowledge management per se is not a portal-specific or even an IT-specific discipline. It has been around in many different forms since ancient times, treasured and refined by the likes of philosophers, priests, authors, teachers, and politicians. Even today, most companies are bound to have human-centric KM schemes with certain individuals credited with being an oracle, a guru, or a font, or having a "good gut feel for this stuff." There is even a technical name for such nontechnical KM. It is referred to as "noncodified" KM, since it does not involve meticulously maintained databases or sophisticated, computerized tools. Computer-based KM systems, in contrast, are heavily codified schemes, whereby extracted knowledge is stored in readily and repeatedly accessible form.

A corporate portal has significant applicability in both codified and non-codified KM scenarios. This is important to remember. Those who rely on and further noncodified KM invariably have an insatiable thirst for raw information. They also like to communicate and collaborate with peers to validate and refine their perceptions. Corporate portals with their personalized information feeds, ready access to IT data, and powerful collaborative schemes can provide these corporate "intellects" (who, however, may not necessarily be the corporate "visionaries") with the tools they need to thrive and flourish. Nonetheless, it is the codified, computer-based KM systems, also now increasingly referred to as business intelligence systems, that most people think of when it comes to KM and portals.

Computer-based KM schemes are a set of loosely integrated (i.e., capable of working independent of each other) electronic processes that relate to the capture, creation, analysis, distillation, organization, dissemination, utilization, and safeguarding of knowledge. The express goal of these processes is to enhance and continually refresh the corporate knowledge base. The key functions necessary to realize a KM system can be summarized as follows:

1. Culling data from various and disparate prespecified internal and external sources—including obtaining dynamic data from the Web as well as the corporate portal using automatic "push" mechanisms

2. Optionally integrating with a workflow-management process to ensure that all pertinent data are captured, that these date are updated each time, and that no data fall between the cracks

3.   Transforming the data (e.g., adding XML qualification) to realize some level of standardization and consistency

4.   Organizing and storing the data (including links to its source) in a data warehouse

5.   Extracting and transforming the necessary data from the data warehouse

6.   Performing first-level analysis using popular tools (e.g., Excel or a database-specific capability as with Oracle)

7.   Sharing first-level analysis results to obtain feedback on how the data can be refined

8.   Applying advanced, customized analytical tools such as OLAP and data mining

9.   Sharing results from the advanced analysis, getting feedback, and refining the analysis methodology if necessary

10.   Publishing the latest insight and encouraging discussion

11.   Finding means to gainfully leverage new insight by modifying business processes

12.   Protecting the extracted knowledge for future use

13.   If appropriate, ensuring that some of this knowledge becomes company "lore" so that it can be of use to the widest possible audience

The good news is that proven, total-KM (or business intelligence) suites are now available from some well-respected names in the ERP field, such as SAP, IBM, Oracle, and PeopleSoft—where PeopleSoft uses the term "Enterprise Performance Management" to describe their BI-related product suite.

This description from SAP's Web site shows, verbatim, the firm's take on BI:

mySAP Business Intelligence gives you a complete, end-to-end solution that satisfies the diverse needs of end users, IT professionals, and senior management alike. The key capabilities of mySAP Business Intelligence include:

- ■ *Web-Based Reporting and Analysis—Provides tools for reporting and analysis delivered through a powerful, Web-based interface that is secure and fully interactive.*

- ■ *Information Delivery—Delivers timely, relevant information within and beyond the enterprise. Reports and alerts are delivered through HTML, wireless devices, and Microsoft Excel.*

- *Excel-Based Reporting and Analysis—Enables you to use Microsoft Excel as a fully functional interface for all reporting and analysis needs. Minimizes user training and lowers total cost of ownership.*

- *Advanced Analytics—Provides statistical and mathematical functions and multidimensional analysis to extract hidden insight via customer segmentation, in-depth data analysis, and much more.*

- *Mobile Business Intelligence—Delivers interactive business intelligence to a full range of mobile and wireless devices with on-demand access to critical information.*

- *Business Content—Leverages best practices to deliver prepackaged business content tailored for different user roles in different industries. Includes report templates and metrics to accelerate deployment and tap into valuable expertise.*

- *Portal Integration—Integrates seamlessly into mySAP Enterprise Portals, allowing you to deploy and collaborate on real-time information using SAP Portal's unification and iView technology.*

- *Data Warehousing—Ensures accurate and timely integration of data from all sources. Includes a robust operating environment with data transformation, warehouse management, and near-line storage.*

The foregoing description of SAP's BI solution immediately brings into focus a few interesting and representative facts about today's off-the-shelf BI offerings. Foremost among these is that it offers all of the key functionality associated with the KM process—including data warehousing, two-stage analysis, and data delivery. The next thing to note is the built-in portal integration, confirming that, as with ERP, portals are a strategic platform for enhancing the scope, reach, and value of KM.

At this juncture, before becoming portal-specific, it is important to note that "knowledge" is diverse, multifaceted, and function specific. A company's V.P. of sales, the CFO, and the CTO will, indubitably, work off different knowledge "bases" and furthermore seek vastly different types of new knowledge. Although there will be some knowledge of value to all, the knowledge that will most further the cause of a company has to be very precise and function related. The knowledge sought by the V.P. of sales is likely to be derived from data pertaining to customer relationships, market trends, product sale statistics, sales performance, sales forecasts, and competitor activity.

On the other hand, the CTO is likely to be looking for knowledge that has to be distilled from data pertaining to technology, product announcements, and market forecast. While the CFO will always be eager to learn about the latest insight of the V.P. of sales and the CTO, the knowledge of real import to the CFO is likely to have its roots in financial, supply-chain, manufacturing, backlog, inventory, and market-trend data. The bottom line is that when it comes to KM, you really need different horses for different courses. PeopleSoft, for one, stresses this function-specific role of KM by offering its Enterprise Performance Management modules to be used with various ERP applications.

Although the same infrastructure (e.g., data warehouse) could be used to support multiple KM applications, each application will have vastly different needs when it comes to types of information, sources of information, and data analysis. Even though they all share a common foundation, each KM application will be specialized and highly customized, possibly down to the level of individual users. Thus, an HR-specific KM application could offer different types of in-depth analysis for different managers within the HR group (e.g., performance and attrition analysis, marketplace salary trend analysis, recruitment, and workforce availability analysis).

6.2.1   KM and corporate portals

Corporate portals, as mentioned previously, can facilitate both codified and noncodified KM. Portals include as standard functions many of the core services necessary to implement successful KM applications, key among these being collaborative tools; wide-ranging information dissemination features; and powerful security for access control, data syndication capabilities, and personalization. Thus, as with other ERP applications, there can be significant synergy in integrating KM functionality with a corporate portal. However, as with other ERP applications, KM and portals, in the end, still involve separate initiatives and endeavors.

Although the glut of ready information available via the Web makes KM more compelling than ever, a company's attitudes about KM are likely to predate its interest in implementing a corporate portal. If your company already has one or more KM applications, then, as with ERP, the first thing that needs to be done in terms of the portal is to ensure that these KM applications can be accessed via the portal. If the KM applications run on host systems or already have Web interfaces, the portal integration should be relatively simple, as with other, similar host applications. However, some KM applications rely on a client/server model, with desktop processing power being used to do some of the data analysis, modeling, and reporting. Adapting such client/server KM applications for use via the portal could be more challenging.

In the case of company employees already using the client/server KM applications, it might actually just be simpler and logical to leave them as they are to begin with and just treat them as resembling desktop productivity applications (e.g., Word, Excel, or PowerPoint). The users will still be able to use the portal for some KM-related collaborative information publishing and data-transfer functions, but the client/server applications per se will be invoked and executed outside the Web browser windows used to interact with the portal. If these KM applications are used only by a small number of users (e.g., less than 50), it would be difficult to justify the cost and effort of trying to implement a fully integrated solution.

The basic flaw of this approach is that these KM applications cannot be readily offered to external users (e.g., select partners) via the portal. If external access makes business sense, the easiest solution might be to evaluate a

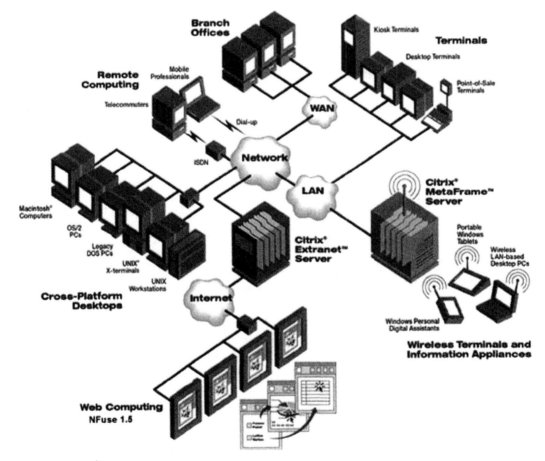

Figure 6.9   *The latest application-delivery architecture postulated by Citrix Systems, showing how "client" applications running on a Citrix server can be conveniently accessed by a wide range of legacy, desktop, terminal, kiosk, Web, and wireless clients.*

Web-oriented "terminal server" scheme such as Citrix's Nfuse, which allows the client component to execute on a server and deliver its results in a browser window. Figure 6.9 shows Citrix's latest application-delivery architecture with its support for a very diverse range of legacy, desktop, terminal, kiosk, Web, and wireless clients. The other option would be to determine whether a Web-enabled version of the product is available.

Once you have portal-accessible KM applications, the issues vis-à-vis these applications and the portal are really the same as those pertaining to ERP applications. One major difference, however, could be that companies are unlikely to be as amenable to sharing their KM applications with external users as they are with ERP applications. The tangible cost-reduction possibilities of e-business make ERP "sharing" hard to resist. KM, however, is different. It is not an e-business process per se. Although it can influence, shape, and monitor e-business, unlike with, say, SCM, partners and suppliers do not have to access your KM tools in order for you to gain the necessary knowledge. That is the rub when it comes to KM applications.

Knowledge is a valuable and leverageable asset. Letting select partners and associates have ready access to all the relevant KM tools might not be entirely prudent from a business standpoint. It might just be better and safer to share selected insights using collaborative tools, customized portal-view pages, teleconferences, or face-to-face meetings. This, however, is a line-of-business decision as opposed to a portal-related issue. The same is true about the use of KM within the company. Determining the best ways to exploit KM has to be a line-of-business decision. A portal can provide the infrastructure for KM applications, but it should not be a determining factor as to how and why KM should be used within a company.

6.3   Data collection for knowledge management

The adage about never being able to be too rich or too thin can easily be extended to cover information within the context of KM. Since codified knowledge is extracted from raw information, it is never possible to have too much of the *right* information, provided, of course, you have the right analytical tools (e.g., data mining) and the processing power (e.g., multiprocessor UNIX servers) to crunch through all of that. Knowledge extraction, in the end, is like any other extraction, distilling, or mining process. How much you can get out depends on the quantity and quality of what you start with.

The Web obviously has changed all the parameters and expectations when it comes to information availability. It is hard to accurately quantify, rationalize, or even visualize the amount of information on the Web. There are, however, two inescapable facts. The amount of information is staggering, and it is growing at an enormous rate. The rate at which information is being added to the Internet is unprecedented. The amount of new information being added to the Internet in one day, at present, exceeds the volume of new information acquired by a large city library over the period of a year 20 years ago.

In mid-2000, it was estimated that there were approximately 500 million Web pages on the Internet. In May 2002, the Google search engine is searching through 2 billion Web pages, and Google will be the first to admit that this 2 billion does not represent the entire, active universe of pages. This universe is estimated to be growing at the rate of a million documents a day (although the 2000 to 2002 growth rate appears to have been double this). Although this information is not comprehensive, structured, or arbitrated, it is a compelling pool of raw data in the context of KM. Web page content, however, is not the only source for data pertinent to a company's quest for knowledge. There are all of those thousands upon thousands of Usenet discussion forums that cover every conceivable topic and interest known to mankind—and then a few more.

You can use Google also to search through these discussion forums or groups. Companies are finding that searching these Usenet groups for specific keywords (e.g., company name, product name, competitor names, market sector) can unearth a wealth of "unedited," unfiltered information about public perception pertaining to areas of interest to the company. This is so much the case that many large companies now have people in their marketing divisions searching these Usenet groups on a daily basis for comments, views, and opinions about the company and competitors.

For example, Google currently has 1.2 million messages containing the keyword Cisco, 10.1 million that refer to IBM, 20.2 million pertaining to Microsoft, and 3,190 about the portal server vendor Plumtree. Figure 6.10 shows the first page of results for a Usenet search for references about Microsoft. In total, Google is at present searching through 700 million messages to find these references. In many ways these "from-the-heart," "disguised identity" messages, when properly analyzed, serve as a true leading indicator of market and public opinion about a company. From a KM perspective, the Usenet message pool is another valuable source of Internet-based information.

The role of corporate portals when it comes to culling Internet data for KM is ambiguous at best. Given that a portal sits on the interface between a company and the Web and contains a lot of software, many people assume

Figure 6.10 *A Google search for the term "Microsoft" in Usenet group discussion messages that resulted in 20,200,000 active messages being found. Information in Usenet messages is thus becoming a valuable leading indicator for knowledge-management applications.*

that a portal has to be a good tool through which to collect data available on the Internet. This is not necessarily the case. A typical corporate portal will include the following functionalities that certainly facilitate some level of data gathering:

- Secure, high-bandwidth Internet connection

- Collaborative tools to enable hassle-free acceptance of large volumes of subscribed data, in multiple different formats, from data originators (e.g., mailing lists, customer lists, purchase transactions, home purchase records) as well as data from partners, distributors, agents, and associates

- Search engines that could be used to search the Web on a global or selective basis (this is done using a public search engine; possibly acting on a customized, subscription basis might be more efficacious)

- Ability to receive syndicated news and content feeds in a variety of formats

- High-speed connections to "back-end" IT systems

- Rules engines that could be used to control the nature and scope of the data gathering

- Content-management capability to index and categorize collected information

Nonetheless, Internet data gathering for KM is not a standard function normally associated with corporate portals. It is more of an IT application—or even multiple applications—that may utilize some of the capabilities available via the portal, such as the collaborative tools and the syndicated content. Depending on the amount and sophistication of the information sought, these data-gathering applications (which in essence could be scripts) may actually require regular interactive human intervention to set new search criteria, add new data sources, and check the veracity of the data being collected. In some instances, it may just be easier to assign somebody in marketing to do a regular troll of the required data sources manually, invoking the necessary search engines or file-transfer processes.

So far this discussion about a portal's role when it comes to collecting data from the Internet for KM applications has focused on the information outside the portal per se (i.e., the actual Internet). However, each corporate portal in its own right is also part of the Internet, with its own complement of information. For example, the collaborative tools provided may include bulletin boards and discussion group capabilities for external users, including customers, prospects, and partners, among others. In addition, the portal is bound to include a "contact us" capability. These external "interfaces" are likely to contain information of value in the context of KM (e.g., definite trends in customer comments or requests).

Then, as discussed previously, there are all the data about user visits and what pages were viewed. There could also be transactional data, although the information contained in the transactions may be better collected from the source application as opposed to the portal interface. The bottom line is that a corporate portal will inevitably contain its own pool of data that could be highly pertinent to KM. In the case of this information, it will obviously be the responsibility of the portal and its manager to make sure that it is readily available to the KM applications.

6.4   Data mining

The data collected for use by KM applications will be stored in a data warehouse, which is, in effect, a big relational database. In the case of data associated with transactional or batch applications, these data would first have to be extracted from operational databases. Data from other sources would also be loaded into the warehouse in a common format. All these data would then be "merged, purged, and enriched" to remove duplicate entries, consolidate related records, and supplement missing fields (e.g., a social security or birth date missing for a person in one record could be located from another record pertaining to that person). The data could then be further reformatted and transformed to facilitate the subsequent analysis.

This analysis, as discussed earlier, will usually happen in two stages. There will be some initial analysis using simple query and reporting tools to gain an overall, high level "map" of the data. These tools are ideal to gain information obtainable via simple, prespecified queries such as average monthly sales, number of portal visits, company backlog for the last year, or new accounts acquired during the last quarter. Once the data based on this initial, first-cut analysis have been deemed to be appropriate and representative by the vested parties (e.g., director of corporate research, V.P. of marketing), then the more complex analysis can begin.

OLAP and statistical analysis are the first of these complex analysis methodologies. OLAP allows professionals (e.g., business analysts or marketing directors) to drill down to the next level of detail spanning multiple dimensions to determine the degree of relationship between two factors (e.g., product shipments to particular zip codes, credit-card transactions over $150 at sporting good stores, portal visits that lasted longer than two minutes from users from Sri Lanka).

OLAP, however, does not provide much value beyond easily correlated information fields. With OLAP, any complex information deduction required will have to be done by the human. Thus, OLAP, for example, will not be able to identify that during the summer months, supermarket shoppers in the northeastern United States, if shopping on a Friday or Saturday, when the temperature is above 70°F, will frequently buy large quantities of hamburgers, hot dogs, potato chips, onion dip, and beer. That type of incisive and insightful analysis is possible only with data mining.

Data mining is a computerized system that utilizes complex artificial intelligence (AI)–inspired algorithms to sift through large amounts of data and highlight convoluted but highly relevant relationships and patterns buried within the data. Jesus Mena, the CEO of WebMiner, Inc., and the author of *WebMining for Profit*, a companion book in this Digital Press Data Management series, provides a great example of the power and insight provided by data mining. Mr. Mena's company was using data mining techniques to analyze the shopping habits of the consumers of a particular supermarket chain. Thanks to data mining, the analysts discovered an intriguing trend. Whenever a particular product was purchased, the number of items in the shopping basket tripled from the average of 6 up to 18 items. This basket-size enhancing product was not milk, diapers, or pizza. It was pickles. That is knowledge. And that is the beauty of data mining.

The January 31, 2002, issue of the *Darwin* magazine (www.darwinmag.com) has an equally impressive example of data mining, this time involving Fingerhut Corp., the Minnetonka, Minnesota–based $2 billion mail-order company. In the 1950s, Manny Fingerhut was making and selling protective seat covers for cars. He knew that his best customers were those who had just bought a new car. The arrival of a mail-order catalog for neckties got him thinking. He rented a list of new car registrations and mailed the people on this list a simple advertising circular. This highly targeted mail-order campaign was a huge success, and Mr. Fingerhut soon had annual sales approaching $1 million.

Fingerhut has never forgotten the power of targeted direct marketing. To this end, the company maintains a huge data warehouse with nearly 50 years' worth of data and has approximately 200 market analysts. Recently, using data mining techniques, Fingerhut discovered that customers who change their residence triple their purchasing in the 12 weeks following their move—with a peak in buying activity within the first four weeks. There was even a pattern in the purchases. Customers who had recently moved bought furniture, telecommunications equipment, and decorations but stayed away from jewelry and home electronics. For a mail-order company, this is indeed valuable knowledge, since change of address information that would point to this target customer base can be obtained in multiple ways.

Data mining uses algorithms with names such as CART (classification and regression trees), CHAID (chi-squared automatic interaction detection), MARS (multivariate adaptive regression), ID3 (interactive dichotomizer), C4.5 and C5.0—these latter two are successors to ID3. Data mining, given the volume of data involved and the complexity of the algorithms, is processing intensive. Parallel processing, involving multiple processors, is usually the preferred approach for performing data mining. Today's powerful UNIX servers, with their multiple processors, large memory capacity, and high-speed I/O, are thus ideal for this purpose. Data mining solutions are available from the likes of Salford Systems, ANGOSS, IBM (DB2 Intelligent Miner for Data), Oracle (Darwin), Rulequest, and Attar. It is also worth investigating outsourced solutions from the likes of Acxiom.

6.5   Web mining

Web mining refers to the process of collecting and carefully analyzing information about the behavior of Web users, including using data mining technology, to gain competitive advantage, foster customer loyalty, increase e-commerce, and craft market strategy. The possibilities of understanding user preferences and dislikes by analyzing the portal usage patterns (e.g., most-visited and least-visited pages, average time per page, most downloaded documents, number of repeat visits by the same user within a week) have already been discussed more than once. But this whole process can be taken further, especially if your business model is gravitating toward e-business.

Rather than just relying on "log file" statistics, collated and reported via a good usage tracking application such as WebTrends, you can implement more "intrusive" methods (e.g., cookies, voluntary divulgence, and Web "bugs"), always keeping in mind that you could be walking a fine line between corporate zealousness and invasion of privacy, as discussed in section 2.3.2. Cookies are a widely used mechanism to store specific information about portal users (e.g., automatic personalization), their preferences, and past behavior, including purchasing or browsing preferences. Amazon is an avid user of cookies.

Cookies are first generated by a Web server and then stored on the hard drive of a user's computer for subsequent use. They are transferred between the Web server and the user's Web browser using standard HTTP, interspersed between the HTML-based Web page transfers. Each time a user access a site that uses cookies, the Web server will request the user's browser to "up-load" the cookie associated with that site. If a cookie is present from prior visits, it will then provide that site with information collected during those visits, including user IDs and passwords—hence their applicability when it comes to personalization. The server can then send back an updated cookie on a regular basis, along with a requested Web page view.

Obviously you don't have to store user preferences and habits on a cookie. You could just use the cookie for identification. Once the user's identity is known, the user's behavior can be recorded, cataloged, and stored on the portal using the content-management tools. A more insidious variant of a cookie is sometimes referred to as a Web "bug," which masquerades as a graphic on a Web page or even e-mail. The "bug," which typically works in conjunction with a Java applet, a JavaScript, or a cookie, will send information about the user to a server, whenever the graphic is viewed. The downside of all these schemes unbeknownst to the user is the specter of "the big Web server in the sky watching you" syndrome it creates among users.

Openly soliciting information from the user, in the form of a portal registration or a document download request, does not impinge on the thorny privacy issue as much. However, the bottom line is that a corporate portal, because of the need for security and personalization, is going to try to get users to explicitly identify themselves in some form or another—whether it be a casual "login" (i.e., just user ID without a password), a strict authentication, or the use of cookies. Once a user is identified, the amount of information that you can track about that user, relative to the portal experience, will probably be limited only by the amount of disk space you want to allocate for all this tracking information.

This really becomes a KM issue, tinged to an extent with respect for privacy. But if your company wishes to exploit Web mining, then you have no choice but to start collecting the portal usage behavior deemed to be necessary for this. It is possible that in the end the information sought is exactly the type made available by the popular usage-tracking and analysis products. If so, you are all set. If not, then you will have to implement JavaScripts, Java, triggers, and other various means to track the user behavior necessary to collect.

So far this discussion on Web mining has revolved around user information culled from your portal. However, most Web sites and portals, not to mention third-party Web advertising companies, have already been collecting user behavior data for quite a long time. In other words, as with all information related to the Web, there is a surfeit of potential information available about Web users. If the behavior of the same users can be tracked across multiple sites (e.g., via an IP address or the same registration "alias"), you could, especially with data mining, determine some fascinating and nonintuitive insights similar to that of pickle purchases increasing the number of items in a shopping basket. Suffice to say, the possibilities in this realm are enormous—and even frightening. However, obtaining user behavior patterns on other sites and portals is not a function of the corporate portal. All the corporate portal can and should do is to provide information related to its user base.

6.6 KM information dissemination and collaboration

A corporate portal is unparalleled when it comes to being the perfect platform to disseminate knowledge, promote knowledge sharing, encourage discussion about captured knowledge, and ensure active participation by vested parties during the data culling and refining process. Thanks to security, personalization, content management, rules engines, and collaborative tools, all of the necessary infrastructure and mechanisms are in place for all of these activities. Security, personalization, and the rules engine can ensure that access to the knowledge base is stringently controlled. This alone represents a major step forward from prior methods. Rather than having to institute ad hoc access control mechanisms, you can now have a standard framework for personalized knowledge delivery.

The beauty of using portal-centric personalization for knowledge dissemination is that this scheme can be effortlessly—but systematically—extended, without caveats, to include external users (e.g., partners, suppliers, distributors, and associates). Sharing selected knowledge in this way will enhance a business relationship, increase empathy, and promote loyalty. It could also be bilateral. Sharing knowledge with partners will motivate them to share some of their proprietary knowledge with you. You could even offer them the use of your collaborative tools (e.g., Web conferencing capability), whereby they can formally present and discuss their knowledge.

It may sometimes be important and beneficial to share certain knowledge with customers and prospects. For example, you may have discovered some very strong customer loyalty statistics particularly relative to industry norms. This could be a very powerful marketing statement. Again, using the built-in personalization capabilities such knowledge of interest to customers can be cleverly delivered to them in the right instance. A feedback mechanism, instituted with the collaborative tools, could be used with such knowledge sharing to solicit customer reaction and comment. Such information could be fed into the data warehouse.

The collaborative capabilities of a portal will continually facilitate and enrich the KM process. Vested parties, regardless of their physical location, can interact in real time to discuss and refine the data being collected. First-cut analysis could be done in real time with all the parties seeing the charts and models together. You can have immediate reaction without the inevitable delays if this information was sent via e-mail attachments for future perusal. Analysts could do online presentations for traveling executives prior to key meetings so as to ensure complete understanding of the insights being presented—and avoid embarrassing questions. Since the only requirement for such a "presentation" is suitable Web connections, all parties can be flexible as to time and locations. The executives could be in various hotel rooms while the analyst runs through the presentation from home. The possibilities are immense and unconstrained.

6.7   Q&A—A time to recap and reflect

Q: How does knowledge differ from information?

A: Knowledge is based on information. Insight gained from information is knowledge. Knowing that a bank lost 400 customers during the past year is information. Finding out that 93 percent of them were charged a $20 service fee because their balances fell below a pre-specified threshold within three months of their decision to cancel their account is knowledge. Information is power. Knowledge is absolute power tempered with security.

Q: What is knowledge management from a corporate perspective?

A: The express goal of knowledge management (or business intelligence) is to enhance and continually refresh a corporation's knowledge base. Computer-based (or codified) knowledge-management schemes are a set of loosely integrated electronic processes that relate to the capture, creation, analysis, distillation, organization, dissemination, utilization, and safeguarding of knowledge. Corporations will also invariably have noncodified knowledge management systems based on individuals with specific insights.

Q: How will XML help knowledge management in the future?

A: Corporate knowledge is extracted from the capture and analysis of various forms of information. Today much of this information is either in proprietary, application form, or if in textual form, in an unstructured, unqualified format. Thus, there is lack of data-format compatibility as well as ambiguity. XML can resolve all these issues. It can ensure data uniformity and self-definition. It can thus provide KM applications with a larger pool of readily accessible and interpretable data.

Q: Can Web services help knowledge management?

A: Most assuredly, yes. Knowledge management thrives on new and innovative analysis, modeling, visualization, and data mining techniques. With Web services companies could start offering new techniques as subscription-based, on-demand programmatic services that will work with the popular KM (or BI) products. Thus, if you want some powerful and dramatic 3D rendering of data for a presentation, you will be able (down the road) to obtain this functionality as a Web service for a one-time fee.

Q: What are ERP applications?

A: Enterprise resource planning (ERP) applications are a comprehensive range of customizable, modular, off-the-shelf, feature-rich applications with wide platform coverage that address every facet of corporate business. Their goal is to provide a compelling and economical alternative to home-grown, decades-old, mission-critical applications. Today there is a wide repertorire of ERP applications that address human resource management, supply-chain management, accounting and finance processing, manufacturing support, project management, product life-cycle management, customer relationship management, supplier relationship management, sales-force automation, and business intelligence.

Q: Why has Web-based supply-chain management been so successful?

A: SCM is all about data interchange, fast access to information, collaboration, flexibility, and cooperation. These are all the things that a Web-based system is good at providing. The Web provides SCM with universal, "zero-cost," high-speed connectivity, popular networking standards, device independence (e.g., wireless support), and standard-based security (e.g., SSL). Corporate portals build on this to deliver personalization, collaboration tools, and content management. SCM has thus become the standard bearer for the effectiveness of b2b e-business.

Q: What is the relationship, if any, between ERP and corporate portals?

A: Though they intersect and impinge with each other in multiple ways and at multiple levels, ERP applications and corporate portals are separate initiatives—each can exist without the other. ERP, for a start, predates corporate portals by quite a stretch. However, there is inescapable synergy when you integrate ERP with a corporate portal. Such integration also opens up the door to successful e-business.

Q: What is data mining?

A: Data mining is a computerized system that utilizes complex artificial intelligence (AI)–inspired algorithms (bearing namcs such as CART, CHAID, MARS, ID3, C4.5, and C5.0) to sift through large amounts of data and highlight convoluted but highly relevant relationships and patterns buried within the data.

Q: What is Web mining?

A: Web mining refers to the process of collecting and carefully analyzing information about the behavior of Web users, using techniques such as cookies to potentially enhance a corporation's overall knowledge base by discovering trends—using data mining techniques if necessary—about customer preferences, buying trends, and Web surfing patterns.

Q: What are cookies?

A: Cookies are a widely used mechanism to store specific information about portal or Web site users. This information can be used to personalize the user experience relative to that site. Cookies can, however, keep track of user preferences and past behavior, including purchasing or browsing preferences. Thus, there can be privacy issues with cookies. A cookie is first generated by a Web server and then stored on the hard drive of a user's computer for subsequent use. They are transferred between the Web server and the user's Web browser using standard HTTP, interspersed between the HTML-based Web page transfers. Each time a user accesses a site that uses cookies, the Web server will request the user's browser to "up-load" the cookie associated with that site—hence their applicability when it comes to personalization. The server can then send back an updated cookie on a regular basis along with a requested Web page view.

7

Supply-Chain and Customer Relationship Management

It doesn't matter how many pails of milk you spill.
Just don't lose the cow.

—John M. Capozzi

It is kind of funny in a sad way, but since the demise of the dot-coms, many IT professionals tend to get somewhat defensive and resort to a sotto voce tone when asked about their e-business plans. There really is no need for this. The failure of dot-coms cannot in any rational way be attributed to weaknesses in the e-business process or, for that matter any deficiencies in the portal paradigm. Dot-coms failed because they were built on hope that was tempered with hype. Their business models were unrealistic from the get-go. Given this fundamental flaw, neither e-business nor portals were in a position to save them. This has nothing to do with the power and promise of e-business. E-business is not alchemy. It cannot turn lead into gold (though some would argue that it sure did turn stock options into gold). What it can do, very effectively, is make a viable business more efficacious, competitive, responsive, visible, and dynamic.

E-business is all about doing business or, to be more precise, transacting selected business processes, over the Web. E-commerce is a subset. Consequently, e-business applies to all aspects of a business, from human resources management to salesforce automation. However, two vital business endeavors are at present indelibly associated with e-business, given the amount of media attention they have received as the processes that epitomize the potential of e-business. These two endeavors, obviously, are supply-chain management (SCM) and customer relationship management (CRM), with the former, as mentioned in Chapter 6, assuming the status of the alluring poster child for e-business.

The emphasis on these two processes is not a coincidence. Both are ideally suited to exploit the possibilities presented by the Web as well as by corporate portals, XML, and Web services. In many ways the coupling of these two processes with e-business were indeed inspired marriages that had to have been made in cyber heaven. SCM and CRM can be done outside the Web, and many are still doing it the way they have always done it, using call centers, faxes, telephone calls, and onsite visits. However, outreach, on a truly global scale, is a pivotal factor if one wants to make these endeavors flourish and exceed all prior expectations.

Discovering new customers is a large part of CRM. So is keeping existing customers informed, engaged, and loyal. In the case of SCM, locating new suppliers, manufacturers, distributors, and possibly even new markets (e.g., the Baltic countries) through global visibility, can make a big difference to a company's success, profitability, and future. The Web, combined with corporate portals, is unique and unsurpassed when it comes to providing "near-zero cost" global reach and visibility. This alone makes the Web and portals extremely valuable, if not indispensable, when it comes to CRM and SCM. However, this is still only the tip of the iceberg when it comes to how the Web and portals empower CRM and SCM.

In addition to global outreach and visibility, some of the other requirements needed to successfully satisfy both CRM and SCM operations include ready access to structured corporate/product information, secure access to personalized account details, ability to quickly perform authorized transactions (e.g., pay bills, order goods, or check inventory status), a secure message exchange mechanism, and prompt updates of pertinent information from the "host" company. In addition, SCM, as discussed in Chapter 6, can also benefit from "partners" and their IT applications having direct, authenticated access to relevant ERP applications for authorized data access or data updates. The Web and corporate portals can address all of these requirements elegantly, without compromise, and quite cost effectively.

Corporate portals really are an unmitigated win-win proposition when it comes to CRM and SCM. Engage, transact, fulfill, and service are the four golden precepts of CRM. Corporate portals can significantly help both the customer base and the company in all four of these areas. Financial, telecommunications, travel, high-tech, and mail-order companies were quick to recognize this and cleverly exploited portals as a way to bolster their CRM efforts while aggressively reducing their traditional call-center operations. Figure 7.1 captures the entry page of Verizon's portal and highlights the features related to the engage, transact, fulfill, and service aspects of CRM.

Figure 7.1   *The portal of the giant telecom provider Verizon with some of its CRM-related engage, transact, fulfill, and service functions highlighted with an annotated dotted ellipse.*

Table 7.1 attempts to crystallize the natural synergy between CRM and portals by showing the positive win-win for both sides, functions that a corporate portal can deliver vis-à-vis CRM, using only a few of the overall capabilities that can be offered through a portal. Table 7.2 then sets out to provide just a glimpse of what XML and Web services can do when it comes to CRM and corporate portals.

The bottom line is that there is definite synergy, not to mention a process-igniting critical mass, when you combine CRM with corporate portals. The ERP application vendors are fully cognizant of this synergy and are quick to promote it. SAP, for example, lists this as one of the six major business benefits for its mySAP Enterprise Portal offering, referring to "improved customer, partner, and supplier relationships thanks to collaboration within and beyond organizational boundaries." In this case SAP is focusing only on the collaborative aspects of the portal. PeopleSoft takes this further by offering a CRM "portal pack" that sets out to provide tight

Table 7.1 *Just Some of the Win-Win Advantages Offered by Corporate Portals When It Comes to CRM, Categorized into Engage, Transact, Fulfill, and Service Phases*

	Corporate Portal Function	Customer Advantage	Advantage to Company
Engage	1. Provide company, product, and service information 2. Include company "propaganda," promotions, testimonials, and news 3. Supply company contact information	1. Ready, unpressured, pick-and-choose, 24/7 access to much of the required information—hopefully internationalized for global consumption 2. Form own opinion about company, based on diverse information sources, without having to deal with a company "representative" 3. Access to appropriate country-specific contact information	1. Minimize call-center costs, collateral (e.g., brochures) costs, and collateral mailing costs; deliver more information at a lower overall cost 2. Reduce advertising and PR costs, deliver more targeted messaging, promote corporate branding, and generate corporate empathy 3. Reduce call-center costs, be more responsive, increase in-house productivity by directing all "calls" to the right place
Transact	1. Offer products and services via e-commerce 2. Enable online account payment 3. Provide online account information	1. Enhance convenience, avoid frustrations of call centers 2. Enhance convenience, avoid frustrations of call centers, avoid postage and check costs 3. Avoid call-center delays, 24/7 access, privacy	1. Minimize call-center costs and overall costs of sales 2. Slash payment-handling costs, get faster access to funds with fewer errors 3. Reduce call-center costs, promote customer loyalty, increase competitiveness
Fulfill	1. Provide online product-shipment tracking 2. Offer online credit-management functions (e.g., request higher credit line, etc.)	1. 24/7, worldwide convenience, feel in control 2. Impersonal (i.e., don't have to talk to rep), 24/7 access	1. Enhance customer satisfaction, reduce call-center costs 2. Promote customer loyalty, increase competitiveness, reduce call-center costs
Service	1. Provide online, electronic support as first line of defense for customer problems	1. 24/7, first-cut support that might solve some problems (e.g., need new software driver or patch)	1. Reduce support cost, 24/7 coverage, increase customer satisfaction, promote customer retention

and intuitive integration between CRM applications and a corporate portal via a set of prebuilt "pagelets" (i.e., PeopleSoft's equivalent of a portlet, as discussed in Chapter 3). These pagelets support all of the necessary data views and self-service transaction processing needs between a portal and the CRM applications.

Then we have SCM, which is a much broader issue than even CRM. SCM, in effect, embraces all facets of a business. It is about being on top of the processes involved in the flow of goods, services, and information between the "host" company and its suppliers, manufacturers, wholesalers, distributors, agents, outlets, and customers. Note that SCM, despite the connotations of its name, is not focused just on the "supply-side" aspects of

Table 7.2 *Just Some of the Potential Roles for XML and Web Services vis-à-vis CRM in the Context of Corporate Portals*

	Corporate Portal Function	Role for XML	Role for Web Services
Engage	■ Provide company/product information ■ Provide online currency conversion for internationalization on request ■ Provide stock prices in local currency relative to a local market index on request	■ Use XML to qualify data to promote internationalization and reuse of information.	■ Subscribe to a Web service to obtain real-time rates ■ Rely on a Web service to deliver this information
Transact	■ Offer products via e-commerce ■ Enable online account payments	■ Maintain product data in XML to facilitate reuse in other applications (e.g., SCM) ■ Start maintaining customer records and accounts in XLM to facilitate future e-business extensions	■ Invoke different Web services to obtain currency conversions, shipping rates, customs requirements, and delivery estimates ■ Rely on Web services to obtain credit-card approval or electronic check clearing
Fulfill	■ Offer online credit management	■ Start keeping credit information in XML so that it can be readily used in the future with other e-business applications	■ Subscribe to multiple Web services from different credit bureaus to obtain real-time credit risk scores
Service	■ Offer online electronic support	■ Start maintaining support documentation in XML so that it can be readily exchanged with partners and "OEMers'" and others	■ Use Web service to generate real-time problem-tracking system

Figure 7.2
A corporate portal becomes an information switch between all the parties involved in SCM or CRM, providing necessary access to the information and the collaborative tools they need.

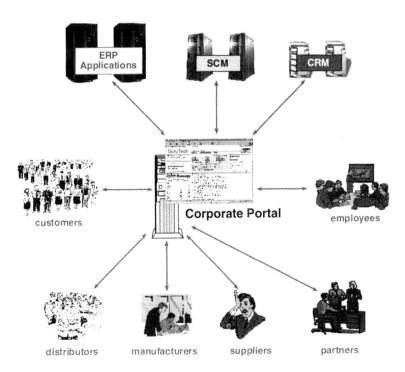

a business. It covers the complete gamut, from supplier to end user, from product build to after-sales product service. Thus, there is a definite overlap and bidirectional relationship between SCM and CRM. Customer satisfaction is contingent on the performance of the supply chain, while supplier demand is contingent on customer interest and loyalty.

Companies thus have to continually juggle CRM and SCM to optimize business goals, leveraging cost-saving methods such as "zero-stock," and just-in-time production made possible via contemporary SCM to keep costs down and enhance competitiveness. Portals with their powerful personalization capabilities are again in the ideal position to accommodate this overlap. The portal becomes a virtual "switch." Customers, employees, partners, suppliers, distributors, and remote locations are all connected with the necessary data and applications—with SCM and CRM being key among them—via the portal, as shown in Figure 7.2.

7.1   Supply-chain management using portals

SCM is all about keeping a constant electronic finger on the pulse of a business as the dynamics of that business ebb and flow in response to customer, supplier, market, competitor, or in-house changes. It is about gaining an edge when it comes to staying ahead of the game. You want to become even more competitive. It is about being able to be reactive, responsive, and responsible when it comes to exploiting new business opportunities or taking evasive action on early detection of an unexpected "curve ball." If CRM is all about engage, transact, fulfill, and service, then the key words for SCM are plan, respond, communicate, and execute. With contemporary SCM you want to increase the value of your company, products, and services. To do this you need to:

- Reduce product costs through more competitive supply/component sourcing (e.g., using an XML-based scheme to locate new suppliers), more cost-effective manufacturing, maintaining lower inventories, continually fine-tuning "logistics" (e.g., shipping, warehousing), and improving overall efficiency of the overall product life-cycle process

- Increase market visibility, especially in new geographies and demographic sectors (e.g., appeal to a different age or ethnic group)

- Minimize the time and cost of the sales cycle by mounting online campaigns, conducting personalized offers to known prospects and existing customers, permitting hassle-free online purchasing, and enticing qualified distributors

- Attract new customers by offering compelling products, better service, lower prices, and faster availability, among other things

- Retain existing customers through responsive customer support, superior service, 24/7 online help desks, customized special offers, and loyalty programs (e.g., frequent-flyer miles)

- Strike a fine balance between supply and demand through better forecasting aided by diligent and creative use of knowledge-management tools to analyze past performance and emerging trends

- Increase overall company productivity by maximizing the efficiency of all business processes by eliminating duplication of effort (e.g., multiple entries of the same transaction), streamlining operations, reducing paperwork in favor of electronic processes, expediting transactions (e.g., e-mail rather than normal mail), reducing costs (e.g., e-mail rather than overnight delivery), facilitating rapid decision making (e.g., access to powerful knowledge-management systems), and rekindling esprit de corps across and beyond company lines

By now it seems somewhat unnecessary to belabor this point, but corporate portals are ideally suited to address many of the functions listed above. Let's just take one example, in this case the last function mentioned—esprit de corps—and see how a portal helps this cause. Esprit de corps stems from morale and motivation. It has to do with a sense of community, belonging, ownership, pride, and camaraderie. These are all things that a corporate portal excels in making happen.

A corporate portal is a water cooler, notice board, newspaper, the company gossip (i.e., think e-mail), and a town meeting rolled into one—and functioning 24/7. You can provide personalized company news, success stories (e.g., a big sale), feel-good stories (e.g., triplets born to a V.P. of marketing in Taiwan), upcoming events, special employee offers, employee appreciation gestures, and notification of awards—all quickly, affordably, and incessantly. A corporate portal can and should be a positive and constructive propagandist and a virtual, low-cost motivator. This is just the "passive," information push aspect of the portal. Then there is all the community building possible with the collaborative functions, starting with bulletin boards and extending all the way to instant messaging capabilities.

7.1.1   The portal as the external interface for SCM

Motivation and morale boosting, as discussed previously, does not have to be limited to employees. It can, in the context of SCM, be very effectively extended to suppliers, manufacturers, partners, and distributors, both existing and prospective. The personalization possible with portals can further enhance the impact of such initiatives. Just as with employees, the portal can be used to convey a positive and buoyant image about the company that makes the outside people feel good about dealing with the company.

Remember that from an SCM context many of the outside people accessing your portal to get information or access authorized applications are likely to be doing administrative and clerical roles. Other than through the portal, they will not have ready access to what your company is all about. They would not have the benefit of meeting executives of your company and hearing them talk about prospects and the future. But the portal can mitigate this. The portal can make them feel proud to be doing business with your company. The implications in terms of attracting new "partners," whether it be suppliers, distributors, manufacturers, or investors, are also enormous and far reaching.

The bottom line is that the following features, which in terms of today's technology are best delivered via a corporate portal, are invaluable in increasing the reach, value, and efficacy of SCM in the context of external "users" in the chain:

1. Extensive access to structured, indexed, and searchable information

2. Personalized content and services for external "associates"

3. Powerful, multitier security via authentication bolstered by digital certificates

4. Single sign-on option, once authenticated, to facilitate convenient but authorized access to multiple applications and services

5. Systematic and wide-ranging collaborative tools for interactive as well as asynchronous communications

6. Customizable "push" and alert mechanisms (via the collaborative tools if necessary) to enable timely notification of key events or breaking news

7. Content-management capabilities, replete with digital signature support, to avoid discrepancies and misunderstandings about the status and disposition of documents (e.g., contracts)

8. Consistent and controlled access to all relevant SCM, ERP, and business process–control applications

9. Selective access to knowledge-base and knowledge-management tools

10. Integrated usage monitoring and statistics to determine and analyze interests, behavior, and frequency of visits of the external users

7.1.2   Leveraging portals to realize adaptive SCM

For SCM to make a true difference it has to be a living, breathing, and pulsating multidirectional, to-and-fro process. Ideally, parts of it need to be autonomic (i.e., rapid, automatic, "preconditioned" responses to external events, as discussed in section 5.3.2 in the context of self-managing systems). But vigilance, interaction, and responsiveness are what in the end pay true dividends in this field. SCM and the portal are just tools and processes. It is people with their attitudes and their skills that make the difference.

Implementing an SCM system does not mean that you have SCM. People have to first buy into the system. Change is hard, and old habits die hard. People will want to continue to do things the way they have done them in the past, even though they realize that there are better, more efficient, and more cost-effective ways of doing things. So accounts will still insist on using faxes to receive invoices, and purchasing agents will insist on mailing purchase orders, even after they have been trained how to use e-mail, scanners, and Adobe Acrobat to streamline and computerize the whole process. So there is an undeniable human element to all of this that has to be won over, conditioned, and focused. A portal, through its uniformity, user friendliness, compelling content, and helpful personal services, will play a positive role in helping to overcome this initial resistance.

The goal is to move toward what is now being referred to as adaptive SCM. "Adaptive" in this sense means real time. Today, especially with the Internet, news travels fast and wide. Markets change at lightning speeds. Even as CNN is reporting a fast-breaking news event, stocks are already on the move in reaction to the news, and people are scrambling to buy some new supplies or trying to cancel existing contracts. Significant opportunities are seized or lost in split seconds. That is why real-time, adaptive SCM is so pivotal.

Portals are key to making this real-time aspect of SCM happen. Portals, by keeping users engaged, can make sure that they are around and available to react and respond to SCM issues in real time. This is another reason why portals need to be considered an integral part of contemporary SCM. SCM and portal-server vendors both recognize this and consistently talk about how these go together, hand in glove.

A portal becomes the focal point for all computer-related activity. Though a user may be using other applications, surfing the Web, or reading e-mail, all of this will be done within the portal framework. Thus, you have the opportunity to immediately notify the user if something changes or

Figure 7.3
A clear and concise diagram by PeopleSoft defining the key processes that make up the supply-chain operations model between suppliers and the eventual end customer.

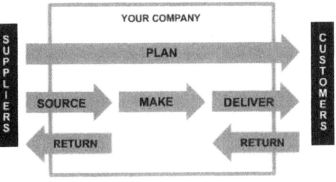

requires immediate attention vis-à-vis SCM. It can be the SCM equivalent of AOL's famous "you have mail" message.

The portal, through collaborative tools, pushes technology (e.g., scrolling message bar), and alerts can try to make sure that users respond to critical SCM issues in real time. Though it should not be used for punitive purposes, the usage-monitoring capabilities of a portal, especially during the early part of the system adoption process, could be used to gain a feel of how responsive users are being to the needs of adaptive SCM. This intelligence could be used to fine-tune some processes and also work out what "altering" schemes are most effective.

The supply-chain process, as very clearly shown by the PeopleSoft model shown in Figures 7.3 and 7.4, consists of five key steps between the supplier and the end customer. These are as follows:

1. *Plan*—this is the strategic, cerebral aspect of SCM that extends across the entire gamut of operations from concept to after-sales product support, replete with all of the necessary feedback mechanisms and metrics to monitor successful execution.

2. *Source*—this is about locating the optimum suppliers and then implementing all of the necessary pricing, delivery, quality control, payment, and logistics processes to obtain the necessary supplies at the right time, at the right place, and at the right price.

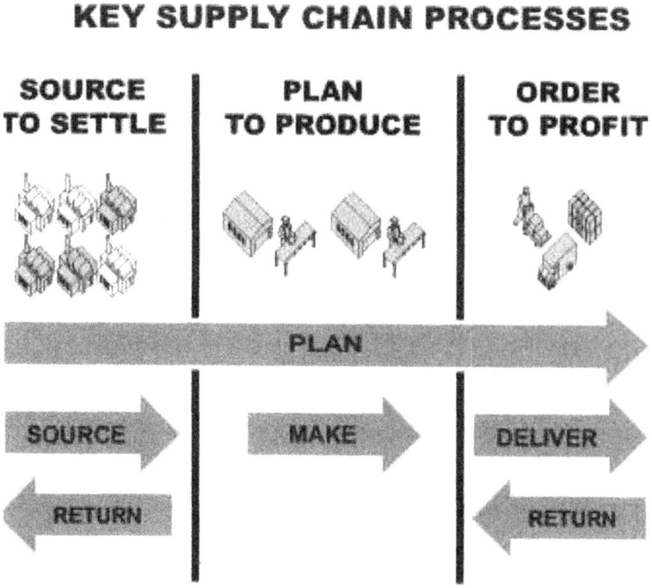

Figure 7.4
A second diagram from PeopleSoft following on from that shown in Figure 7.3 and highlighting the constituent parts of key supply-chain processes.

KEY SUPPLY CHAIN PROCESSES

| SOURCE TO SETTLE | PLAN TO PRODUCE | ORDER TO PROFIT |

PLAN

| SOURCE | MAKE | DELIVER |

| RETURN | | RETURN |

3. *Make*—this refers to the manufacturing phase with all the issues related to manufacturing schedules, availability of supplies, testing, packaging, and delivery that require extensive monitoring and analysis, relative to predefined metrics, to ensure that production, quality, and productivity expectations are being met.

4. *Deliver*—this is the getting-the-goods-to-the-customer "logistics" phase, which involves customer order coordination, warehousing, dealing with distributors, finding the best carriers, and the like.

5. *Return*—this is the only "backward" process in SCM and involves dealing with customer issues, in particular defective, undelivered, or delivered-too-late goods.

Table 7.3 takes these five key SCM steps and sets out to summarize the primary portal-related functions that pertain to that step, along with an indication as to what roles can be played by XML and Web services.

Table 7.3   *The Five Key Steps of Supply-Chain Management and How and Where Corporate Portals, XML, and Web Services Can Help*

Supply Chain Management Step	Key Functions That Can Be Provided by a Corporate Portal	Potential Role for XML	Potential Role for Web Services
1. Plan	Content management; knowledge management; Internet access; collaboration; ERP access including product life cycle and CRM	Use XML to start structuring product data—if possible using standards like Product Data Markup Language (PDML)	Knowledge management functions (e.g. data mining), obtaining country specific regulations
2. Source	Publicize company requirements to attract new suppliers; personalized content, access and services for specific suppliers; Internet access; selective ERP access; content management; controlled knowledge management access; collaboration; support for wireless devices for mobile users; portal usage statistics to track supplier 'activity'	Use XML, in particular standards such as RosettaNet, XML Common Business Library, commerce XML (cXML), Trading Partner Agreement Markup Language (TPAML) VISA XML Invoice Specification etc., to standardize and streamline requirements as well as contracts/ invoice processing	Currency conversions; unit conversions; shipping rates; shipping schedules; local custom and excise rates

Table 7.3   *The Five Key Steps of Supply-Chain Management and How and Where Corporate Portals, XML, and Web Services Can Help (continued)*

Supply Chain Management Step	Key Functions That Can Be Provided by a Corporate Portal	Potential Role for XML	Potential Role for Web Services
3. Make	Publicize company requirements to attract new manufacturers and distributors; personalized content, access, and services for specific manufacturers and distributors; Internet access; selective ERP access; content management; controlled knowledge-management access; collaboration	Leverage XML to convey product details and automate contract, order, and invoice processing	Currency conversions; unit conversions; shipping rates; shipping schedules
4. Deliver	Publicize company requirements to attract new logistics firms; personalized content, Access, and services for specific associates; Internet access; selective ERP access; content management; controlled knowledge-management access; collaboration; support for wireless access		Lists of international holidays; local weather [that could impact shipments]; Shipping rates; shipping schedules; custom clearance regulations
5. Return	24/7 online first-line support; post return policies; offer automated returns handling application; CRM integration; usage statistics to track customer activity		Shipping rates; return label printing

7.2   Supplier relationship management via portals

Supplier relationship management (SRM), most bluntly put, is the matter of treating suppliers with the same importance and deference once reserved for customers. Thus, in addition to the maxim that the customer is always right, one now has to at least start contemplating that the supplier might be right most of the time, although this may be very hard for some to concede. But suppliers, more so than ever, are becoming vital to the success of a company, as more and more companies inexorably move toward a product build model increasingly reliant on multiple, diverse components, sub-assemblies, and OEM modules as well as "outsourced" services (e.g., assembly, testing, delivery). Consequently, an increasing amount of the value provided to customers by today's product-oriented companies are contingent in turn on the goods and service they receive from their suppliers. The recent high-profile, acrimonious, and unsavory fallout between the Ford Motor Company and Bridgestone/Firestone attests to this—although this was an exceptional case that is unlikely to have been helped by any amount of SRM software.

Thus, SRM is, in effect, CRM for suppliers. SAP captures this "SRM is the flip side of CRM" concept in Figure 7.5. It is also worth comparing this SAP diagram with i2's value chain diagram that was shown in Figure 6.7. Some of the key things to note are that SRM resides at the supplier-to-company boundary and that the host company (i.e., your company) is a customer and as such a candidate for CRM from the supplier's perspective. SRM uses many of the techniques hitherto associated with CRM but now in the context of managing, monitoring, and bolstering supplier relationships.

SAP, with its enviable grasp of the ERP sector, cites this example as to the need for and value of SRM. According to SAP, for many of today's business, purchased goods and services represent over 60 percent of the value of a sale. Thus, if the business can get a 4 percent reduction in the cost of these purchased goods and services from their suppliers, it would be the equivalent of increasing sales by nearly 10 percent. Thus, effective SRM can have a profound impact on profitability and corporate bottom lines.

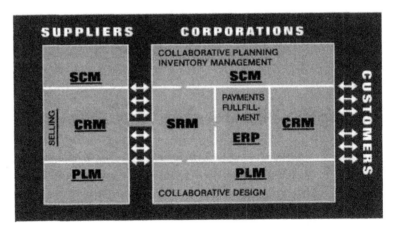

Figure 7.5   *A cut-to-the-chase diagram from SAP that shows the relationship between SRM and CRM from the perspectives of a host company and one of its suppliers as well as SRM's relationship to other ERP applications—where PLM is product life-cycle management.*

Whereas CRM was categorized as consisting of engage, transact, fulfill, and service, portal-centric SRM consists of six separate processes or phases. These are as follows:

1. *Source*—locate appropriate suppliers via past associations, recommendations, repute, request for quotation (RFQ), and auction processes.

2. *Engage*—enter into a formal, contractual relationship with suppliers selected from the engage cycle.

3. *Procure*—this is the start of the spend cycle, when one starts to obtain goods and services from the suppliers.

4. *Settle*—what used to be the paperwork nightmare involving purchase orders, invoices, payments, and the like is now made easier, thanks to XML and portals.

5. *Design*—this is an engineering-oriented collaboration phase, in which engineers and product managers from the host company work closely with their counterparts at the supplier to ensure better "fit," smooth integration, and optimum problem-resolution procedures.

6. *Analyze*—this is the knowledge-management and introspection phase, in which the true worth of a supplier relationship can be continually monitored, analyzed, and documented per multiple criteria, such as price, delivery, quality, and service.

If one just takes a quick glance at the foregoing list of processes, it is possible to forget that these functions, in this context, are focused purely on the supplier-host company boundary. But that is what SRM is all about. It is an adjunct to SCM that deals just with a subset of the overall SCM process. Figure 7.6 takes the PeopleSoft SCM diagram shown in Figures 7.3 and 7.4 and annotates it to show where SRM fits in, just in case there are any lingering misunderstandings.

XLM can, and should, play a role in all six of the foregoing steps. So can Web services. The XML "dialects" and possible Web service examples shown in Table 7.3 provide a framework to display the possibilities in this arena, keeping in mind that many of the XML "dialects" mentioned are also applicable vis-à-vis SRM. The same is true when it comes to Web services. SAP, for example with its SRM offering, talks about the concept of "indirect procurement," which is SAP's way of talking about XML-centric relationships with suppliers in the context of SRM.

Figure 7.6
*The PeopleSoft
supply-chain
operations reference
model shown in
Figure 7.3,
updated to show
where supplier
relationship
management
(SRM) fits in and
the six key steps
associated with
SRM.*

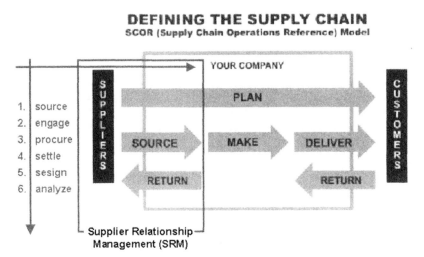

DEFINING THE SUPPLY CHAIN
SCOR (Supply Chain Operations Reference) Model

1. source
2. engage
3. procure
4. settle
5. sesign
6. analyze

Supplier Relationship
Management (SRM)

Obviously there is nothing that says that the six steps identified for SRM are in any way unique to the supplier-host relationship. These same steps and the functions associated with them can and should be applied to manufacturers for what could be called manufacturer relationship management (MRM). The same would be true for distributors—namely, DRM. If your company's sales process is handled via a "channel," where this channel can consist of a direct salesforce, distributors, and partners, then the distributor and partner relationship management aspect of this channel will also fall into the DRM category.

What is important is the cognizance that within the overall SCM continuum there are separate relationships and processes that also have to be managed in addition to CRM at the consumer end of this continuum. Siebel Systems, a leader in CRM, takes this even further and offers an employee relationship management (ERM) suite. Others address this more in terms of HR applications and intranet portals. But the theme is loud and clear. Today's business world is all about the adroit handling of relationships, exploiting computerized applications, as much as possible, to help facilitate, manage, and monitor all the efforts on this front.

In general, it should be possible to use a good SRM application suite to also handle other relationships, in particular those with manufacturers, distributors, and even partners. If you think about it, all of these steps, including design, still apply to distributors and partners, where design in this context would focus on the technical aspect of pre- and postsales support.

Just as with SCM, the goal is to have an adaptive SRM process where there are real-time, meaningful, collaboration, engagement, decisions, and interactions with all the suppliers. This real-time process should be backed up by up-to-date information being provided by the SRM, SCM, and associated ERP (e.g., accounts payable) applications. Knowledge-management tools will, in addition, play a key role, not just in analysis but also helping with insights pertaining to the whole issue of supply and demand as well as pricing trends.

Just as with SCM and CRM, a corporate portal is indubitably the optimum platform for instituting a mutually beneficial SRM system that covers all suppliers and possibly even manufacturers and distributors. The portal will already possess the necessary infrastructure in terms of collaboration tools, content management, ERP access, and personalization for making this happen. This is so much the case that most of the leading SRM vendors (e.g., PeopleSoft, SAP) automatically talk about SRM in the context of portals or invariably cite SRM as yet another "killer" application for portals. At this juncture in the book, it should be clear how corporate portals provide a whole new personalized and secure collaborative environment for all of these types of applications that require both internal and external access.

7.3 Customer relationship management via portals

If considered on a global basis, covering as wide a spectrum of businesses as possible, much of what is purported to be CRM is still being handled by traditional call centers. Most of the software associated with CRM was developed to be used in call-center environments. This call-center association should immediately provide a connection as well as a context for how corporate portals and CRM intersect with each other. From a customer-support perspective, augmenting and possibly even replacing a traditional call center has always been one of the major rationales for corporate portals.

A corporate portal, as postulated at the beginning of this book, is a fully automated emulation of a highly proficient, well-motivated call center. Thus, from the get-go, corporate portals were expected, of necessity, to play a pivotal role when it comes to CRM. Nonetheless, one needs to keep in mind that a corporate portal will deprive customers of the human touch that is eventually always available with a call center—albeit typically after a long and frustrating delay usually exacerbated by being forced to play roulette with a voice-response system.

The human interaction is important to some, which is why you can never totally eliminate the call-center aspect. There will be some users, sophisticated and computer savvy at that, who every once in a while will feel a compelling urge to talk with a human "rep," even though they know how to do it electronically via the portal. Executing a "big" financial transaction could be one of these instances.

Despite using the portal for most of their trades, because of the lower cost, speed, and convenience, some investors still feel more secure dealing with a human to transact an "important" trade even though many know, at the back of their minds, that the human "rep" is basically using the same tools and applications available via the portal. It is to satisfy this need for human interplay that some portals, such as the Lands' End portal shown in Figure 2.13, actually offer an integrated "talk to a human" feature.

The absence of human interaction, however, does not usually stop a corporate portal from significantly enhancing the customer experience. The end goal of CRM is to build up an ever-increasing base of satisfied and loyal customers. Corporate portals, by design, are sympathetic to the time pressures affecting most people living in "high-tech" (a.k.a. modern) societies. Corporate portals are convenient, operate 24/7, and eliminate frustrating ("you are on hold") delays. They also provide more information and permit direct execution of transactions—unhampered by a rookie call-center rep who might not be as fluent in the language—let alone as knowledgeable about the company or its products—as you would wish. Thus, corporate portals, in essence, offer faster and more incisive service at a lower cost, where the cost element comes into play when dealing with fee-based transactions, such as investment trading, travel reservation, and, in some instances, e-commerce promotions. Then there are all the personalized content and service possibilities that further cement the user's empathy with the portal. The bottom line is that it is difficult, if not impossible, to deny that corporate portals increase user satisfaction and thereby foster corporate loyalty.

Though one of the primary rationales for corporate portals in the context of CRM is to mitigate the frustrations and inefficiencies of call centers, voice interaction can sometimes be a very powerful and valued feature offered by a portal. The difference here is that the voice interaction is all with software applications as opposed to harried customer reps. Voice in this instance becomes another option for data input, output, or both when interacting with a portal view or portlet. It is thus voice-to-Web-page or Web-page-to-voice rather than the traditional voice response unit approach used in conjunction with call centers.

This voice option is of particular relevance to mobile wireless users. While portal servers can excel at elegantly integrating wireless devices, the ergonomics of wireless devices, in particular the tiny keyboards, are often not conducive for conducting portal transactions that require appreciable amounts of data entry—for example, trying to locate and book a flight reservation. Being able to interact with voice could make all the difference in such scenarios. Voice response unit technology has been extended to work with portals. If you have an interest in this type of voice integration, start out by looking at IBM's WebSphere Voice Response with DirectTalk Technology as an example of what can be realized with today's off-the-shelf solutions.

While this user satisfaction and loyalty boosting is invaluable, this is not the only role for a portal vis-à-vis CRM. As summarized in Table 7.1, a well-implemented, full-functioning corporate portal provides win-win CRM related to functions across all four customer-facing phases of CRM—engage, transact, fulfill, and service. But there is much more that a portal can do. Understanding customer needs and behavior so that you can better serve the customer base is another vital facet of CRM. Portals can be of significant help with this endeavor in numerous ways.

The roles that a portal can play relative to the whole gamut of knowledge management were discussed in Chapter 6. Much of this related to obtaining, categorizing, analyzing, and disseminating customer and market-trend information obtained from nonportal sources. But then there is all that highly pertinent, company-specific data on user preferences and behavior that can be extracted from the way users actually behave when they visit the company portal. While the importance of this user monitoring and tracking function has been discussed in the context of capacity planning, portal management, and Web mining, it also has a CRM-specific dimension.

The amount of user behavior and preference intelligence that can be garnered from a portal can be prodigious and unparalleled in terms of its granularity, acuity, immediacy, and pertinence. With today's portal usage–tracking technology, the market reaction to an important announcement can be gauged in real time by monitoring portal "hits"; ideally, there will be unmistakable spikes corresponding to the news becoming available in different geographies, time zones, and media outlets. You can drill down to the next level of detail by seeing what the portal visitors were interested in relative to the announcement.

Did most just glance (i.e., say less than ten seconds) at the announcement synopsis, or did most go directly to the full announcement? How many users requested downloads of the related collateral within two minutes of reading the full announcement? If you have instituted a cookie- or logon-based scheme for personalization, you have the added advantage that you can correlate behavior and preferences with identifiable users—ideally, customers. The possibilities, when these portal usage data are subjected to knowledge-management and data mining tools, are immense and exciting.

The tracking of user preferences via the portal does not have to be all indirect and implicit. With a portal you have the option of soliciting feedback and comments in numerous ways. For a start you can always have a standard e-mail–based feedback option that appears on all portal views, in the same place and in the same way for uniformity. You will also have a "contact us" option. But you can go further, limited only by resolve and resources as opposed to technology.

You could, for example, have "rate us" options against key items of content or even with self-service applications. You could politely request that users participate in a voluntary survey on a random basis or after x number of visits. IBM, for one, does this very effectively with some of its closed user-group portals (e.g., the ones for analysts and registered consultants). Thus, overall possibilities abound. Consequently, user behavior capturing, in multiple forms, is yet another feather in the cap for portals when it comes to CRM.

Then there is all of the CRM, as well as related ERP, application access coordination possible via the portal for internal users as well as selected external partners (e.g., distributors). The bottom line is that portals are rapidly becoming an integral aspect of CRM. They serve a unique dual role in this context. Not only do they help create better customer relations but they are also a powerful tool in managing and monitoring customer relationships.

7.4 Synthesizing all of the portal-related applications

By now it should be abundantly clear that ERP applications and portals, though able to synergistically complement each other, are still essentially independent endeavors with one being able to proceed without the other. But it must also be clear that portals provide a unique and compelling way to standardize, control, and streamline application access. Then there is also XML, which was devised to provide consistency, standardization, and integration among these applications.

Given this continually revolving and evolving interplay between the various ERP applications, portals, and XML it was inevitable that somebody would try to come up with a mechanism to show how all of this can be formally, but flexibly, integrated together. In the old days this mantle would have automatically fallen upon IBM. But IBM hasn't had much luck with architectures of late. The market dynamics have also changed.

There are important, high-rolling new players, some of them totally focused on ERP. Siebel Systems, a $2 billion e-business application provider and an undisputed leader in CRM applications, is one of these. Given its vested interest in CRM and other ERP applications, Siebel, for one, would obviously like to see some semiformal framework for XML-centric ERP integration. Well, to the firm's credit, Siebel decided to be proactive. In April 2002 Siebel put forward a standards-based, vendor-independent application-integration solution referred to as a universal application network (UAN).

UAN, which is heavily XML-centric, is purported to be the very first initiative of this type—with vendor independence being the very crux of this claim. To emphasize this vendor independence, UAN, right from the start, openly relies on solutions from other vendors to achieve its goals. Some of the vendors currently included in this UAN initiative include IBM, TIBCO, WebMethods, Vitria, and SeeBeyond.

The goal of UAN is to enable enterprises to deploy end-to-end, industry-specific business processes made up of prepackaged out-of-the-box applications from different vendors. It relies on XML and Web services to realize this interapplication integration. It is a kind of "integration bus," referred to as the transport layer in the UAN architecture, for bringing together different applications from different vendors, as depicted in Siebel's "XML superhighway" diagram shown in Figure 7.7. Note that Siebel, in marked contrast to SAP, Oracle, and PeopleSoft, does not market an explicit portal server per se; does not promote the concept of a single, consolidated portal; and furthermore shows a "company Web site" as opposed to a company portal.

Siebel's underlying premise for UAN is simple and incontrovertible. Siebel maintains that it is no longer possible for any single vendor to deliver the entire range of applications required by an enterprise, especially in the context of e-business. Consequently, enterprises have no choice but to entertain best-of-breed applications from multiple vendors and then try to work out how to best achieve integration across all of them. This is what UAN is trying to address from a business-process standpoint and via the data "self-description" and data interchange promise of XML.

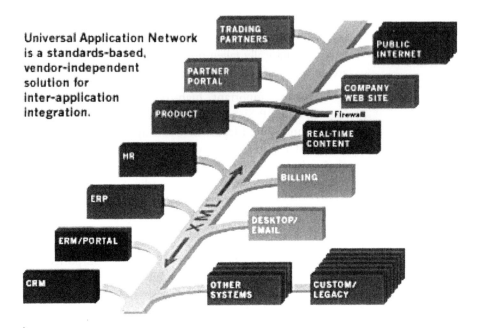

Figure 7.7   *Siebel's "XML superhighway" diagram for its universal application network (UAN) application-integration proposal. Note the employee relationship management (ERM) portal (second from bottom left) and partner portal (second from top left) but the absence of a corporate portal per se.*

7.4.1   Building blocks of the universal application architecture

UAN consists of three basic building blocks: the business-process library, the business-process design tool, and the integration server.

The business-process library is a collection of prepackaged, end-to-end, industry-specific business processes. A business process could be creating new customers, generating a quote for an order, making a billing inquiry, or obtaining a customer credit rating, among other things. Figure 7.8 depicts the concept of an end-to-end business process, in this case an insurance company's "new policy" process as illustrated by Siebel, and Figure 7.9 shows the overall architecture of UAN. In the case of UAN, these business processes will be based on XML and Web services standards to guarantee platform, vendor, and application independence. UAN expects a business process to consist of three components: business-process flows, common objects, and transformation maps.

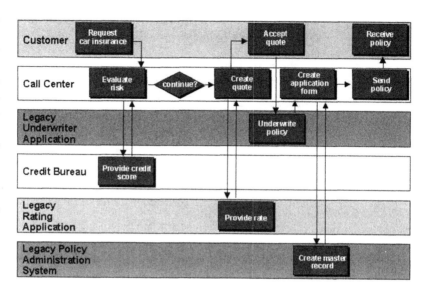

The business-process design tool is a classic "point-and-click," "drag-and-drop" graphical tool for developing and modeling custom business processes—if the necessary ones are not in the business-process library. As with everything to do with UAN, it is XML-based and has the capability to import (and export) business-process definitions using XML. The design tool can be used to create all three of the components that constitute a

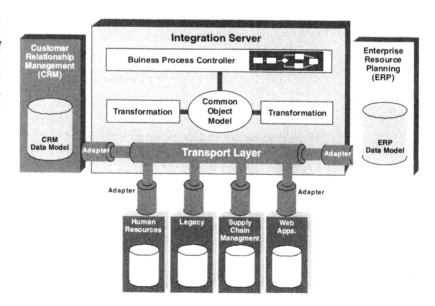

UAN business process—namely, business-process flows, common objects, and transformation maps.

Siebel, true to its promise to be vendor agnostic in this venture, defers to the acknowledged market leaders to provide this functionality rather than trying to define anything of its own. Thus, Siebel cites IBM's CrossWorlds InterChange Server, TIBCO's BusinessWorks (part of ActiveEnterprise), Vitria's BusinessWare, SeeBeyond's Business Integration Suite, and web-Methods' Platform as potential integration servers for UAN. Note that these are not application servers such as IBM's WebSphere Application Server or BEA's WebLogic. They are one step higher within the "food chain" and ideally have some cognizance of business processes.

It is the integration server, as shown in Figure 7.9, that is responsible for making sure that all the UAN components can communicate with each other. Although the exact composition of the integration servers will differ from vendor to vendor, UAN assumes that at a minimum they will all offer:

1. A full-function messaging service

2. Adapters that connect specific applications to the UAN transport layer

3. A common object model, based on XML and the nascent XML schema definition language (XSD), for defining common objects, including customer-developed objects

4. Transformations, based on XSLT, that map between an application's specific data model and the common object model

5. A business process controller that provides controlled step-by-step execution of a business process

The UAN business process flows are heavily reliant on the emerging Web services flow language (WSFL). WSFL, designed by IBM, is an XML-based language intended to describe the role and make-up of Web services as part of a business-process definition. Hence its significance vis-à-vis UAN. Per WSFL, Web services compositions can come in two forms. The first type, known as flow models, specifies the anticipated usage pattern of a set of Web Services so that it completes a specific business process. The second type, known as global models, specifies how a set of Web services interacts with each other in terms of an interaction pattern between them.

Common objects are meant to be composites of application data models—ideally, compliant with industry-specific standards such as those being instituted by the Open Applications Group (www.openapplications-.org). The Open Applications Group is a nonprofit consortium focusing on best practices and processes based on XML content for e-business and application integration. It claims to be the largest publisher of XML-based content for business software interoperability in the world. The common objects will be based on XML and XSD. Per the UAN paradigm, these industry-standard common objects will have an ID that uniquely identifies the objects across different applications to obviate the need for point-to-point, application-to-application mappings.

Transformation maps provide the mapping between application-specific data models and the common objects. Siebel provides the following example. Within Siebel eBusiness Applications, the data model for "country" might specify "USA," whereas the common model expects it to be "United States." Transformation maps, based on XSLT, will take care of such incompatibilities.

Given that it is trying to synthesize rather than create anew, UAN is credible. It also bends over backwards to deal in industry standards only—in particular, XML. It thus has the potential of gaining industry and market acceptance. Given its openness and flexibility, it can be many things to many people. However, given today's competitive market, others will still feel compelled to put forward their variants of UAN. The bottom line is that with UAN there is at least a start, based firmly on XML, at coming up with efforts to integrate all of the growing numbers of ERP-related applications.

7.5   Other pertinent portal-related applications

Most companies and most people got their first experience of corporate, as opposed to public, portals via employees-only intranet portals that were widely implemented during the latter part of the 1990s. One of the first types of applications to be offered on these intranet portals, and subsequently one of the most popular categories, was human resources (HR) applications. HR applications, which ranged from simple online vacation-request applications to complex, multiple-choice benefits-management applications, were another classic win-win proposition.

Right off the bat, they offered unprecedented convenience to the employees while at the same time slashing administrative costs for the company. They improved efficiency and productivity across the board. They helped mitigate employee frustration. During a period of considerable turmoil across the corporate world, self-service HR applications gave users some sense of control of their affairs. HR applications put an end to inefficient paperwork and the delays, errors, and confusion that went with it. HR applications reduced the time taken to reimburse expenses and change dental plans. All in all, they were instrumental in changing vital, constantly used internal processes to make them more streamlined and expeditious and significantly more economical per transaction.

HR applications are thus a mainstay when it comes to corporate portals. They are a big draw vis-à-vis portals. They continue to be enormously popular and extensively used. There might even be situations in which management may want to know if there are ways to limit the usage of some applications. In the heady days of the mid-1990s, when company stock options really could make you rich, some companies, particularly in the high-tech arena, were genuinely concerned that there could be a drop in productivity given how much time employees, across the company, were spending online, checking their option strategies using the applications that had been provided for simple option management. This, ironically, should no longer be much of an issue!

Today there is a surfeit of HR-related applications that cover the entire gamut of employee-oriented functions in addition to the well-known operations and productivity-enhancing tools such as online expense filing, electronic benefits management, and online timesheets. HR, as with SRM, has benefited from CRM. Within the relationship management paradigm, employees have to be a key asset—in some cases even more important than customers. Thus, just as with customers and suppliers, it is important that a company uses formalized, standardized, and measurable techniques to attract, maintain, nurture, and motivate employees.

The possibilities of creating esprit de corps with a portal was already explored at the beginning of this chapter. Today's HR applications, from the likes of SAP, Oracle, Siebel, and PeopleSoft, all set out to make handling all facets of employee relationship management that much more incisive and mutually rewarding. Web services will further enhance the range of scope of HR applications, with employees being able to offer even more customized services. All of the popular HR applications are portal ready, so to speak. Thus, HR applications will definitely be one of the key application types made available on corporate portals.

Another popular application type is likely to be salesforce automation. Personalized content (e.g., by territory, product, or responsibility); fast, universal access; and collaboration tools are key to making salesforce automation successful. Portals obviously excel at all of these, with the "no-hassle" universal access (e.g., wireless support) alone worth its weight in gold. In addition to this are all the exciting possibilities of what can be done in terms of ERP access and application integration.

Besides providing ready access to the relevant CRM, SCM, and KM applications, the portal could also facilitate automated interapplication cooperation to eliminate the need for transaction duplication. On-the-run salespeople will be required to enter a transaction only once. All of the databases and applications that may need to be updated as a result of this new transaction could be taken care of programmatically, possibly even via the development of a new Web service. As with all of the other applications, salesforce automation will increase efficiencies, improve productivity, reduce cost, and bolster salesforce satisfaction.

It will also ensure that all sales-related data are recorded, maintained, acted on, and analyzed in real time. Thus, management can have near-instantaneous visibility to the bottom-line impact of a big new order. This is what John Chambers, the legendary CEO of Cisco, refers to as the Internet-empowered "virtual close" process. Now, thanks to portals and salesforce automation applications, corporations can close and reconcile their books in minutes rather than in the weeks it used to take in the past. The cost saving alone of such automated account keeping are huge and profound.

Product life-cycle management applications are another obvious candidate that can palpably benefit from portal integration. Collaboration and content management play a big role in PLM. So does ready access to SCM, SRM, CRM, and KM applications. By now the message coming across should be loud and clear. It really is difficult to find a contemporary application that does not tangibly benefit from being made portal-capable. Going forward, corporate portals really do represent the best way to provide both internal and external users with controlled, authenticated access to business applications.

7.6 Q&A—A time to recap and reflect

Q: Were e-business applications in any way related to the collapse of the dot-coms?

A: Though dot-coms by the very nature of their Internet-centric operations were big e-business application users, their demise in no way can be attributed to these e-business applications, portals, or the Web. If anything, the inherent efficiencies of e-business applications most likely gave these companies a bit of an edge when it came to defraying their operational "burn rates," which in quite a few instances were spectacular to say the least. If the management really cared, these applications probably also gave them plenty of heads-up warnings about what was happening to their businesses. But as the saying goes: You can only take a horse to water. Thus, e-business applications had nothing to do with the failure of dot-coms.

Q: Why are corporate portals such an attractive proposition for SCM and CRM applications?

A: Global reach at a low cost can make a huge difference to SCM, CRM, and SRM applications. Global reach is what you need to attract and engage new customers, new suppliers, new partners, and new distributors. The Internet and corporate portals provide an unprecedented opportunity, one not likely to be bettered, for achieving truly global visibility at a true cost that really is in the "peanuts" range. Compared with advertising, trade missions, and the challenges of recruiting credible distributors in new geographies, the cost, convenience, and effectiveness of the Internet approach are truly staggering. But low-cost global reach, though pivotal, is just the tip of the iceberg. Portals, right off the bat and at negligibly small "delta" cost, can provide translations, universal access (e.g., support for latest i-phone in Japan), personalization, security, and collaboration. SCM and CRM applications are powerful and proven tools in their own right. Integrating them with portals makes them formidable.

Q: What are the four golden precepts of CRM?

A: Engage, transact, fulfill, and service.

Q: Is there a role for XML vis-à-vis CRM and SCM?

A: Most assuredly, yes. Standardization, consistency, and interoperability are all very important when it comes to making these applications even more effective and successful. XML can definitely play a major role in this area. XML, as repeatedly mentioned, is contingent on common "understanding"—that is, both sides need to know what you are talking about in order to interpret what is being defined via XML. This mutual understanding is achieved through the creation of industry- or process-specific XML "dialects." There are already quite a few de facto standards, especially for conveying product, contract, and invoicing–related data, such as RosettaNet, cXML, TPAML, and VISA XML invoice specification.

Q: What are some examples of the types of CRM-related capabilities that can be provided with Web services?

A: Web services can be effectively used to obtain real-time currency conversion, shipping rates, credit ratings, and delivery status information. They can also be used for getting clearances on electronic checks and credit-card approvals. They could also be used to schedule shipments and provide automated notifications of delivery. Specialized analysis or data mining schemes obtained as Web services could also be effectively used for analyzing customer preferences and behavior within the context of CRM.

Q: What are the five key steps associated with supply-chain management?

A: Plan, source, make, deliver, and return.

Q: What is adaptive supply-chain management?

A: "Adaptive" in this context refers to automation, immediacy, and responsiveness. It is about making SCM a dynamic, on-the-fly, real-time process as opposed to one that people get to when they have time on their schedules. Corporate portals, by keeping users engaged, can play an important role in making the real-time aspect of this come to pass.

Q: What is supplier relationship management?

A: SRM in a nutshell is CRM for suppliers, now that suppliers are such a vital component of the overall corporate value chain. SRM applications set out to help in managing, monitoring, bolstering, and analyzing supplier relationships. Whereas CRM was about engage, transact, fulfill, and service, SRM extends this to include source, engage, procure, settle, design, and analyze.

Q: What is the significance of Siebel's universal application network (UAN) initiative?

A: UAN is a totally XML-centric, standards-based, vendor-independent application-integration scheme for today's e-business applications. Its goal is to enable enterprises to deploy end-to-end, industry-specific business processes made up of prepackaged out-of-the-box applications from different vendors. It relies on XML and Web services to realize this interapplication integration. There definitely is a need for this type of standards-based, vendor-independent scheme, given the diversity of compelling e-business applications available from numerous vendors.

Q: In addition to CRM, SCM, and SRM, what are some other examples of e-business applications that should be considered for access via corporate portals?

A: HR applications are a given. From an employee perspective these HR applications are some of the most sought after and used portal applications. HR applications were the heart and soul of many an intranet portal. Though partitioned, consolidated corporate portals will provide considerably more content, applications, and services, HR applications, given their relevance to employees' well-being, will continue to be heavily used. Salesforce automation is another attractive proposition for portal integration, as is product life-cycle management.

8

Web Services

Great services are not canceled by one act or by one single error.

—Benjamin Disraeli

Web services would be much easier to come to grips with if not for the ambiguous, misleading, and misused name. "Services," in computer circles, means many things to many people. It is used, quite appropriately, to refer to any external entity that does work on your behalf, so to speak. So people are used to such terms as "print services," "directory services," "file services," and "security services," to name a few. It has got to the point where in the context of enterprise networking there is an overall connotation that services are provided by "middleware" à la J2EE, IBM's WebSphere Application Server, BEA WebLogic, IBM MQSeries, and Microsoft BizTalk Server. The problem is that Web services per se are not "middleware."

Web services are, indeed, services, and they are delivered across the Web. But they are meant to deliver high-level services—even modular applications. Start off by thinking of Web services in terms of:

- Credit-card authorization
- International currency-rate converter
- Stock-quote provider
- Package delivery–status locator
- Shipping-rate calculator
- Local weather update
- Local traffic update
- Personalized horoscope
- User authentication—for example, with two-factor authentication

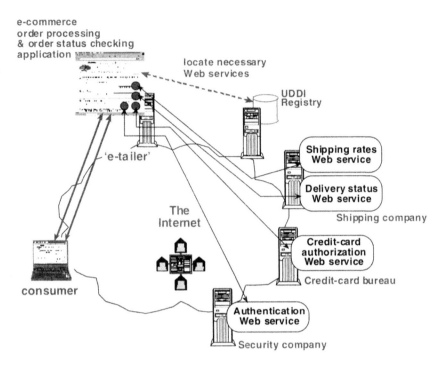

Figure 8.1

The concept of Web services providing specific, specialized service—in this case, to an e-commerce application

Figure 8.1 illustrates the concept of Web services in the context of an e-commerce transaction, in which the e-commerce application calls up various Web services to perform specific, specialized functions. Figure 8.2 emphasizes this theme of Web services providing specific functions by showing just some of the ways that a portal, in this case Lycos's public Internet portal, could exploit Web services. Figure 8.2 also highlights the potential and powerful relationship between portlets (or equivalents) and Web services, showing how you can have a one-to-one Web service to portlet relationship or a many-to-one relationship, where a portlet synthesizes data obtained from multiple Web services.

Providing specific, self-contained (i.e., modular) functionality is the underlying rationale for Web services. It is all about the availability of easily "pluggable" functionality, in view of the fundamental goals of the object-orientation paradigm, to expedite and simplify new application development. Just as with other OO initiatives, it is an ambitious, no-holds-barred proposition with tremendous inherent promise, which, in the case of Web services, might actually come to pass.

To be fair, there are no restrictions or guidelines as to what Web services can or cannot do. Somebody just needs to be motivated, financially, altruis-

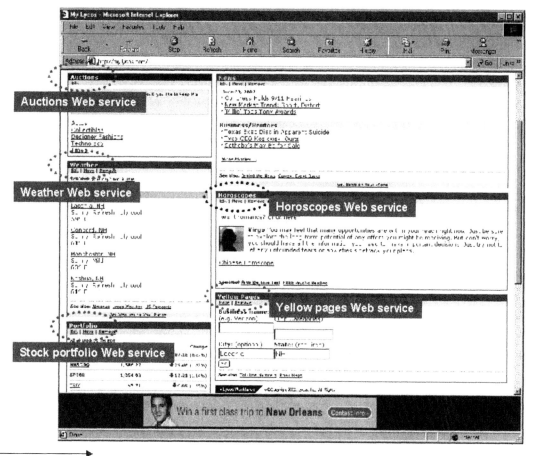

Figure 8.2   *The possibilities of using Web services to provide content and services for portals are immense and hard to ignore. This figure shows just a few examples using a personalized Lycos public Internet portal. It highlights how the individual portlets making up a portal view can be driven by one or more Web services working in the background.*

tically, politically, or egoistically to develop a Web service. Thus, anything is possible. Yes, you could most certainly have a print Web service (e.g., remote printing to a specialized printer), a directory Web service (e.g., white pages or yellow pages), or even a file service. Web services, however, should not be confused with protocols or other system-enabling middleware "services." In particular, Web services should not be thought of as referring to SOAP, WSDL, and UDDI.

SOAP, WSDL, UDDI, and the nascent Web Services Flow Language (WSFL) are examples of innovative and strategic technology used to make Web services possible. Although they are, indeed, middleware services, they are not in themselves Web services; they are enabling technologies for Web services. But there continues to be confusion about this distinction in the media, where it is yet possible to read three articles about Web services in trade journals of which two are talking exclusively about the enabling technologies while the third is actually talking about Web services as modular applications. In addition, it is not unusual to see headlines such as "Intel to support Web services," where the services in question are the enabling technologies as opposed to the high-level, application-oriented services.

Most simply stated, Web services are a platform and programming language–independent way to call and obtain high-level functionality from other programs. They rely on a remote procedure call (RPC) mechanism in the true sense of that phrase, provided you do not get it confused with the heavily used UNIX RPC scheme that popularized this term. Web services as such were meant to be programmatic, as opposed to visually interactive, solutions (i.e., they were for program-to-program rather than for human-to-program consumption). Web services were going to provide new applications with the rich set of functionalities that humans had been enjoying on the Web for so many years. If you go to the list of quintessential Web services mentioned at the beginning of this chapter, this point about the programmatic orientation should come across loud and clear.

Take, for example, package tracking, cited as a good prospect for a Web service. The likes of FedEx, UPS, Airborne, and even the U.S. Postal Service provide online tracking systems, as discussed in Chapter 1 and highlighted in Figure 1.2. But these services are for human use. E-tailers that currently offer shipment tracking typically do so by providing a hot link, usually with the tracking number embedded, to the Web page of the shipper in question. But it is a two-stage operation, in that you do the shipment tracking outside the e-tailer's e-commerce application.

If the shippers provided the tracking function as a Web service, then the e-tailers would be able to plug it into their overall application as a built-in feature. The shippers should not be averse to this since, the e-tailer is unlikely to hide or distort its identity. That way consumers would still know that the shipment they are expecting will arrive via FedEx, UPS, or whichever. What the package-tracking Web service does in this instance is provide function integration to ensure application completeness. This is the classic programmatic model for Web services.

Web services—as must be becoming clear by now and as illustrated in Figure 8.2—can play a pivotal role vis-à-vis portals, whether corporate, public, or employee only. The concept of portlets makes this the tie-in between Web services and portals that much more convenient and compelling. Web services, in effect, can become the modular software "engines" that power a particular portlet, either on a one Web service to one portlet basis (e.g., a stock price portlet) or a multiple Web services to one portlet arrangement (e.g., a "your commute home" portlet that could combine input from three Web services offering information about local weather, traffic conditions, and radio station programming).

Given this inextricable "gravitational" pull between Web services and portlets, it was inevitable that someone would postulate the concept of Web services that came replete with their own presentation services. That would make the portlet integration—not to say portlet—rendering that much simpler, although you are now back to the visual, interactive paradigm. Well, IBM has taken the lead in defining such "Web services for remote portals" (WSRP)—a.k.a. "remote portlet Web services"—and has presented it as a potential standard to OASIS, where OASIS (www.oasis-open.org) is a not-for-profit, global consortium with more than 400 corporate and individual members in 100 countries around the world that drives the development, convergence, and adoption of e-business standards. The introduction of WSRP thus puts a big dent into the initial concept that Web services were meant to be programmatic. But that is the dynamic nature of all things related to the Web.

8.1   The scoop on Web services

Web services are an XML-centric means for integrating modular programs over the Web using open, standardized interfaces that are decoupled from proprietary application programming interfaces (APIs). Their goal is to facilitate simple but pervasive program-to-program interactions around the Web (although IBM's new WSRP initiative is attempting to extend the scope of Web services beyond just programmatic scenarios). Thanks to Web services, different companies will be able to easily interconnect software components to create sophisticated e-business applications. Web services are expected to become the predominant means by which companies will interact with one another on a programmatic basis. Hence their pivotal significance when it comes to corporate portals.

The key, defining attributes of a Web service are as follows:

1.   Modular (i.e., the concept of an "object" that can be snapped together with other modular components)

2.   Self-contained (i.e., it needs to deliver the entire functionality it promises without other external dependencies)

3.   Self-describing (i.e., per the XML precept of self-identification, Web services using WSDL describe their interfaces and what you need to do in order to "bind" with them)

4.   Self-advertising (i.e., they can be easily located on the Web using UDDI)

5.   XML-centric

6.   Platform-independent

7.   Programming language–independent

8.   Easily combined with each other in mix-and-match mode regardless of platform and programming language differences

9.   Standards-based

Even more so than the platform- and programming language–independence, it is the self-advertising and self-description aspects that make Web services truly special and revolutionary. In much the same way that you could today use a search engine (e.g., Google) to find Italian olive oil producers or no-fee dating services, it will be possible to search for Web services that offer the exact service that you seek. This could be done, as of now, when developing a new application or a portlet. When faced with the need for some self-contained, modular functionality, the first and automatic reaction should now be to determine whether this functionality is available as a Web service. This would be realized using UDDI and a UDDI registry. It could be done manually by a human being or programmatically by an application. Figure 8.3 shows IBM's UDDI test registry, where IBM, Microsoft, and HP are currently working together to host the UDDI Global Registry—the cornerstone of UDDI. (Though not essential to the Web services initiative, it is highly conceivable that down the road some search engines such as Google might include UDDI support so that these popular search engines may also be used to locate Web services.)

When searching for a Web service to source, one does not have to limit the search to specific platforms, formats, APIs, or programming languages. Web services transcend all of these issues that up to now remained pertinent concerns when talking about using external software functionality—despite all the huge strides made in object-oriented technology. Web services, thanks to their inherent XML-enforced standardization, are easy to integrate with each other to realize composite functionality. In much the same manner as Lego blocks they are meant to snap together with a minimum of effort.

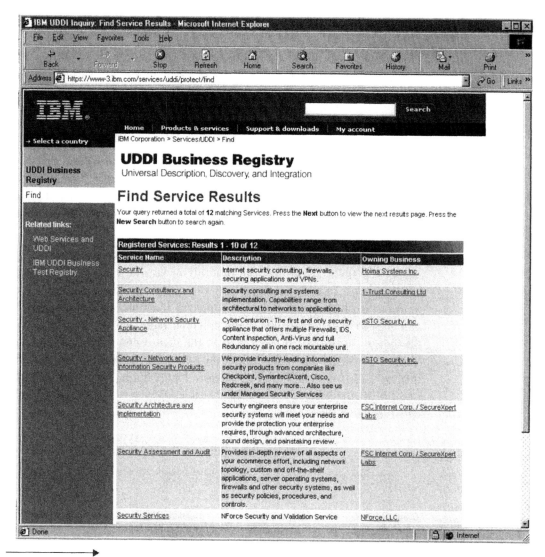

Figure 8.3 *IBM's UDDI Business Registry showing the results for a search on "security."*

This ability to easily obtain incisive software functionality in the form of one or more Web services should positively influence all future discussions and decisions about new application development, particularly as it applies to corporate portals. It is important not to lose sight of this. Web services have the potential to dramatically compress schedules, further enhance the functionality of applications, increase the competitive element of applications, and even reduce cost. This is not idle hyperbole. All of these are the things that Web services are really supposed to deliver.

8.1.1   Pricing, security, reliability, and scalability

This is not to say that there will be no cost associated with acquiring Web services. The pricing model for Web services at present is in its embryonic stage with most people, quite rightly, still focusing their attention on the technical side of things, although IBM—a major shaker and mover when it comes to Web services as well as a company that knows a thing or two about complex, usage-based pricing models—has, to its credit, already started publishing position papers about possible accounting and metering schemes for Web services. What is abundantly clear is that there will be a very wide spectrum ranging from freeware to expensive, premium offerings coupled with many permutations, in the case of the nonfreeware offerings, as to how the pricing will be structured.

The pricing options available will definitely include one-time charge schemes, periodic licensing (e.g., monthly or yearly), and umpteen usage-based options. In addition, it is likely that there could be third-party Web services distributors—although the inherent dynamic discovery capability of a Web service dilutes some of the potential value that can be offered by a distributor. In the case of Web services the main value that a distributor is likely to provide is that of handling the billing and collection. Indubitably, there will also be syndicated Web services. Figure 8.4 highlights some of the possible pricing models that will be available for Web services depending on who is offering the service.

Figure 8.4
Some of the possible pricing models for Web services depending on their source.

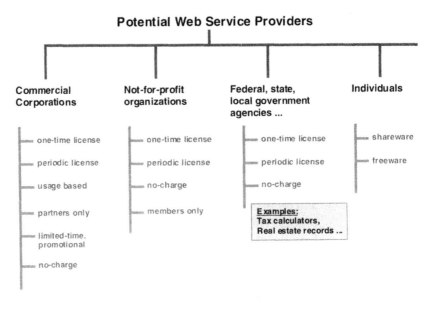

Whatever the pricing model, it will still not detract from the dynamic, "pick the best and most pertinent service you need" principle that is so fundamental to the whole rationale of Web services. It is this concept of dynamic discovery, self-description, and the XML-based, standardized invocation that truly distinguishes Web services from all the other object-oriented approaches (e.g., common object request broker architecture [CORBA] and Microsoft's Distributed Component Object Model [DCOM], which preceded it). Although they will not displace these other technologies, Web services are poised to become the preferred and strategic means for adding modular functionality to new e-business and portal applications.

Security vis-à-vis Web services is an area that is already attracting lots of attention and scrutiny given that there is vast potential for exposure and abuse. A "malicious" Web service can do untold damage since it is the perfect Trojan Horse in that it is brought in to work, hand in glove, with your new applications. So Web services per se need to be obtained from trusted sources and authenticated ideally with digital certificate technology. But then there is the flip-side, where a Web service, once integrated into an application, may need to perform security-related functions (e.g., authenticate users logging on to the application or encrypt data that are being transmitted).

That would mean that the Web service itself will be required to perform security-related functionality. In fact, obtaining such security-related functionality in the form of proven, ready-to-roll external modules has been repeatedly cited in this book as a valuable and compelling use for Web services. In reality, the issues here are really no different from those involved in acquiring any other piece of important software. The only caveat is that in the case of Web services you have the possibility of obtaining the software on the "open market," so to speak, exploiting the dynamic discovery capabilities of UDDI.

But this is where common sense has to step in. It probably would not be prudent to source a security-related Web service from an unknown company claiming to be located in Timbuktu. This point really does not have to be belabored in this context, because it really falls within the normal guidelines of software development and corporate security. Despite all their self-describing and self-advertising "magic," a Web service, cut to the chase, is but another software service. You should not let the dynamic sourcing aspect cloud your judgment when it comes to validating, testing, and proving what you are getting. The bottom line is that it probably would not be totally conducive to career prospects to obtain vital, mission-critical Web services from unknown sources. Just keep in mind that old adage about not getting fired for buying IBM; if necessary, substitute your own favorite name in place of IBM as long as you retain the essential meaning.

As with any other software, Web services should not be immune from concerns about reliability, performance, scalability, and manageability, particularly in the context of portal applications. There is nothing in the Web services "standards" that say that these software components have to be any different from other products offered by software vendors in these areas! To assume that Web services will somehow miraculously break the mold when it comes to all the standard RAS issues (i.e., reliability, availability, and serviceability) that have hounded software for the past four decades would be a case of taking optimism to unheard-of heights. In terms of these RAS issues, a new Web service, at best, will not be that different from a new release of Netscape for the Mac. Rigorous and diligent testing is thus recommended to make sure that there are no hidden surprises.

Ultimately, then, Web services are indeed the new genre of self-describing and self-advertising building blocks for distributed e-business applications. They are based on open standards that are extremely XML-centric. While it will certainly be possible to dynamically source them across the Internet, many are unlikely to be freeware. As with any other piece of valuable software, there is likely to be a charge to cover development, maintenance, support, and future releases. The pricing model will, however, vary widely, depending on the supplier as well as on the functionality being sought. The dynamic sourcing aspect should also not cloud traditional concerns about security, reliability, performance, and the like. Once dynamically sourced, a Web service, like any other piece of mission-critical software, should be researched, tested, and validated.

8.2   The role of XML

Web services are so contingent on XML that some people refer to them as XML Web services. One can actually say that XML and SOAP are the basic technologies that make Web services possible. SOAP itself is a mechanism for using XML documents to exchange messages. XML's scope, potential, and promise, however, extend well beyond that of making Web services possible. XML permits incompatible systems, belonging to different organizations, to interchange data with each other in a meaningful and productive manner. Hence the oft-heard claim that XML is the lingua franca for e-business.

XML provides a common platform and programming language–independent scheme for sharing data in an unambiguous and consistent man-

```
<!-- Copyright 2000 The HR-XML Consortium (TM) -->
<!-- version 1.0  October 17 2000 -->
<!-- 11/05/2000
Changed all elements to UpperCamelCase
 -->
<!ELEMENT PersonName  (FormattedName* , GivenName* , PreferredGivenName? , MiddleName? , FamilyName* , Affix* )>

<!ELEMENT FormattedName  (#PCDATA )>
<!ATTLIST FormattedName  type (presentation | legal | sortOrder )  'presentation' >
<!ELEMENT GivenName  (#PCDATA )>

<!ELEMENT PreferredGivenName  (#PCDATA )>

<!ELEMENT MiddleName  (#PCDATA )>

<!ELEMENT FamilyName  (#PCDATA )>
<!ATTLIST FamilyName  primary  (true | false | undefined )  'undefined' >
<!ELEMENT Affix  (#PCDATA )>
<!ATTLIST Affix  type  (academicGrade |
                        aristocraticPrefix |
                        aristocraticTitle |
                        familyNamePrefix |
                        familyNameSuffix |
                        formOfAddress |
                        generation )  #REQUIRED >
```

Figure 8.5 *A proposed DTD from the HR-XML Consortium for describing a person's name in XML form for HR applications. Here the term "#PCDATA," which appears often, refers to "parsed character data," which is a fancy way of saying that this is a string of text. This and other DTDs and schemas can be found at xml.org.*

ner. However, for this data sharing to occur there must be mutual understanding at both ends. In essence, the success of XML is dependent on the use of mutually understood, common "vocabularies" on both sides. This is where the industry- and application-specific XML standards sponsored by the likes of OASIS come in —for example, ebXML (for "electronic business XML" for e-business) and tpaML (for Trading Partner Agreement Markup Language), as described in Chapter 7. Industry-specific XML "dialects" are also being promoted by the likes of RosettaNet.org, a self-funding, nonprofit consortium of major IT, electronic components, and semiconductor manufacturing companies. These standards and "dialects" are in DTD schema form. Figure 8.5 shows a proposed DTD available at xml.org submitted by the HR-XML Consortium, Inc., for describing a person's name in XML for HR applications.

8.2.1 Mandatory XML health warning

At this juncture it is only fair to point out that there are some who worry that XML, despite the towering tsunami of industry support behind it, may not live up to its now exalted expectations. They worry that XML is too verbose and cumbersome and continually hampered by the need for the common vocabularies. These points are brought neatly to focus in Figure 8.5, which illustrates the amount of XML required to describe a person's name for the purposes of HR applications. For those who have been involved in networking for a while, there is a valid and unnerving parallel in terms of a hugely supported technology that eventually turned out, at the eleventh hour, to be a damp squib. This was ATM. Not automated teller machines, which continue to thrive, but the asynchronous transfer mode (ATM) standard for networking.

In the early 1990s ATM was as endorsed, promoted, and hyped as XML is today; to be fair, however, the Web was not then in full swing, as it is now, to add its reach, ubiquity, and clout to the fray. Nonetheless, the whole industry, the market, analysts, and media were totally convinced that ATM was the basis for the future of networking well into the second decade of the twenty-first century; the only issue that had to be settled was whether it would extend all the way to the desktop, and, if so, whether "desktop" ATM would work at 25-Mbps or 155-Mbps. IBM alone would spend in excess of $3 billion developing ATM products. IBM was so gung-ho about ATM that at the unveiling of its first ATM switches in 1993, senior IBM executives stated, unequivocally, that ATM's significance to IBM over the next 15 years was likely to be equivalent to what the S/370 mainframes had been during the previous 15 years.

As predictions go, this was not as bad as the claim in 1943 by IBM's founder and then chairman Thomas Watson, who said: I think there is a world market for maybe five computers. But it was close. IBM is lucky if it has made $1 billion in ATM revenues during the past nine years. ATM, though still used in some wide area network (WAN) scenarios, including the Internet, was totally eclipsed in the mid-1990s by Fast Ethernet and Gigabit Ethernet, which came from left field and blew away ATM. What adds piquancy to this comparison between ATM and XML is that ATM, like XML, was a complex, "high-overhead" technology. It insisted on "slicing and dicing" all data into 53-byte cells before switching them across the network.

Fast Ethernet and Gigabit Ethernet came along with technology that was much more intuitive and easier to adapt to existing infrastructures. That is what people also worry about when it comes to XML. Some believe that when push comes to shove, businesses will go with simpler, industry-specific schemes for e-business rather than incur the overhead of XML. Time will tell. It is, however, important also to note that the future and the prospects for Web services are not totally tied to those of XML. That would appear to be incongruous at first sight, given the tight coupling between the two, but Web services in essence are consumers of XML. Web services, if anything, make XML somewhat easier to deal with.

Though all the Web services–enabling technologies, such as SOAP and WSDL are XML-based, e-business application developers do not have to deal with these low-level "protocols." In the case of Web services, application developers need contend only with XML in terms of providing input to a Web service and receiving the output from a Web service. To appreciate what is being said here let's look at an example. Consider a Web service that provides a credit-card authorization function. To do this, the Web service will need, at a minimum, the following information: credit-card number, expiration date, and cardholder's name. In some cases it might also need additional verification information such as the person's zip code.

The Web service will likely return a "yes" or "no" code to denote the status of the authorization, and in the case of a "yes" return code, an authorization code as well. According to the inviolable edicts of Web services, the inputs (i.e., credit-card number and other data) and outputs (i.e., return code and possibly authorization code) for this Web service have to be in bona fide XML form. The WSDL definition for the Web service will specify the exact "parameters" for this XML in terms of an XML schema. However, these input and output data will, in this instance, be the sum total of the amount of XML needed for this transaction. The rest of the e-business application does not have to rely on XML. So developers can, if they need to, use XML only when they have to invoke Web services. Thus, one can, in theory, still gainfully exploit Web services without making a wholesale commitment to XML.

8.2.2   Some of the mechanics of XML—DTDs and schema

Data are included in an XML document as strings of text. The data are bracketed by XML text markup, which sets out to describe those data (i.e., give them context). The basic building blocks of an XML document are called "elements," where an element is a specific unit of data along with the XML markup describing those data. The XML markup, in much the same way as HTML, is in the form of tags, with the tags appearing within angle brackets. An XML element is thus delimited by two tags: a start tag and an end tag. The element per se typically consists of these two tags with text (i.e., data) in the middle. In some cases there can be more XML markup between the original start and end tags.

XML thus takes a flat stream of text that represents data of some sort and transforms it into a set of self-describing objects that can be easily and consistently manipulated by recipients. Since XML documents are always in text form, they can invariably be read and deciphered by humans. However, in order for an application to be able to successfully process an XML document, it needs to know what the various elements represent. In other words, the application needs to know what the tags mean. Since the meaning of a tag can differ significantly between different organizations, countries, and industry sectors, an application really needs to know what each tag means within a specific "application domain." This is the rub when it comes to XML.

Just because you have a well-formed XML document does not guarantee that it can and will be correctly interpreted by any and all applications. An analogy widely used in the mid-1980s to explain the need for networking protocols and architectures can now be used again to highlight XML's reliance on shared understanding at both ends of the transaction.

The analogy being referred to relates to that of making a direct-dial phone call between London and Moscow. Though you will, with luck, get a connection, there is no guarantee that you will be able to hold a meaningful conversation unless both of you happen to know a common language, whether it be Russian, Esperanto, English, or French. The same is true with XML, although XML, to its credit, does provide mechanisms to facilitate this mutual understanding. The two main schemes for this are DTDs and XML schemas. In some special cases it is possible to have a DTD-less XML document, provided the elements are structured in some type of self-explanatory manner.

A DTD is a formal description of a particular class of XML documents in XML Declaration Syntax. XML borrows the concept of DTDs from SGML. A DTD specifies what structures are permissible within an XML document. A DTD thus spells out what names are to be used for the different types of element, where they may occur, the attributes that can be assigned to elements, and how they all fit together.

If a DTD is being used, every element that can appear within an XML document needs to be declared within that document's DTD with an element declaration statement. The basic structure of an element declaration statement looks like:

```
<!ELEMENT element_name (content_description) ('?' | '*' |
'+')>
```

where the '?', '*', and '+' are "wild-card" references; '?' indicates that the pre-ceding name (or associated content description) can occur zero or one times, '*' denotes zero or more times, and '+' denotes one or more times. Thus, a simple DTD for an XML document containing contact informa-tion may look like:

```
<!ELEMENT person (name, company*)>
<!ELEMENT name (salutation?, first_name, middle_name*,
last_name)>
<!ELEMENT salutation (#PCDATA)>
<!ELEMENT first_name (#PCDATA)>
<!ELEMENT middle_name (#PCDATA)>
<!ELEMENT last_name (#PCDATA)>
<!ELEMENT company (#PCDATA)>
```

The term "#PCDATA," which is often seen in DTDs, refers to "Parsed Character Data" (i.e., essentially a string of text). If an element is defined as being of type #PCDATA, then it cannot have subelements (or child ele-ments). For example, if you define an element "phone_number" as being <!ELEMENT phone_number (#PCDATA)> you will, within the corre-sponding XML document, have to just define the phone number as a string of text. You could not, in this instance, subdivide it further into separate elements corresponding to "country_code," "area_code," "extension," and the like.

A DTD would typically be stored as a file (with a ".dtd" suffix), separate from the XML documents it describes. It could also be included within the XML document it describes. The location of the DTD that describes a given XML document is specified within that document via a Document Type Declaration. A typical Document Type Declaration would appear as:

```
<!DOCTYPE contact_info SYSTEM "http://www.wownh.com/
dtds/contactinfo.dtd">
```

The <!DOCTYPE > declaration usually follows the <?xml version= ...?> statement that kicks off an XML document. If the DTD is to be included within the XML document, then it is embedded as a part of the Document Type Declaration statement, as follows:

```
<?xml version="1.0" encoding="UTF-8"?>
<!DOCTYPE person (
  <!ELEMENT person (name, company*)>
  <!ELEMENT name (salutation?, first_name, middle_name*,
  last_name)>
  ....
)>
```

```
<person>
 <name>
  <salutation>Mr.</salutation>
  <first_name>Anura</first_name>
.....
.....
</person>
```

There is now a relative rich body of public DTDs for various industry sectors and applications (e.g., loan processing within the financial sector, property description within the context of real estate, engineering change [EC], change management as it applies to supply-chain management). A collection of public DTDs for various industry sectors can be found at www.xml.org/xmlorg_registry. This site is maintained by The Organization for the Advancement of Structured Information Standards (OASIS), which is now endorsed and supported by the United Nations (UN). Public DTDs can also be found at wwLINUXw.schema.net and on Microsoft's BizTalk site at www.biztalk.org.

DTDs just specify the structure of an XML document. Since the roots of DTDs go back to SGML, their forte is describing conventional text documents. Consequently, DTDs do not have a mechanism for expressing the content of elements in terms of data types. Thus, a DTD cannot be employed to specify numeric ranges for an element, to define limitations of what can occur, or for checks on the text content. Furthermore, the syntax of DTDs is relatively complex and cumbersome, as you can see if you look at some of the public DTDs available at the above-mentioned Web sites. In addition and ironically, DTDs are written in their own special syntax rather than in XML per se. The bottom line is that DTDs are now being usurped by XML schemas per a W3C recommendation, which can be found at http://www.w3.org/TR/xmlschema-0/.

XML schemas are written in standard XML. They can provide a far more comprehensive and rigorous description of the contents of an XML document in a modular, typed, and object-oriented manner. Since they permit data types to be rigorously specified, developing a good XML schema will require more thought and work than was required to create a DTD. This is especially so if the XML document being described contains complex data types. As with DTDs, industry- and application-specific XML schemas are already available, and many new ones are in the process of being defined.

8.2.3   **XSLT and the XML APIs**

Once you have an XML document, people invariably want to be able to display it on various devices, with Web browsers and intelligent cell phones being in the lead in this respect. But it does not end there. A lot of work is currently taking place on VoiceXML for voice-based applications, such as the voice-response systems used by call centers. XML documents are typically displayed on a browser or cell phone by associating a style sheet with the XML document. In some cases this can be achieved by using standard cascading style sheets (CSSs). Using XSL, however, is the more strategic approach, given that CSS uses a non-XML syntax. It is hoped that the next generation of browsers will contain sufficient XML functionality to enable them to reasonably display most XML documents without the need for auxiliary style sheets.

XSL defines the format for an XML document. XSL is divided into two parts: XSL formatting objects (XSL-FO) and XSL transformations (XSLT). XSL-FO is deemed to be an XML application that can be used to precisely describe the layout of a page in terms of blocks of text, graphics, and horizontal lines. Most people, however, don't create XSL-FOs. Instead, they write an XSLT style sheet that transforms the XML in the document into the corresponding XSL-FOs.

XSLT is also called an XML application. It specifies how one XML document can be transformed into another. XSLT works through the use of XSLT style sheets, which are sometimes referred to as XSLT documents. XSLT styles heets contain templates and constitute an XML document in their own right. XSLT works by comparing the elements in an input XML document being converted with the templates appearing in the style sheet. When it finds a match, it creates a corresponding output per what is specified in the template.

You can have multiple style sheets for the same XML document: one for displaying the document in HTML form within a browser and another for displaying it in some type of WML form on an intelligent phone. Internet Explorer 5.5 has a built-in XSLT processor, which enables it to accept XML documents and its corresponding style sheets and process the necessary XSLT transformations on the fly. If the browser does not support XSLT transformation, a separate XSLT processor will have to be used (e.g., the "open-source" Apache Software Foundation's Xalan (in Java or C++) from www.apache.org).

XHTML is an XML-based variant of HTML 4.0 and is an official W3C recommendation. It reformulates HTML 4.0 to ensure that it lives up to XML's syntax requirements. There are three DTDs available that describe HTML 4.0 in terms of XML. The big thing with XHTML is that it imposes strict discipline on HTML. For a start, unmatched tags are not allowed. Therefore, all start tags have to have matching end tags. All attribute values now have to appear within quotes. Whereas HTML is not case sensitive, XHTML, consistent with XML's being case sensitive, enforces case sensitivity in the case of tags, deeming <p> to be valid and <P> to be invalid. Most of today's browsers, irrespective of their vintage, can adequately render most XHTML documents.

A free XML editor that will allow you to display and manipulate XML documents per their XML structure is available from Microsoft. Other, but not free, XML editors are available from XML Spy at www.xmlspy.com and Corel/SoftQuad at www.xmetal.com. These editors come in two forms. XML Spy, like Microsoft's Notepad, deals directly with XML code and expects you to know XML. On the other hand, XMetaL hides the XML from you. You concentrate on the structure of the document using word processor–like techniques. The editor, behind the scenes, generates the XML on your behalf.

These types of automatic XML "generators" are similar to MS FrontPage or MacroMedia DreamWeaver in the context of HTML. These user-friendly HTML tools allow you to compose Web pages using visual, drag-and-drop, graphical techniques. The HTML is generated automatically by the editor without the user's having to know anything about it. If you plan to use XML extensively, you might want to get one of each of the two different editor types. Use the automatic generation one to get you started. Then use the XML-centric editor to refine, optimize, and customize the automatically generated XML.

At present there are two popular XML APIs, known as document object model (DOM) and simple API for XML (SAX). These APIs allow applications to read XML documents independent of the XML syntax. These APIs are geared toward different applications. DOM is geared for display-type applications involving XML-oriented browsers and editors. SAX, on the other hand, is targeted for interactions among programs.

The bottom line when it comes to XML, is that it is nothing more and nothing less than a metamarkup language. In this role it is indubitably the kingpin—the most endorsed and talked about standard of its type. XML, however, is not a programming language, a database scheme, or a networking protocol. XML documents can be and are transported across networks using standard, widely used protocols such as FTP, HTTP(S), SOAP, and SMTP. Databases (e.g., DB2 V7) will support XML data and even permit data to be described in XML form. But the database per se will not be in the form of a large XML document.

8.3   SOAP and WSDL

SOAP is the preferred and most popular communications protocol for XML Web services. It is a simple and lightweight mechanism for exchanging structured and typed information between peers in a decentralized, distributed environment using XML or variants of XML such as WSDL. SOAP thus provides a peer-to-peer protocol for facilitating intercompany communications within the context of Web services—for example, conveying UDDI requests and responses.

SOAP, per se, does not define any application semantics such as a programming model or any implementation-specific guidelines. Instead, it specifies a simple scheme for expressing application semantics through the provision of a modular packaging model and an encoding mechanism for encoding application-defined data. This abstract, implementation-neutral specification allows SOAP to be used in a large variety of diverse networking systems, ranging from those relying on messaging systems (e.g., MQSeries) to UNIX systems that prefer remote procedure calls (RPCs).

SOAP specifies how XML documents can be used as messages. The SOAP specification, which is now at version 1.2 and can be found at w3.org, consists of five main parts. These are as follows:

1.   A syntax for SOAP messages, which are messages defined in terms of XML documents

2.   An operational model for exchanging SOAP messages between SOAP nodes

3.   SOAP encodings, which are a set of rules as to how data will be represented within SOAP messages

4.   Recommendations for using SOAP over HTTP

5.   Instructions on how to make RPCs using SOAP messages

A SOAP message, as shown in Figures 8.6 and 8.7, consists of an outer SOAP envelope that may contain two subelements—an optional header and a mandatory body. The envelope is the top element of the XML docu-

```
Example 1
<?xml version='1.0' ?>
<env:Envelope xmlns:env="http://www.w3.org/2001/12/soap-envelope">
 <env:Header>
  <m:reservation xmlns:m="http://travelcompany.example.org/reservation"
         env:actor="http://www.w3.org/2001/12/soap-envelope/actor/next"
         env:mustUnderstand="true">
   <m:reference>uuid:093a2da1-q345-739r-ba5d-pqff98fe8j7d</reference>
   <m:dateAndTime>2001-11-29T13:20:00.000-05:00</m:dateAndTime>
  </m:reservation>
  <n:passenger xmlns:n="http://mycompany.example.com/employees"
         env:actor="http://www.w3.org/2001/12/soap-envelope/actor/next"
         env:mustUnderstand="true">
   <n:name>John Q. Public</n:name>
  </n:passenger>
 </env:Header>
 <env:Body>
  <p:itinerary xmlns:p="http://travelcompany.example.org/reservation/travel">
   <p:departure>
     <p:departing>New York</p:departing>
     <p:arriving>Los Angeles</p:arriving>
     <p:departureDate>2001-12-14</p:departureDate>
     <p:departureTime>late afternoon</p:departureTime>
     <p:seatPreference>aisle</p:seatPreference>
   </p:departure>
   <p:return>
     <p:departing>Los Angeles</p:departing>
     <p:arriving>New York</p:arriving>
     <p:departureDate>2001-12-20</p:departureDate>
     <p:departureTime>mid morning</p:departureTime>
     <p:seatPreference/>
   </p:return>
  </p:itinerary>
  <q:lodging xmlns:q="http://travelcompany.example.org/reservation/hotels">
   <q:preference>none</q:preference>
  </q:lodging>
 </env:Body>
</env:Envelope>
```

Figure 8.6   *An example from the SOAP 1.2 specification from w3.org showing the makeup of a SOAP message, using a travel reservation record as the example. Note that the SOAP message consists of an overall outer "container" known as the envelope, which, in turn, houses a header section followed by a body section.*

ment representing the SOAP message. This envelope defines an overall framework for expressing what is in a message, who (i.e., which process) at the receiving end should deal with it, and whether the request contained in the message is optional or mandatory. The contents of the header and body, as highlighted in the travel reservation example in Figure 8.6, are application specific and not defined by the SOAP specification.

The header is optional. It is there to facilitate future extensions without requiring changes to the existing specification. One possible use for the

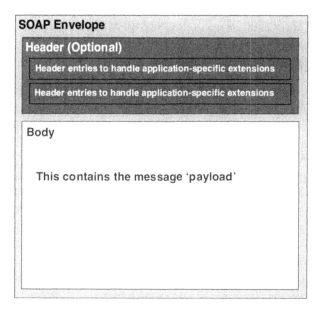

Figure 8.7

The overall syntax of a SOAP message.

headers is to provide information for "intermediary" SOAP nodes, which in the future, may get involved in a SOAP delivery from the sender to the ultimate recipient. The body is the mandatory element within a SOAP envelope. Thus, there is an implication that this is where the main information conveyed in a SOAP message must be included.

The SOAP encoding scheme is based on a simple system similar to that used by programming languages and databases. A SOAP encoding type is either a simple (scalar) type or a compound type constructed as a composite of several parts, each with its own type. The SOAP encoding rules thus define a serialization mechanism that can be used to readily and unambiguously exchange instances of application-defined data types in a platform-independent manner. The SOAP bindings are the conventions for encapsulating a SOAP message within or on top of another protocol (i.e., the underlying protocol) for the purpose of transmitting these messages between peers using SOAP envelopes. Typical SOAP bindings include carrying a SOAP message within an HTTP message, in an e-mail, or simply on top of TCP.

To use SOAP in the real world, you need SOAP implementations of the SOAP specification. This will not be an impediment, given that there are over 70 SOAP implementations at present covering all popular hardware and software permutations. In general, developers will not set out to directly generate and receive SOAP messages. Instead, they would opt to use a SOAP toolkit, as available from Microsoft or the Apache Software

Foundation, to help them create, parse, and manage SOAP messages. The highly popular Microsoft SOAP Toolkit 2.0 intercepts standard COM calls and converts them to SOAP messages, and the Apache toolkit does the same for Java function calls.

Web Services Description Language (WSDL), typically pronounced "whiz-dull," is a platform-independent XML derivative for generically describing network services as a set of end points that function by exchanging messages containing either document-oriented or procedure-oriented information. With WSDL, these operations and messages are described abstractly in an implementation-neutral manner and then bound to a concrete network protocol (e.g., SOAP) and message format to define an end point. In addition to SOAP, WSDL can be used with HTTP and MIME (i.e., multipurpose Internet mail extensions, the popular and official Internet standard that specifies how messages must be formatted so that they can be exchanged between different e-mail systems). If we take SOAP as an example, then a WSDL document (or schema) is in effect an XML document that describes a set of SOAP messages and how those messages are to be exchanged.

Similar to HTML in the way it describes the format of Web pages, WSDL provides a means for incisively describing contemporary Web-oriented communications protocols and messaging schemes. The XML-based WSDL is thus a handbook for describing communications environments in terms of a set of communication end points that are capable of exchanging messages between them. The goal of WSDL is to ensure that automated processes (e.g., e-business applications running on client PCs) can automatically determine the exact networking capabilities of remote systems (e.g., mainframe) without human intervention or prior definitions.

A WSDL document describing a communications setup will define the available services as collections of network end points, or ports. The key WSDL constructs, per the current WSDL specification available at w3.org, are as follows:

1. WSDL types—a container for data type definitions using some type of system

2. Message—an abstract, typed definition of the data being communicated

3. Operation—an abstract description of an action supported by the service

4. Port type—an abstract set of operations supported by one or more end points

5. Binding—a concrete protocol and data format specification for a particular port type

6. Port—a single end point defined as a combination of a binding and a network address

7. Service—a collection of related end points

8.4 UDDI

The goal of UDDI is to create a platform-independent, Web-centric, open framework for describing services, discovering businesses, and integrating business services (i.e., creating and maintaining a worldwide machine-readable "phone book" for e-businesses). UDDI enables businesses (or individuals) to describe themselves in a standard and consistent manner so that other businesses can easily determine whether they could profit by conducting e-business with that company (or individual). It will make the search process for Web services smarter and more incisive than is possible with today's search-engine technology (although as mentioned earlier it is likely that some of the major search engines will incorporate UDDI support in the future).

UDDI incisively addresses the self-advertising aspect of Web services; WSDL describes a Web service, while UDDI handles the publishing of this description. UDDI is also responsible for facilitating the dynamic location of Web services—the so-called "find" function. The third thing handled by UDDI is referred to as the client "bind" functionality. This has to do with facilitating the dynamic invocation of a Web service.

The UDDI Publish function deals with how and when the purveyor of a Web service registers the service per se as well as itself as the provider of the service. The UDDI Find function addresses how a client application locates the description of a Web service or a provider of Web services. The UDDI Bind function then deals with how a client application connects and interacts with the appropriate Web service after locating it on the Web by means of its description.

UDDI was officially unveiled as a result of the joint efforts of IBM, Microsoft, and Aribia in September 2000. The second version (V2) of the UDDI specification was made available at UDDI.org in June 2001. Key new features in V2 include the following:

1. The ability to accurately describe complex organizations in terms of representative, real-world organizational structures that include business units, departments, divisions, and subsidiaries.

2.   Enhanced support for global trading and internationalization in
      the form of support for multiple languages, providing companies
      the option of describing their business and services in more than
      one language.

3.   The inclusion of additional categories and identification schemes,
      including industry-specific categories (e.g., chemical and pharma-
      ceutical), to give companies even more flexibility and freedom
      when it comes to accurately describing their businesses. In addi-
      tion, these new categories can be validated during registration
      through third parties such as industry associations.

4.   The availability of richer searching options to facilitate complex
      searches. You can now search the UDDI registry for e-business–
      related products and services you are looking for using more
      expressive query parameters spanning more fields and involving
      more complex combinations of fields.

The UDDI Global Registry, the cornerstone of UDDI, is already operational. IBM, Microsoft, and Aribia, the three "founding fathers" of UDDI,
were going to host this registry. But then Aribia opted out and HP offered
to take its place. The companies that will host the global registry will be
called UDDI Operators. Microsoft and IBM are thus UDDI Operators. A
UDDI registry will maintain three types of data, published by business type
and classified per terms borrowed from telephony—white pages, yellow
pages, and green pages.

The white pages maintain business "listing" information, such as company name, contact details, and alternative names by which the company
may be known. Yellow pages, like the phone-book equivalent, classify companies by various criteria (e.g., industry, geography, and services offered).
The green pages then get into the technical aspects of what a company offers.
This will be where Web services will be published, at least to begin with.

8.5   Java or Microsoft .NET?

Of the multibillion-dollar heavyweights with a major vested interest in
making Web services a commercial success, Microsoft is conspicuous as
being the only one with a stated aversion to Java. The rest, which include
IBM, Sun, HP, Oracle, and BEA, are avid proponents of Java, with SAP
doing its best to keep a foot in each camp. Thus, right from the start a holy
war was in the making as to what would be the optimum "platform" for
Web services—Microsoft's emerging .NET initiative or the already strident

J2EE implementations. At the beginning there was much rhetoric and chest thumping from both sides as the market tried to fathom what Web services was all about.

Microsoft made a tactical faux pas to begin with when everybody was still murky about exactly what a Web service was. Microsoft announced that its first .NET-related endeavor, referred to as HailStorm, was going to be an XML-based scheme to collaborate and correlate Web-based transactions within the context of Microsoft's already existing Passport program, which enables you to securely store all the user IDs, passwords, addresses, and credit-card details you need these days to be an active and productive Web citizen. This got portrayed as an example of a .NET Web service.

The real problem was that shortly after the unveiling of HailStorm there were a spate of highly publicized security breaches involving Microsoft servers, Internet Explorer, and Passport. The Java zealots immediately seized on this to claim that .NET-based Web services were going to be security risks. Sun and others went as far as creating something called the Liberty Alliance Project to provide a Java equivalent of Passport—obviously sans the security flaws.

But now, a year to 18 months after the initial public roll-out of the potential promise of Web services, most people are beginning to appreciate that the Java versus .NET arguments, in the context of Web services, are really nothing more than an extension of the overall Java versus Microsoft NT battle. It was really a rehashing of the now familiar issues, now ascribed to Web services, such as scalability, security, reliability, and—here is the kicker—platform independence.

Web services, by definition, are supposed to be platform and programming language independent. This alone should have precluded the earlier debates about the platform issue. Web services work on a client/server basis with Web services subscribers and Web services providers. Given the platform independence creed, it must be possible to have Web services working freely across all possible client/server permutations. This is what now starts to make the old debate look so puerile. The Java camp may argue that J2EE is the only viable means for creating, executing, and publishing Web services and that the role of any Microsoft technology should be confined to that of a client that subscribes to Java-based Web services.

This approach of "let's develop and deploy Web services only on Java platforms" is not going to work. It is as simple as that. Microsoft NT and now .NET servers are hugely popular within the development community, and one yet again feels obliged to point out that many a popular e-business application debuted on NT. Moreover, Microsoft is making a concerted attempt to provide compelling development tools to facilitate the creation of Web services, such as Visual Studio .NET, which is based on what is by now a very familiar and popular Microsoft software development methodology.

The bottom line is that both Java and .NET have to play a role in making Web services real and pervasive. Facile arguments and artificial barriers as to how and where to develop and deploy Web services will ultimately be a waste of time and effort because software developers, typically, tend to do what they want. If they feel that .NET will allow them to develop Web services faster and easier, they will find a way to use .NET. Trying to stop it would be like trying to stop the sea tide from coming in. So, in this respect, it's time to go with the flow. If, as repeatedly stated in this book, yours is an NT shop, then pursue .NET. If, on the other hand, you use NT only at a department server level, go with J2EE. Either way, know that it will be possible to gainfully use Web services deployed on a different platform.

8.6   Q&A—A time to recap and reflect

Q: Are SOAP, WSDL, and UDDI examples of Web services?

A: No. Not in the true sense of the word. SOAP, WSDL, and UDDI are enabling technologies for Web services. They themselves are not Web services.

Q: In that case, what are Web services?

A: Web services are reusable, highly XML-centric, self-contained, self-describing, self-advertising units of business work—that is, remotely invocable, high-level functions for future e-business applications.

Q: What are some good examples of e-business–related functionality that can be obtained in the form of Web services?

A: Credit-card authorization is an obvious one. So is online package tracking à la the interactive services already available from FedEx, UPS, Airborne, and so on. It would also be possible to have a Web service that will dynamically calculate shipping rates based on weight, dimension, and destination. Currency conversion and stock quotes are other possibilities, as are user authentication and obtaining weather reports.

Q: How do Web services describe themselves?

A: That is done using Web Services Description Language (WSDL), which is a derivative of XML. The WSDL-based descriptions of Web services (known as schemas) are published in a UDDI registry so that they can be dynamically located across the Web.

Q: Do Web services come with their own presentation GUI for user interaction?

A: Web services were originally meant to be programmatic—that is, they worked only on a program-to-program basis. As such they did not come with their own GUI. But that is changing. IBM has put forward a proposal for "Web services for remote portals" (WSRP), whereby some Web services will come replete with their own presentation services. This would make Web service integration with portals that much easier.

Q: Can Web services be used with portlets in the context of corporate portals?

A: There is a natural and intuitive fit between portlets and Web services. Web services can become software "engines" that drive individual portlets or add functionality to the service being provided by a portlet. It can be a one-to-one, Web service to portlet relationship or a many-to-one relationship in which a portlet utilizes the functionality offered by multiple Web services. It would also be possible for multiple portlets to call on the same Web service for a specific function—say, user authentication.

Q: Will there be usage charges associated with Web services?

A: Yes, most Web services will have some type of cost associated with them. Though dynamic, and easily sourced over the Web, a Web service, nonetheless, will be a piece of important software with intrinsic value. Although there will be some freeware offerings, most industry-strength Web services will be available only for a fee. That fee may be a one-time charge, a periodic license, a usage-based scheme, or an indirect fee through some form of affiliation. An example of the latter would be shipping companies providing their large clients with sophisticated package tracking Web services, at no charge, in return for the client's using their shipping services whenever possible.

Q: Is there a possibility that XML may not live up to its exalted expectations?

A: There is a small probability of this. XML, despite its flexibility and extensibility, is verbose, cumbersome, and totally dependent on the presence of mutual cognizance at either end. This mutual cognizance is achieved via the formulation of common "vocabularies" using DTDs or schemas; in fact, schemas are gradually usurping DTDs. Some managers, quite rightly, worry that XML is too unwieldy. They would prefer to see something "lighter" and not as involved. This might not happen given that XML itself came to be to serve as a lighter version of SGML. However, those who remember asynchronous transfer mode (ATM) know that a heavily fancied and universally endorsed industry standard can still falter and fall at the eleventh hour.

Q: What is SOAP?

A: SOAP is the preferred and most popular communications protocol for XML Web services. It is a simple and lightweight mechanism for exchanging structured and typed information between peers in a decentralized, distributed environment using XML or variants of XML such as WSDL. SOAP specifies how XML documents can be used as messages. A SOAP message consists of an envelope that may contain an optional header and a mandatory body component; the message payload is carried in the body component.

Q: What is the optimum platform for developing and deploying Web services?

A: Platform and program language independence is a central tenet of Web services. Currently, J2EE and Microsoft's .NET are the two major alternatives when it comes to developing and deploying Web services, although it would also be possible to contemplate UNIX or LINUX platforms without having J2EE on top of them. However, the bottom line is that a Web subscriber should be able to readily locate and invoke a remote Web services without having to know what type of platform the service is resident on. Both Java and Microsoft are going to great lengths to support and promote Web services. Microsoft technology is very popular with developers, so many will develop .NET-based Web services. But that should not be an issue, unless security or scalability gets in the way, because these Web services could be used by subscribers on any other platform.

9

Living and Breathing Portals

It is a fine thing to be honest, but it is also very important to be right.
—Winston Churchill

The manifold advantages derived by a company through having a proficient corporate portal are unmistakable, proven, and, above all, irrefutable. Among other things, a corporate portal will, unequivocally:

- Greatly increase corporate reach vis-à-vis new prospects and "partners" at a near-zero cost

- Reduce operational costs, particularly those associated with call-center operations

- Bolster customer loyalty by eliminating delays, frustrations, and inefficiencies

- Improve in-house productivity through online tools (e.g., HR applications), faster access to pertinent data, powerful collaboration capabilities, and reduction in workflow interruptions

- Enhance corporate competitiveness through the ability to very cost effectively provide more information and services than was possible with non-Web mechanisms

- Accelerate decision making through rapid access to pertinent data sources and process streamlining

- Expedite and cost reduce business processes via external e-business links, tightly integrated with such IT applications as supply-chain management and supplier relationship management

- Invigorate the entire customer relationship management operation, across the engage, transact, fulfill, and service cycles, from both a customer and a company standpoint

- Increase business volumes via low-cost, all-electronic self-service functions that do not need to be "reprocessed" in-house

- Help attract and source new suppliers, distributors, manufacturers, and partners that can improve the SCM business model, on a global basis, at a very low cost

- Significantly simplify, expedite, and lower the cost of b2b dealings with all "partners" and associates

Corporate portals thus make a lot of sense, whichever way you look at them, whether it be cost containment, improving the corporate image, solidifying customer loyalty, growing the business, or facilitating b2b transactions. They are not fads nor do they represent a technology that is being hyped purely for the sake of avaricious commercial gain on the part of the vendor community. The Internet is brimming with heavily used, highly effective, feature-packed corporate portals.

The Fortune 1000 crowd were quick to see and seize the business opportunities afforded by corporate portals. For those whose business relied heavily on call centers (e.g., financial institutions, travel companies, insurance companies, phone companies), corporate portals were a miraculous panacea in that they allowed organizations to offer slick self-service functions that dramatically reduced operational costs while giving customers faster, more comprehensive, and wider service.

Corporate portals are about as close to a free lunch as you can aspire to in today's world. The Fortune 1000 class corporate portals are flourishing, and these corporations are now relentless in their efforts to steer the calls that still go to their call centers toward the portals. Invariably, the first message that greets customers or prospects who call the call center is something along the lines of: Have you tried contacting us on the Web at www.whatever.com where you can get quick access to your account information and pay your bills online. This announcement, with its promotional incentives for using the portal, was invariably included in all statements and bills to make sure that customers truly appreciated that the company really wanted them to start using the corporate portal.

The resistance to consolidated, partitioned corporate portals has come from corporations at or below the "mid-tier" ranking vis-à-vis corporate revenues. Recent reports by analyst firms suggest that less than 40 percent of such companies have externally accessible portals, the relevant phrase being "externally accessible." This has been the rub. Corporations of all sizes have been more than comfortable with providing employee-only intranet portals and maybe even b2b etxranet, partner portals for selected partners. The problem has been the fear of letting the outside world just come in, at will and without any barriers, through a portal. Security, despite the strides made with digital certificates and two-factor authentication, continues to be a concern. So is that of providing a compelling, convincing, and reassuring "face" to the general public.

Management and IT professionals understand, viscerally, that implementing a shoddy and unreliable portal could cause more damage to a company's image and credibility than not offering an externally accessible portal at all. Furthermore, they also appreciate that implementing and sustaining a good corporate portal is a major, relatively costly, and never-ending undertaking. In many instances corporate portals were intended to be the next major IT undertaking once companies had a chance to recoup their energies and budgets after completing the Y2K conversions. However, the dotcom implosion and the global economic slowdown intervened. IT budgets, at best, were frozen. Most were mercilessly pared as companies had no choice but to reduce their workforce, tighten their belts, and wait for the economy to slowly recover.

However, as companies head past 2002, all the indications are that corporate portals, yet again, will be high on the IT priority list alongside various initiatives to incorporate XML into various parts of the overall business process. Some of the forces that will necessitate this reelevation of the emphasis afforded to portals include:

- The continuing need to contain, if not reduce, corporate operational costs

- The need to seek and open up new international markets to increase business opportunities

- The need to maintain a competitive edge within the market

- The need to satisfy the requirements for SCM, SRM, or CRM programs as new versions of these applications became increasingly portal-centric, XML focused, and Web services oriented

- The need to address requests by busy, always-on-the-run customers for direct online self-service functionality in place of time-sapping call centers

- A concerted effort by the vendor community, led by IBM, Oracle, BEA, and SAP, to promote portals as a critical infrastructure mechanism to facilitate Web services–centric b2b e-business, especially given the close tie-in between Web services and portlets, as described in Chapter 8

In the end, when it comes to corporate portals, the question is never going to be "if." It will always be "when," with budgets and resources invariably being the gating factor. But portals are destined, inexorably, to be the next logical step in the office automation evolution that has been taking place since the advent of the PC two decades ago. In the late 1980s and early 1990s the availability of affordable desktop computing resulted in the far-reaching business process reengineering crusades. Though traumatic at the time, the continuing increases in corporate productivity, so often cited by the U.S. Federal Reserve as one of the catalysts that drives economic growth, can be directly traced back to the processes instituted as a part of these crusades to eliminate duplication, streamline workflow, automate processes, and encourage collaboration.

This PC-driven business process reengineering, if you think about it, was really a consolidating and retrenching effort following the so-called PC explosion. Starting in the mid-1980s groups and individuals began using PCs in tactical, ad hoc ways to automate various tasks. There was no overall cohesion. This necessitated the discipline and workflow integration brought about by business process reengineering. Today a similar two-stage evolution is happening in the context of portals. Since the mid-1990s, analogous to the PC explosion, the ever-growing significance of the Internet has compelled corporations to institute various efforts to capitalize on the reach and cost economies provided by the Internet. Now corporate portals, in much the same way as the business process reengineering crusade, are stepping up to the bar to provide a meaningful framework in which to consolidate all of these Web-related activities.

9.1   Laying the costs down for a corporate portal

Obtaining a positive ROI on a corporate portal, within say a 24- to 36-month period, should typically not be an issue. The palpable cost saving made possible by a corporate portal in the areas of call-center operations, supply-chain management, electronic document transfer, and direct transaction processing alone should guarantee positive ROI returns within a three-year window. And this is without even factoring in the harder to quantify but still very real and significant "indirect" dividends returned by a portal (e.g., increased productivity, heightened customer loyalty, better employee morale, superior company image, broader company reach, and the sharpened competitive edge).

Being able to credibly and succinctly demonstrate that a portal can deliver a positive ROI within a relatively short period is vital, since the company investment required to realize a good portal is likely to exceed cursory, preconceived management expectations. There will be "sticker shock." Some might have thought that the existing company "home page" Web site already had most of the features expected from a portal and that all that was needed was to activate these currently unused capabilities. Consequently, there will be a need to explain and educate prior to even trying to justify the anticipated costs.

The one-time up-front costs for implementing a good corporate portal will include many different cost elements. These costs will be outside and distinct from those associated with operating, sustaining, and expanding a portal once it has been successfully activated for production use. They will also not include any costs associated with other IT applications, including CRM and SCM applications, since the need and justification for such ERP applications are not related in any way to providing a corporate portal. Key elements of the implementation-related costs will include:

- Significant planning costs spanning both in-house personnel and outside expertise in the form of one or more consultants to pontificate, play devil's advocate, and add external perspective

- Portal server and enabling software costs (e.g., application server and possibly Web server upgrade)

- Ancillary portal-related software costs (e.g., content management adjuncts, collaboration tool upgrades. additional management tools, and usage pattern–monitoring software)

- Security services, including digital certificates, authentication technology, and more firewalls

- Design tools

- Portal-related software development and XML tools (e.g., Java or C++ tools and XML editors)

- Design costs, in-house or external, for the overall theme, structure, look and feel, and layout for individual portal views

- Portal-related development costs for scripts, custom portlets, and new self-service applications

- Web-to-host technology if it is not already present in some form

- Possible upgrades to ERP applications to facilitate easy portal integration (e.g., HTML interface)

- Syndicated content (e.g., world news, industry news)

- Web services licenses or subscriptions (e.g., local weather, stock quotes)

- Hardware platform and storage for the portal

- Internet connection upgrades

- Possible network infrastructure changes to assimilate the portal with the rest of the IT systems

- Portal set-up costs

- Content, application, and services integration costs

- Portal-testing costs

- Portal-specific training for administrators, operators, and portal "maestros"

- In-house portal introduction costs (e.g., presentations, demos, newsletters, instructions, etc.)

- Costs to bring the portal to the attention of the outside world (this is really a marketing and company PR–related cost, but it is included here because it should not be overlooked)

- Maintenance licenses contracted to at product-acquisition time

- Cost of the portal team "nucleus"

The last item here, the so-called portal team, is worth elaborating on, since it will be the sustaining force that drives the entire portal initiative. A contemporary portal cannot realistically be implemented and run by part-time help. There is just too much to be done, usually in real time, especially when the portal is up and running. In addition, it is imperative to have somebody who is totally accountable for the portal from a technical perspective so as to eliminate fingerpointing and aimless vacillation when something goes wrong.

Thus, you have to have a portal "commander in chief," who supervises, specifies, and controls the overall portal mechanics and processes to avoid problems. Consequently, it would be imprudent to set off on a portal project without appointing at least two dedicated senior professionals to be responsible for pulling together the whole thing, with one of these being the "commander in chief." Two is the bare minimum. This nucleus portal team will grow with the portal.

Nonetheless, the members of this team are unlikely to be able to do everything themselves—assuming you want the portal up and ready in a reasonable amount of time. They will need assistance from other in-house resources (e.g., graphics, IT programmers, systems programmers) and typically they will also resort to external resources (e.g., design studios, contract programmers). What is key is the coordination and control of these resources. This is where the commander in chief and the nucleus team come in.

9.2   Budgets and mandates

Given the list of items mentioned previously, it is easy to see that a corporate portal cannot be envisaged without access to a sizable budget, which also must include a fairly large recurring component to take care of ongoing operations costs, necessary product upgrade costs, and contingency sums to cover extensions and enhancements to the portal. Determining the required budget for a portal is a major task in itself, given all the variables involved. Diligent planning to make sure that nothing is being forgotten is the key—so much so that it is safe to say that the three vital prerequisites for ensuring the success of a corporate portal are planning, planning, and even more planning.

This is not as flippant and facetious as it may sound. The importance of planning when it comes to a portal cannot be overstated. There are plenty of IT projects that one can dive into with little or no planning, working out the details and kinks as you go along. A corporate portal, however, is not one of these projects. A corporate portal is best implemented and run according to a well thought out, thoroughly sanity checked and approved master plan. As mentioned earlier in this book, it often makes sense to develop a formal business case, replete with cost and "revenue/benefits" projections, to guarantee that a set of people have no choice but to engage their minds in all that is involved in making a portal real.

The final portal budget, once approved by management, must also be accompanied by an unequivocal mandate vis-à-vis the company's total commitment to the portal effort. The reason for this is that a portal falls into a category of technology best described as being "electro-political" in that a portal can never be made totally successful purely via technology. Even the best architected and engineered portal, implemented with the finest products that money can buy, will nonetheless fail if it does not have the backing of the right people within the company. For example, a V.P. of marketing or sales who for whatever reason is "antiportal" may be able to continually thwart efforts to increase the portal's reach and effectiveness.

A portal, as mentioned earlier, more than any other IT project will require active cooperation from many different organizations within a company if it is to deliver on its promise. Given the CRM, SRM, and SCM aspects, a portal will require unstinting support from groups such as sales, marketing, purchasing, accounts, engineering, finance, manufacturing, HR, business development, business analysis, and IT. In essence, the whole company, in one way or another, must be behind the portal initiative. It cannot just be a skunk-works project being driven, in isolation, by IT or marketing. Senior management must continually promote it and emphasize its significance to the company with a single voice. This is the mandate.

Therefore, the things that you must have in place before you start to venture down the portal-implementation path are:

1. An approved master plan, possibly in the form of a bona fide business case

2. A realistic budget

3. An attainable schedule with specific milestones

4. A trustworthy nucleus team with a designated commander in chief

5. A mandate from management

6. Publicity within the company as to what the portal is all about and its significance

7. Unconditional support from all department heads

8. A cast-iron constitution, aided where necessary by prescription drugs, to weather the travails ahead

9.3   Taking the plunge

Once you have the items listed in the previous section in place, you have no choice but to firmly grasp the thistle and go about implementing a corporate portal. If you have done as much planning as urged, then you should not be having too many compunctions at this stage. The planning stage should have given you plenty of time and motivation to confront your worst fears. By now you should be feeling fairly comfortable and confident.

It isn't as if you are venturing into hitherto uncharted water—this is something that you should constantly remind yourself of. Corporate portal technology is highly proven and extensively implemented. If and when you have doubts, you should visit other portals, and by now you must have looked at quite a few not only to get inspiration and pointers but to see what they are doing and how well they are doing it.

The chances are that you did speak to yours peers in other companies about their experiences when it came to implementing portals during the planning and budgeting phases. With luck you might have even attended one or more user group meetings at which portal implementation was addressed. At this juncture, you will be dealing with the vendors of your choice. They should be able to put you in touch with other customers if you want to discuss a particular issue with a corporate peer as opposed to a vendor representative or consultant. It should also be noted that by now the portal server vendors have encountered pretty near all eventualities when it comes to corporate portal implementation, with the nascent Web services possibly being the exception. You should not hesitate to exploit their experience and expertise. And then there are also the consultants.

The bottom line is that there is no shortage of the technology, products, or expertise needed to make your corporate portal into an unmitigated success. It is just a question of making sure that you have access to what you need; that is why the planning phase was so invaluable. Most of the issues related to resources and where to get them should have been addressed at that juncture. Now is the time to work the plan with growing optimism. Others have gone down this path before you and have been kind enough to leave you plenty of visible tips on the Internet as to what you should do if per chance you occasionally stumble or get disoriented. The satisfaction of getting to the end of this road and seeing a slick, fully operational corporate portal should be enough incentive to weather the inevitable minor storms along the way.

9.4 Q&A—A final chance to recap and reflect

Q: Is it even remotely conceivable that corporate portals are but a passing fad?

A: Absolutely and categorically not. Corporate portals are here to stay. In the case of the larger, Fortune 1000 class companies, they have already become an indelible and vital business-critical process. Corporate portals are becoming the preferred and highly cost effective means for providing customer relationship management—not to mention supplier relationship management and supply-chain management. Corporate portals have become the next logical step in the office automation evolution that has been taking place for the past two decades. Business process reengineering in the early 1990s consolidated and formalized the uncoordinated strides that had been made in desktop and client/server computing as a result of the PC explosion. Now, a decade later, corporate portals are set to provide a similar consolidation and formalization process, but this time to all of the uncoordinated Web-related initiatives instigated by corporations. Hence the concept of a corporate portal being a focal point for Web-related activity regardless of whether the transactions are coming in from the Web into the company or going out of the company into the Web.

Q: What are the crucial "four Ss" for maintaining a successful corporate portal?

A: Security, scalability, synchrony, and speed, where synchrony in this context is used to refer to the art and science of keeping portal content up-to-date, accurate, coordinated, and linked.

Q: What are some of the primary benefits of a corporate portal?

A: A corporate portal, among other things, will indubitably increase corporate reach, reduce operational costs, bolster customer loyalty, enhance corporate competitiveness, accelerate in-house decision making, invigorate the entire customer relationship management operation, increase business volumes, help attract suppliers, and lower the cost of b2b dealings with all partners.

Q: What are the three vital prerequisites for ensuring the success of a corporate portal?

A: Planning, planning, and more planning.

Q: Is it possible to have a positive ROI from a corporate portal?

A: Yes. In addition to valuable but difficult quantify "dividends" (e.g., heightened customer loyalty, higher business volumes, increased corporate reach, enhanced productivity, and better employee morale), corporate portals provide tangible cost savings in the areas of call-center operations, supply-chain management, customer transaction processing, and automated b2b interactions. Given the size of the potential cost savings, particularly in the case of minimizing call-center costs, it is often possible to achieve a positive ROI within three years despite the significant up-front and operational costs associated with a good corporate portal.

Q: What are the eight things you must have in place before you start to contemplate embarking on the actual portal implementation phase?

A: First and foremost, you have to have a detailed and approved master plan. It would be even better if you created this plan in the form of a business case. The next thing that you must have is a realistic budget commensurate with the goals set in the master plan. You also need a feasible schedule with specific milestones so that you can monitor and track your progress. The progress that you make is going to be driven by a trusted nucleus team with a designated commander in chief, who is accountable for the technical success of the portal. However, no matter how good your team is, they will not be able to make the portal an unmitigated success purely via technology. The success of a corporate portal is contingent on the support and cooperation of people from across the company. So you have to have mandates from senior management as to the importance of the portal. This mandate must be publicized across the company, and unconditional support must be obtained from all department heads to avoid delays and frustrations down the road. However, given that there will be some inevitable bumps along the way, it also behooves you to have appropriate over-the-counter and prescription medication at hand.

Q: Why is there a need for XML?

A: XML is a platform and programming language–independent scheme for sharing data among applications and corporations in an unambiguous, consistent, and extensible manner—albeit through the use of somewhat verbose vocabularies that need to be understood at both ends. XML can thus eliminate the proprietary nature of commercial applications, and it ensures that data from one application can be understood by a totally different application, even if the two applications are from different, competing vendors. XML sets out to sweep away the incompatibility issues that have in the past precluded easy data interchange between disparate applications.

Q: What are Web services?

A: Web services are a new genre of Web software that is heavily XML centric; they are based on protocols such as SOAP, WSDL, and UDDI. They represent reusable, self-contained, self-describing (i.e., via WSDL), self-advertising (i.e., via UDDI) units of business work. They are thus remotely invocable, high-level functions for future e-business applications. They provide a standard, strategic, and consistent way to package business processes (e.g., credit-card authorization, user authentication) and make them readily available over the Web to interested and authorized parties.

Q: What are the key functions provided by a portal?

A: The key functions typically offered by a corporate portal include content aggregation, content syndication, search services, collaboration schemes, and access to applications.

Q: What things should you take comfort in during the portal implementation process when you occasionally run into a problem?

A: Even though it may feel like it at times, you are not the first and you are not alone when it comes to implementing corporate portals. It is a well-trodden and sign-posted trail by now. The technology, with the possible exception of that related to the nascent Web services, is well proved and extensively used. There is also no shortage of experience and expertise. You should be able to talk to peers at other companies—where necessary, through introductions from the vendors you are dealing with. Many of the vendors are also likely to have user groups in which portal implementation issues are discussed. There are likely to be bulletin boards and Usenet groups about your portal server, especially if it is from one of the heavyweights. Then, of course, there is the support and succor you can get from your vendors, always keeping in mind that most portal vendors have considerable experience by now in this realm. And, of course, there are consultants aplenty, who will, for a fee, be happy to help you with almost anything. If you are still all at sea after exhausting all these possibilities, you can always try to contact me at anu@wownh.com to see if I, by some miracle, have any ideas as to what you should do.

Selected Glossary

ActiveX   Microsoft's strategic object-oriented technology, which applies to COM and object linking and embedding (OLE) technologies.

Adaptive SCM   SCM in real time.

Aggregation   Assimilation of information from various sources per a user's personalization criteria.

Application server   Service-rich (e.g., load-balancing) software platforms for executing contemporary applications written in languages such as Java and C++.

ASP   Microsoft's server-side scripting technology for creating dynamic Web content.

Authentication   Process of identifying and validating a person.

Autonomic computing   Self-managing, self-healing systems epitomized by IBM's Project eLiza technology.

BI portals   In-house portals customized to aid decision making via the provision of access to diverse business information and tools to analyze the information.

BPM   Software systems that enable companies to create, model, map, and manage their business processes.

Breadcrumbs   Navigational trail of the pages traversed within a portal.

CA   A trusted authority that issues digital certificates.

Capacity on demand   Ability to dynamically invoke processor and I/O resources on the fly and on a usage basis to handle peak loads.

Clustering   Combining multiple machines to increase processing power and resilience.

Collaboration   Tools such as e-mail, bulletin boards, and calendering to facilitate fast interpersonal interactions and communications.

Collaborative portal   In-house portals that specialize in offering collaborative capabilities.

Cookie   Widely used mechanism to store specific information about portal or Web site users.

Corporate portal   A secure, Web-based, easy-to-use, focal point of access to a diverse range of potentially personalized corporate information, services, applications, and expertise to both internal and external users.

CRM   Everything to do with adroitly handling all interactions that a company has with its customer base.

CSS   Styles heet that tells Web browsers certain document formatting preferences (e.g., font type, font size, and margin settings).

Data mining   Computerized system that utilizes complex artificial intelligence (AI)–inspired algorithms to sift through large amounts of data and highlight convoluted but highly relevant relationships and patterns buried within the data.

Data warehouse   Organized and stored data with links to their original sources to be used by KM applications.

Digital certificate   Electronic credential that vouches for a person's identity.

Digital dashboard   Microsoft "speak" for a portal.

Digital signature   The "tamper-detection" seal for digital certificates and other digital documents.

DMZ   A subnetwork containing Web and portal servers, protected from both the internal network and the Internet via firewalls.

DOM   One of two popular APIs for reading XML documents. The other is SAX.

DTD   The original XML mechanism for describing the structure of an XML document that is based on a 20-year-old modeling concept pioneered with SGML.

EAI   Another term for host integration.

e-business   Doing business processes over the Web.

e-commerce   A subset of e-business related to buying or selling products or services over the Web.

EIP   An old generic name used in the main to refer to in-house, intranet portals.

EJB   Server-side version of JavaBeans fortified with access to various Java services (e.g., Java directory and naming).

Enterprise portal   Ambiguous term that could mean either a partners-only portal or a consolidated, partitioned corporate portal serving both internal and external users.

ERM   CRM for employees.

ERP   Rapidly becoming a generic term to describe all the mission-critical, business-related IT applications essential for running a contemporary corporation.

Firewall   Security technology to control and monitor access to and from the Internet (and other networks).

Gadget   A term popularized by Plumtree Software that is analogous to a portlet or Web part.

Horizontal portals   Portals, typically general-interest public Internet portals, that cover a broad spectrum of topics and services.

Host integration   Technology that permits the proven business logic in existing host applications to be reused when creating new e-applications or Web services.

Host publishing   Host application-access Web-to-host solutions that work by converting host terminal data streams to HTML (or XML) via a server-side component.

HTML   Language used to describe the format of a Web page.

HTTP   The transport protocol most often used between Web servers and Web browsers.

IDS   Electronic "burglar alarm" for IT systems.

Internet call center   Another name for a corporate portal or one that is targeted just at customers, prospects, and partners.

Intranet portal   Employee-only, in-house portal accessible only via the company's intranet.

IPSec   Framework of open standards developed by the IETF to ensure the secure exchange of packets at the IP layer.

J2EE   The server-side Java platform targeted at supporting enterprise-class applications.

Java Highly popular, widely endorsed, platform-independent programming scheme introduced by Sun Microsystems circa 1995.

JavaBeans Client-side Java objects to facilitate reuse of program components.

JSP Java equivalent of Microsoft's ASP.

KM Tools to help turn information into useful knowledge.

Mirrored portal Immediate-takeover, hot-backup scenario in which the portal servers are a considerable distance apart and, under normal operational conditions, serve user populations divided up by their geographic location.

.NET Microsoft's latest Web and e-business–related global initiative, which also embraces Microsoft's efforts in the Web services arena.

OASIS Not-for-profit, global consortium to promote e-business standards.

Partitioning Virtual and dynamic system clustering on the same machine by dividing the machine's resources into multiple virtual machines.

PDF Adobe Systems's highly popular scheme for creating lavishly formatted documents that are platform independent.

Personalization Customizing portal content and services to the needs of specific users.

PKI Incisive framework for facilitating secure but easy-to-use public key encryption and digital signatures.

Portal A Web-based, easy-to-use focal point of access to a diverse range of content, services, resources, and applications.

Portal server Software for facilitating the implementation, deployment, and running of portals.

Portal view An entire portal "Web" page, which is typically made up of multiple, autonomous "windows" representing portlets (or their equivalent).

Portlet Content channel or application window within an overall portal view.

Public key cryptography Data encryption scheme that uses a pair of associated keys, known as public and private keys, for encryption and decryption.

Public portal Typified by AOL, Yahoo!, Lycos, and Excite, where the primary business of the portal per se is to run the portal for revenue and profit.

RAID Using multiple disk drives to create a single logical disk.

RPC   Means of obtaining run-time functionality in real time from another application.

SAN   Dedicated, high-volume disk storage solution built around a high-speed, Fiber Channel technology network.

SAX   One of two popular APIs for reading XML documents. (The other is DOM.)

Schema   The new strategic XML approach for precisely describing the structure of an XML document where a schema per se is also an XML document.

SCM   Managing the entire business process starting from sourcing supplies to build a product and extending to handling faulty returns.

Self-service portal   Another name for an Internet call center.

Single sign-on   Obviating the need to individually sign on to separate applications or services once a user has been authenticated by the portal.

Skins   Look-and-feel themes for a portal view or an entire portal.

SMTP   The most prevalent protocol used for Web-based e-mail operations.

SOAP   The preferred, lightweight communications protocol for Web services that permits the exchange of structured and typed, XML-centric information between peers.

SRM   CRM for suppliers.

SSL   Widely used client/server security scheme, developed by Netscape, that operates at the transport layer and provides authentication and data privacy.

Synchrony   Keeping portal content up to-date, accurate, coordinated, and linked.

Syndication   Obtaining specific context from external sources.

Thin client   Software, typically in Java or ActiveX form, that can be dynamically downloaded to a client from a Web server. Also used to describe wireless clients in some circles.

TLS   The latest version of SSL.

Two-factor authentication   Scheme whereby users must identify themselves using two unique factors—one that they know (e.g., a PIN) and the other being something they physically possess (e.g., a magnetic stripe card).

UAN   Siebel's XML-centric, standards-based, vendor-independent application integration scheme.

UDDI   A far-reaching electronic registry that enables Web services to fulfill their goal of being self-advertising.

UDDI global registry   The actual implementation of the distributed UDDI registry.

UDDI operators   The companies such as IBM, Microsoft, and HP that together host and maintain the UDDI global registry.

Vertical portal   A portal that has a specific focus of interest, as opposed to being broad based; thus, corporate portals are vertical portals since their focus is confined to corporate interests.

Vortal   A vertical portal.

Web mining   Process of collecting and carefully analyzing information about the behavior of Web users.

Web parts   The components, equivalent to portlets, that make up a Microsoft digital dashboard.

Web services   A new genre of heavily XML-centric Web software items that represent reusable, modular, self-describing, and self-advertising units of business work.

WebSphere   IBM's "umbrella" brand name for most of its offerings pertaining to the Web, e-business, Java, and Web services.

Web-to-host   Technology to integrate pre-Web "legacy" applications with the Web.

Wireless portal   Specialized portals, during the early days of wireless clients, used only for supporting handheld devices.

WSDL   Platform-independent XML derivative for generically describing Web services.

WSFL   Proposed standard by IBM for an XML-based language to describe the role and make-up of Web services as a part of a business process definition.

WSRP   IBM's proposal for Web services with their own built-in GUIs.

XML   A platform and programming language–independent scheme for sharing data among applications and corporations in an unambiguous, consistent, and extensible manner through the use of mutually understood vocabularies.

XSL   Defines the format for an XML document using style sheets.

XSL-FO   XML's rather sophisticated equivalent of HTML when it comes to document formatting.

XSLT   The scripting language component of XSL.

Zero foot print   Totally Web browser–based application-access solutions that do not require any other application-specific software on a client.

Acronyms

AI	Artificial Intelligence
AOL	America Online
API	Application Programming Interface
ASP	(Microsoft's) Active Server Pages
ATM	Automated Teller Machines or Asynchronous Transfer Mode
b2b	Business-to-Business
b2c	Business-to-Consumer
b2e	Business-to-Employee
BASDA	Business and Accounting Software Developers Association
BI	Business Intelligence
BPM	Business Process Management
CA	Certificate Authority
CART	Classification and Regression Tree
CGI	Common Gateway Interface
CM	Content Management
CoD	Capacity on Demand
COM	(Microsoft's) Component Object Model
CORBA	Common Object Request Broker Architecture
CRM	Customer Relationship Management

CSS	Cascading Style Sheets
cXML	Commerce XML
DC	Digital Certificate
DCOM	(Microsoft's) Distributed Component Object Model
DES	Data Encryption Standard
DMZ	Demilitarized Zone
DN	Distinguished Name
DTD	Document Type Definition
ebXML	Electronic Business XML
ECC	Error Checking and Correction
EIP	Enterprise Information Portals
EIS	Executive Information Systems
EJB	Enterprise JavaBeans
ERM	Employee Relationship Management
ERP	Enterprise Resource Planning
FTP	File Transfer Protocol
GeoRM	(IBM's) Geographic Remote Mirror
GIF	Graphical Interchange Format
HAEGO	(IBM's) High Availability Geographic Cluster
HDML	Handheld Device Markup Language
HR	Human Resources
HTML	HyperText Markup Language
HTTP	HyperText Transfer Protocol
IDS	Intrusion Detection System
IIOP	Internet Inter-ORB Protocol
IIS	(Microsoft's) Internet Information Server
IKE	Internet Key Exchange

IP	Internet Protocol
IPSec	IP Security
ISO	International for Standardization Organization
J2EE	Java 2 Enterprise Edition
JNDI	Java Naming and Directory Interface
JPEG	(images formatted per) Joint Photographic Experts Group (standard)
JSP	Java Server Pages
KM	Knowledge Management
LDAP	Lightweight Directory Access Protocol
MARS	Multivariate Adaptive Regression
MIME	Multipurpose Internet Mail Extensions
NAS	Network Attached Storage
NDS	Novell Directory Services
NITF	News Industry Text Format
OASIS	Organization for the Advancement of Structured Information Systems
OCS	Open Content Syndication
ODBC	Open Database Connectivity
OEM	Other Equipment Manufacturer
OLAP	Online Analytical Processing
OO	Object Orientation
ORB	Object Request Broker
PCDATA	Parsed Character Data
PDF	Portable Data Format
PKI	Public Key Infrastructure
PRISM	Publishing Requirements for Industry Standard Metadata
QoS	Quality of Service

RA	Registration Authority
RAID	Redundant Arrays of Inexpensive Disks
RAS	Reliability, Availability, and Serviceability or, in some context, Remote Access Server or Services
RFQ	Request For Quotation
RMI	Remote Method Invocation
ROI	Return On Investment
RPC	Remote Procedure Call
RSS	Rich Site Summary
SAN	Storage Area Network
SCM	Supply-Chain Management
SGML	Standard Generalized Markup Language
SMTP	Simple Mail Transfer Protocol
SOAP	Simple Object Access Protocol
SRM	Supplier Relationship Management
SSL	Secure Sockets Layer
SSO	Single Sign-On
TCP	Transmission Control Protocol
TLS	Transport Layer Security
tpaML	Trading Partner Agreement Markup Language
UAN	(Siebel's) Universal Application Network
UDDI	Universal Description, Discovery, and Integration
UN	United Nations
URL	Universal Resource Locator
USPS	United States Postal Service
W3C	World Wide Web Consortium
WAP	Wireless Access Protocol

WML	Wireless Markup Language
WSDL	Web Services Description Language
WSRP	Web Services for Remote Portals
WSTP	(IBM's) WebSphere Transcoding Publisher
XHTML	Extensible HTML
XML	Extensible Markup Language
XRF	(IBM's) Extended Recovery Facility
XSD	XML Schema Definition Language
XSL	Extensible Style sheet Language
XSL-FO	XSL Formatting Objects
XSLT	XSL Transformations

Bibliography

Much of the research and reference pertaining to this book was done dynamically on the Web. I only made reference to a very few books. These were as follows:

Elliotte Rusty Harold and W. Scott Means, *XML in a Nutshell.* Sebastopol, CA: O'Reilly, 2001.

Benoit Marchal, *XML by Example.* Indianapolis, IN: Que, 2002.

Michael Morrison, *Teach Yourself XML in 24 Hours.* Indianapolis, IN: Sams, 2002.

Patrick Cauldwell, et al., *Professional XML Web Services.* Birmingham, UK: Wrox Press, 2001.

Jesus Mena, *WebMining for Profit.* Woburn, MA: Digital Press, 2001.

Barry de Ville, *Microsoft Data Mining.* Woburn, MA: Digital Press, 2001.

Anura Gurugé, *Integrating TCP/IP i•nets with IBM Data Centers.* Reading, MA: Addison-Wesley, 1999.

Index

About the Author

Anura Gurugé is an Independent Technical Consultant who specializes in all aspects of contemporary networking—particularly those involving IBM host systems. He has first hand, in-depth experience in Web-to-host, SNA/APPN, frame relay, token-ring switching, ATM, system management, and *x*DSL technologies. He was actively involved with the token-ring switching pioneer Nashoba Networks, which was acquired by Cisco Systems in 1996, and the ATM broadband access company Sonoma Systems, which was acquired by Nortel in 2000. He was the founder and Chairman of the SNA-Capable i•net Forum in 1997. He also ran a boat-based, take-out delivery service in New Hampshire called Waiters on Water.

He is the author of *Integrating TCP/IP i•nets with IBM Data Centers* (1999), *Reengineering IBM Networks* (1996), the best selling *SNA: Theory and Practice* (1984). He co-edited Auerbach's handbooks, *Communications Systems Management* and *Web-to-Host Integration*. He is currently writing a new book, *Web Services: A Guide for Decision Makers*. He also publishes a highly acclaimed 16-page, monthly, electronic newsletter called *i-BigBlue Professionals' Monthly* that deals with most issues related to IBM systems.

In addition, he has published over 290 articles. In a career spanning 26 years, he has held senior technical and marketing roles in IBM, ITT, Northern Telecom, Wang, and BBN. He can be contacted at (603) 293-5855 or anu@wownh.com. His Web sites are: www.inet-guru.com and www.wownh.com.

Printed and bound by CPI Group (UK) Ltd, Croydon, CR0 4YY

08/05/2025

01864877-0001